AF753365

BOROBUDUR as Cultural Landscape

Local Communities' Initiatives for the Evolutive Conservation of Pusaka Saujana *BOROBUDUR*

BOROBUDUR as Cultural Landscape

Local Communities' Initiatives for the Evolutive Conservation of Pusaka Saujana *BOROBUDUR*

Edited by

Kiyoko Kanki

Laretna T. Adishakti

Titin Fatimah

Kyoto University Press

TRANS PACIFIC PRESS

First published in 2015 jointly by:
Kyoto University Press
69 Yoshida Konoe-cho
Sakyo-ku, Kyoto 606-8315, Japan
Telephone: +81-75-761-6182
Fax: +81-75-761-6190
Email: sales@kyoto-up.or.jp
Web: http://www.kyoto-up.or.jp

Trans Pacific Press
PO Box 164, Balwyn North, Melbourne
Victoria 3104, Australia
Telephone: +61-3-9859-1112
Fax: +61-3-8911-7989
Email: tpp.mail@gmail.com
Web: http://www.transpacificpress.com

Copyright © Kyoto University Press and Trans Pacific Press 2015.

Edited by Cathy Edmonds

Set by Toyo Planning Corporation

Printed by Taiyosha Co., Ltd., Kitakata, Gifu, Japan

Distributors

James Bennett Pty Ltd
Locked Bag 537
Frenchs Forest NSW 2086
Australia
Telephone: +61 2 8988 5000
Fax: +61 2 8988 5031
Email: info@bennett.com.au
Web: www.bennett.com.au

USA and Canada
International Specialized Book Services (ISBS)
920 NE 58th Avenue, Suite 300
Portland, Oregon 97213-3786
USA
Telephone: (800) 944-6190
Fax: (503) 280-8832
Email: orders@isbs.com
Web: http://www.isbs.com

Asia and the Pacific except Japan
Kinokuniya Company Ltd.

Head office:
38-1 Sakuragaoka 5-chome
Setagaya-ku, Tokyo 156-8691
Japan
Telephone: +81-3-3439-0161
Fax: +81-3-3439-0839
Email: bkimp@kinokuniya.co.jp
Web: www.kinokuniya.co.jp

Asia-Pacific office:
Kinokuniya Book Stores of Singapore Pte., Ltd.
391B Orchard Road #13-06/07/08
Ngee Ann City Tower B
Singapore 238874
Telephone: +65-6276-5558
Fax: +65-6276-5570
Email: SSO@kinokuniya.co.jp

All rights reserved. No reproduction of any part of this book may take place without the written permission of Kyoto University Press or Trans Pacific Press.
ISBN 978–1–920901–67–7

Borobudur landscape photography (Photo: Suparno)

Village environment in Borobudur as cultural landscape (Photo: Rahmi)

Contents

Figures

Plates

Tables

Authors' Profiles

(in order of writing, *Editor = General editors)

Laretna T. Adishakti (*Editor)
Lecturer, Chairperson of Center for Heritage Conservation (CHC), Department of Architecture and Planning, Faculty of Engineering, Universitas Gadjah Mada, Yogyakarta, Indonesia (Chapter 1, Chapter6)

Kiyoko Kanki (*Editor)
Professor, Department of Architecture and Architectural Engineering, Graduate school of Engineering, Kyoto University, Kyoto, Japan (Introduction, Chapter 2, Chapter 6)

Dwita Hadi Rahmi
Lecturer, Department of Architecture and Planning, Faculty of Engineering, Universitas Gadjah Mada, Yogyakarta, Indonesia (First section of Chapter 3)

Amiluhur Soeroso
Researcher, Center for Heritage Conservation (CHC), Department of Architecture and Planning, Faculty of Engineering, Universitas Gadjah Mada, Yogyakarta, Indonesia (Second section of Chapter 3)

Helmy Murwanto
Lecturer, Department of Geology, Faculty of Mineral Technology, the National Development University (UPN) Veteran, Yogyakarta, Indonesia (Third section of Chapter 3)

Ananta Purwoarminta
Researcher, Research Center for Geotechnology, Indonesian Institute of Sciences (LIPI), Bandung, Indonesia (Third section of Chapter 3)

Punto Wijayanto
Lecturer, Department of Architecture, University of Technology Yogyakarta (UTY), Yogyakarta, Indonesia (Fourth section of Chapter 3)

Jack Priyana
Borobudur Tourism Network (JAKER), Borobudur, Magelang, Indonesia (Fifth section of

Chapter 3)

Titin Fatimah(*Editor)
Lecturer, Department of Architecture, Faculty of Engineering, Universitas Tarumanagara (UNTAR), Jakarta, Indonesia (First section of Chapter 4, Chapter 6)

Wahyu Utami
Lecturer, Department of Architecture, University of North Sumatera (USU), Medan, Indonesia (Second section of Chapter 4)

Tatak Sariawan
Chairperson, Village Tourism Cooperative of Candirejo, Borobudur, Magelang, Indonesia (Second section of Chapter 4)

Suparno
Professional Photographer (previously Staff of Borobudur Conservation Office), Borobudur, Magelang, Indonesia (Third section of Chapter 4)

Kusumaningdyah Nurul Handayani
Lecturer, Department of Architecture, Sebelas Maret University (UNS), Surakarta, Indonesia (Third section of Chapter 4)

Muhammad Hatta
Borobudur Tourism Network (JAKER), Borobudur, Magelang, Indonesia (Fourth section of Chapter 4)

Sinta Carolina
Staff, Center for Heritage Conservation (CHC), Department of Architecture and Planning, Faculty of Engineering, Universitas Gadjah Mada, Yogyakarta, Indonesia (Chapter 5)

Yeny Paulina Leibo
Staff, Center for Heritage Conservation (CHC), Department of Architecture and Planning, Faculty of Engineering, Universitas Gadjah Mada, Yogyakarta, Indonesia (Chapter 5)

The precise roles of authors in their collaborated activities are described in Introduction.

Acknowledgments

This book was planned and produced to introduce the actual situation of the cultural landscape conservation movement in Borobudur. The conservation movement started as local activities with the collaboration of researchers and students. So, first, the authors express special thanks of gratitude to the people of the local communities in Borobudur Sub-district and the non-profit organizations that collaborate with the local communities. The authors also express special thanks to the people within the official sectors, including local governments, regional governments, and, especially, the Borobudur Conservation Office, Ministry of Culture and Education, Republic of Indonesia, which supported the opening and continuation of the Borobudur Field School. Through such vast collaborations, the authors came to know about many diverse subjects.

In planning and editing this book, Kyoto University Press provided much help. Three of the authors, Laretna T. Adishakti, Kiyoko Kanki, and Titin Fatimah, graduated from the doctoral course of the Graduate School of Architecture and Architectural Engineering, Kyoto University, and their research and collaborative works with local communities about cultural landscape conservation originated from their student days at Kyoto University. The authors consulted with Kyoto University Press about this publishing project and took a very long time to write the chapters, and Mr Takagaki, Mr Suzuki, and expert editors kindly guided the completion of this book.

This publishing project is supported by the Japan Society for the Promotion of Science (JSPS) with the Scientific Literature program from a Grant-in-Aid for Publication of Scientific Research Results. This support, particularly the expert editing, was essential.

The authors thank the collaborators who helped write the English manuscripts, especially Ms Granita Zulaycha, who is not listed as an author but who greatly helped in writing the first drafts with the authors from Borobudur local communities (Muhammad Hatta and Jack Priyana).

The authors hope that this book will provide an opportunity to promote further activities and collaborations among the locals in Borobudur, Indonesia, as well as worldwide colleagues who dedicate their time to conserve cultural landscapes according to local initiatives.

Introduction:
Borobudur as Cultural Landscape

Kiyoko Kanki

The idea of 'cultural landscape' has enlarged the activities for heritage conservation not only as the protection of designated components of an area but also as the sustainable development of the integrated features, both tangible and intangible, of an area. Especially, in thinking of conserving cultural landscape, the inhabitants and the related people should be involved in the initiatives by themselves because human activities are essentially related to the features and values of cultural landscapes. The implementation of conservation, therefore, requires an activity-based and local community-based approach for understanding and searching the existing and potential landscape. Here it is requested that all the related people including local communities and local supporters, as well as conservation planning experts, together find dynamically authentic ways to develop the physical environment and lifestyles for the future. How is it possible to realize such ways?

This book commemorates ten years of the International Field School on Borobudur Cultural Landscape Heritage (hereafter, BFS (Borobudur Field School)). The writers and editors have been engaged in BFS as facilitators, lecturers, and participants.

BFS started in 2004 with the objective to re-explore village and town areas surrounding Borobudur Temple, areas that had not been considered as closely connected with the temple. In 2003, just before the first BFS, an argument erupted over a large-scale commercial development near Borobudur Temple and interest in the surrounding areas rapidly increased. Borobudur Temple is located inside a park area, which is now closed and separated from its surroundings, where there was once a village and rural land before the park construction. A series of three temples, Borobudur, Pawon, and Mendut, should be regarded as combined, even if they appear isolated, since, with tourist development increasingly concentrated in the neighborhood of Borobudur Temple and the park, problems in the surrounding environment have become apparent.

In 2003, when the large-scale commercial facility was planned on a site neighboring the closed park, many discussions were held and movements were planned by the local communities and various organizations about the idea that the surrounding areas, including the temples and the park, should be regarded as a connected and whole landscape. The local communities concluded that the development should not be implemented and this decision was in line with the recommendation of the International Council on Monuments and Sites (ICOMOS) in 2003. The opinion by the local communities was based on the idea that the basin topography of Borobudur Sub-district is one complete landscape and that the temples and the sub-district should be regarded as closely related, while ICOMOS used a buffer zoning idea and a circular zoning scheme with Borobudur Temple as the center point (Chapter 1, '*Saujana* heritage planning and the role of community' in Chapter 3).

In this way, Borobudur as a cultural landscape became a point of discussion. Local communities and several organizations stirred interest in the large surrounding areas – of mountains, hills, agricultural fields, villages, towns, and rivers, which include many kinds of historic tangible and intangible items – to increase understanding about the basin topography as the cultural landscape heritage of Borobudur. At the same time, there was interest in the role and potential of local communities and various organizations for the conservation of heritage, as well as the living environment, including sustainability of people's ways of living for the present and future. Some people who supported this idea used to live in the park area before the park construction. Before they were forced to suddenly leave their own village near Borobudur Temple, they had grown up in the nearest environment to the temple and they had memories of coexistence with historic and special surroundings. Even before such movements in 2003, some local communities and organizations had started activities to improve the attractiveness of their villages. Some of the community developments and conservation-oriented activities had begun more than twenty years earlier and had become well known ('Community-based conservation through rural tourism initiatives in Borobudur' in Chapter 4).

BFS was started by people who shared the idea that the large topographic area of Borobudur should be unified as a cultural landscape with close relations with Borobudur, Pawon, and Mendut temples. The first BFS was organized with researchers, non-profit organizations, village communities, university students, local administrations, and several invited guest speakers. This event provided an opportunity for people from different backgrounds to meet each other in an open atmosphere. It also brought together people necessary to the program and to collaborative relationship building. Over a few years, participation increased and several images of the Borobudur cultural landscape became recognizable; for example, the characteristics of each village, the places where traditional as well as contemporary artistic activities can be experienced, how local activities are related to the management of the cultural landscape, and so on.

In such a way, the authors of this book became colleagues. After the first ten years of BFS, we are very interested and eager to discuss with the wider network of landscape studies how Borobudur as cultural landscape can be described, how the diverse activities can be related, and how we can contribute to the sustainability of the cultural landscape, and also how we can create processes and initiatives for cultural landscapes. BFS has been one way in which the authors and our wider circle of colleagues have tried to introduce the idea of cultural landscape in Borobudur, and have increased the diversity of evaluation of the large area related to Borobudur, during these ten years.

A short introduction to each chapter and the role of each author in this book follows.

Chapter 1 is written by Dr. Laretna T. Adishakti, the founder of BFS. She is from the Center for Heritage Conservation Dept. of Architecture and Planning, Faculty of Engineering at Universitas Gadjah Mada, where she majored in architecture and planning. She connected the several initiatives around Borobudur and suggested the Indonesian word *saujana* as the translation for cultural landscape, and the word *pusaka* as the translation for heritage. She has dedicated her time to conserve many kinds of cultural heritage, including during the recovery from recent natural disasters, with international networks of collaborators. Here she describes the history of heritage planning for Borobudur concerning cases subscribed as cultural landscape heritage to show how cultural landscape heritage – *saujana* heritage – has been treated and conserved until now, and to show the expectations and suggestions for the next steps of community-based conservation.

Chapter 2 is written by Professor Dr. Kiyoko Kanki, from Kyoto University in Japan, who has majors in architecture and planning and is a collaborating researcher with Adishakti, with whom she has shared experiences about cultural landscape conservation for more than twenty years and assisted in starting BFS. As BFS was being planned, she was contributing to the world heritage nomination as cultural landscape of the Sacred Sites and Pilgrimage Routes in the Kii Mountain Range in Japan, specifically focusing on local community activities for conservation. As chair of the subcommittee for rural cultural landscape at the Architectural Institute of Japan, she works for community initiative approaches to cultural landscape conservation. Here she discusses the new idea of 'evolutive conservation', which was proposed by the subcommittee to focus on new ways of thinking about authenticity and the dynamism of community history and sustainability of cultural landscapes.

Chapter 3 explains Borobudur as cultural landscape and is written by multiple authors. The first part is written by Dr. Dwita Hadi Rahmi, from Universitas Gadjah Mada, who has a background in architecture and planning. She is a co-founder of BFS and has updated explanations of cultural landscape of Borobudur from multiple viewpoints throughout the history of BFS. Here she describes the characteristics of the cultural landscape of Borobudur as a whole. Dr. Amiluhur Soeroso, also from Universitas Gajah Mada and with a geographic background, takes a geographical approach to the characteristics and ecological features of the cultural landscape of Borobudur. Dr. Helmy Murwanto from the University of National Development "Veteran", Yogyakarta with a major in geology, colaborates with Amanta Puwoarminta from Indonesian Institute of Science(LIPI), describes the geological characteristics of the large basin of Borobudur, specifically the lake that existed in ancient times, and provides a basic understanding of the structure of the Borobudur topography and landscapes. Punto Wijayanto, from University of Technology, Yogyakarta and with a planning major, shows the regional planning system related to Borobudur and proposes improvements of the system in relation to the active local communities. To conclude this chapter, we invited Jack Priyana, from the local non-profit organization JAKER (*Jaringan Kerja Kepariwisataan Borobudur* - Borobudur Tourism Network), to describe the characteristics of Borobudur from his viewpoint as a local inhabitant. He has played the role of facilitator for a long time to maintain communications with many local people and has facilitated relationships among the different organizations. He manages several tourist activities with an alternative tourism policy, and has introduced the potential of each village in the Borobudur cultural landscape. BFS could not have started without his activities for communicating and understanding the potential of each village. He is among the people who were forced to move out of the closed area of Borobudur Temple when the park was constructed, and has memories of the way of living together with the neighboring environment and heritage temple.

Chapter 4 describes the history and potential of local communities and organizations in Borobudur Sub-district. The activities of local communities and organizations must be the driving force for the sustainability of the cultural landscape. The first part of the chapter is written by Dr. Titin Fatimah, who was born and grew up in Borobudur, and went to Universitas Gadjah Mada and the Graduate School of Kyoto University. She was also a student participant at the first BFS. She made precise surveys of the histories of local communities and organizations related to the conservation of the Borobudur cultural landscape, and revealed the outcomes of these long processes. Here she focuses on alternative tourism activities and discusses the possibilities and problems of such activities in supporting cultural landscape conservation. Dr. Wahyu Utami, who is originally from Magelang City, finished undergraduate, master and doctor course from Universitas Gadjah Mada, co-authors the second part of this chapter with Tatak Sariawan from Candirejo village. Tatak is the head of Candirejo Tourism Village Cooperative, which was established by the people of Candirejo village as an alternative tourism-oriented community business. Tatak explains the history of Candirejo village community development and the people's ideas for the tourism industry and village development. In the third part, Dr. Kusumaningdyah Nurul Handayani collaborates with Mr. Suparno, a professional photographer who previously worked at Borobudur Conservation Office. Mr. Suparno has taken many beautiful photographs in Borobudur while being very careful about the tourism impact to the villages. Here we can understand the beauty of the Borobudur cultural landscape scenery, while at the same time understanding ways of coexistence between the ordinary but precious village life and the destructive impact of mass tourism. Finally, Muhammad Hatta writes about his activities as a local guide, as well as his role as facilitator for the capacities of village communities. He is also very active with JAKER. In this way, Chapter 4 is written by main authors who all originated from villages in Borobudur. Although the various activities might be launched by each community to search for and solve problems from the viewpoint of cultural landscape conservation, BFS has provided the location for the participants to experience such activities and to grow up in the local context, and the opportunity to gather the authors and their related networks of activists.

Chapter 5 introduces BFS itself. The authors are Sinta Carolina and Yeny Paulina Leibo from the Center for Heritage Conservation, Universitas Gadjah Mada. They have been the organizing secretaries since the first BFS and know the history of BFS. Here we see the program, schedule, content, venues, and participants of BFS. At the same time, they introduce the field survey areas that have been the BFS focus, which provide evidence for discovering the local and precious heritage, both tangible and intangible, implemented by the abilities of the participants. They suggest images to expand the interests from the surroundings of Borobudur Temple to the larger topographic and integrated region. The authors also present feedback from international and domestic BFS participants.

Chapter 6, the short and final part, shows that BFS and the cultural landscape heritage idea must be further developed and that we are still in the midst of the different ways of coexistence for heritage conservation and community development. Ten years is not short, but it is not long enough. We have only started to discuss the evolutive conservation of cultural landscape heritage, and the Borobudur experience is one case that has tried to manage it.

BFS did not start with a fixed definition of cultural landscape, although the World Heritage operational guidelines already provided an official definition. We liked to start with flexible thinking about what was to be perceived and appreciated according to the idea of the landscape and the evolutive relations between nature and humans. BFS activities have been direct collaborations between academics, including university professors, researchers, and students and local communities, and have had the intention of community empowerment. We started with the idea that the terminology 'cultural landscape' in the active field might be more wide-ranging and better understood as a dynamic phenomenon. We started to consider cultural landscape not only with physical aspects such as building styles or land use distribution, but also through social aspects such as local industries, local ways of lives, community development histories, and so on. Cultural landscape should be regarded as the outcome of coexisting and co-promoted activities by different actors in one area. All the authors hope that this experience in Borobudur will show the next step in Borobudur and provide an opportunity to share wider communications among cultural landscape areas throughout the world.

1 Cultural Landscape and *Saujana* Heritage

Laretna T. Adishakti

Introduction

In the *Operational Guidelines for Implementation of the World Heritage Convention* (UNESCO 1994), paragraph 39 added 'cultural landscape' as a new category of world heritage. This category is a mix of natural heritage and culture. The previous category consisted of natural heritage and cultural heritage. In Indonesia some world heritage is mainly categorized under cultural and natural heritage. There is the World Cultural Heritage of Borobudur, Pawon, and Mendut Temples, Prambanan Temple, and Sangiran, and the World Natural Heritage of Ujung Kulon National Park, Komodo National Park, Lorentz National Park, and the Tropical Rainforest Heritage of Sumatra. In 2012 the United Nations Educational, Scientific and Cultural Organization (UNESCO) listed the 'Cultural Landscape of Bali Province: the *Subak* System as a Manifestation of the *Tri Hita Karana* Philosophy', which, as a cluster site, includes the Supreme Water Temple of Pura Ulun Danu Batur and Lake Batur, the *Subak* Landscape of the Pakerisan Watershed, the Subak Landscape of Catur Angga Batukaru, and the Royal Water Temple of Pura Taman Ayun, which cover 20,974.70 hectares in total.

In 2001 the Director-General of UNESCO started to raise awareness about intangible cultural heritage and encouraged local communities to protect such heritage, as well as the local people who sustain these forms of cultural expressions, through the Proclamation of the Masterpieces of the Oral and Intangible Heritage of Humanity. Many manifestations of intangible cultural heritage around the globe were awarded the title of Masterpieces to recognize the value of the non-material component of culture, as well as to entail the commitment of states to promote and safeguard the Masterpieces. Since 2003 many intangible resources in Indonesia have been recognized by UNESCO as Masterpieces, such as Wayang puppets, *keris* (daggers), batik, Saman dance, *angklung* (musical instruments), and *noken* (bags).

In 2003 Indonesian heritage activists in the Indonesian Network for Heritage Conservation (*Jaringan Pelestarian Pusaka Indonesia*), in collaboration with ICOMOS Indonesia and the Ministry of Culture and Tourism, declared the first Indonesian charter on heritage conservation (the Indonesian Heritage Conservation Charter 2003). This charter stated that Indonesian heritage consists of natural, cultural, and *saujana* heritage (cultural landscape, a mix of natural and cultural heritage). This charter also highlighted the use of *saujana* in a translated cultural landscape – the Indonesian word *saujana* means 'as far as the eye can see'.

Saujana is a manifestation of the interaction between the human and the natural environment, which is reflected in space and time and is always evolving (UNESCO 1994). It

Plate 1.1: The World Cultural Landscape of Bali Province (photo: Adishakti, 2013)

is the social system and the way humans manage the space. The issues of *saujana* have been raised globally in the past three decades. Previously, since the Industrial Revolution, Western thought has always considered nature in opposition to culture (Plachter in Droste, Plachter and Rossler, 1995ed.).

World *saujana* heritage and its power of expressions

This section focuses on two cases of world heritage categorized as cultural landscape for the purpose of establishing an image of *saujana* heritage. I made field observations and learned about world *saujana* heritage from the Wachau Cultural Landscape, Austria, and the Sacred Sites and Pilgrimage Routes in the Kii Mountain Range, Japan, in 2005 and 2011. Some expressions of world *saujana* heritage are vast cross-border areas, visual quality and protected living culture, the self-protection of people, and lifetime advantages.

Vast cross-border areas

Heritage that stretches as far as the eye can see certainly covers a huge area and often crosses borders, ignoring administration boundaries. Its strong natural formation and transformation is reflected in specific communities. It may contain a variety of complex phenomena, including the presence of various heritages, including tangible and intangible cultural heritage.

One example is the Wachau Valley, Austria, which was designated as a world heritage cultural landscape by UNESCO in 2000. It encompasses an area of 4800 hectares, stretching from the city of Melk into the city of Krems along thirty-six kilometers of the Danube River

Plate 1.2: Cities along the Danube River (photo: Adishakti, 2011)

(which has a total length of 2800 kilometers and was immortalized in the classical music *The Blue Danube* by Johann Strauss). The Wachau Valley encompasses the cities of Melk, Spitz, Dumstein, Mautern, Weissenkirchen, Stein, Emmersdorf, and Krems. This world heritage cultural landscape has about 5000 heritage buildings, vineyards, and the Dunkelstainer Forest.

Another example is the Sacred Sites and Pilgrimage Routes in the Kii Mountain Range, Japan, which was enacted in 2003 by UNESCO as a world heritage cultural landscape. These sites are located in the dense forest of the Kii Mountains overlooking the Pacific Ocean and link the three prefectures of Mie, Nara, and Wakayama. The sites encompass an area of 495.3 hectares that consist of three main sites: Yoshino and Omine (44.8 hectares), Kumano Sanzan (94.2 hectares), and Koyasan (63.1 hectares). The pilgrimage route covers 304.57 hectares, consisting of 293.2 hectares of core area and a buffer zone of 11.37 hectares.

Visual quality and protected living culture

The second strength of a world heritage cultural landscape lies in the visual quality and the high spirit of life. Arrangements of space, settlements, buildings, and the natural environment express the quality, including the sustainability of community cultural activities and the interaction with nature – all considerations for UNESCO when inscribing them as world heritage cultural landscapes.

The pilgrimage route along the Kii Mountains shows important historical resources. Monuments and natural resources have formed the unique cultural landscape, and demonstrate the exchange and development of cultures and religions in Asia. Buddhism was introduced in Japan by China and Korea, and its transformation has created a uniquely designed heritage with the coexistence of early shrines and temples throughout Japan.

Not only are the shrines and temples significant, but the trees and woods are also

Plate 1.3: Pilgrimage in the complex of Okunoin cemetery, Koyasan city, Kii Mountains, Wakayama, Japan
(photo: Adishakti, 2005)

Plate 1.4: Pilgrimage route, ancient Kumano street; souvenir shops operating from heritage houses have emerged since this region was declared a world heritage site
(photo: Adishakti, 2005)

Plate 1.5: Characteristics of the visual typology in the Wachau Valley: remains of an ancient castle on the hill, medieval architecture, and vineyards
(photo: Adishakti, 2005)

Plate 1.6: Pedestrians in a medieval city in the Wachau Valley
(photo: Adishakti, 2005)

Plate 1.7: The world cultural heritage of Melk Cathedral built on a rock in the hill city of Melk, one of the cities in the Wachau Valley (photo: Adishakti, 2005)

Plate 1.8: The city center of Krems (photo: Adishakti, 2011)

meaningful. The mixture of natural and cultural resources has been well documented over 1200 years, and includes giant trees that are more than 500 years old and are mostly found in the tomb complex of Okunoin, Koyasan city. Kumano Taisha Shrine also has many old trees, which, according to legend, were planted in 1159. These natural beauties of the Kii Mountains culture have inspired poets and painters.

These pilgrimage routes are very complex and long, connecting various sites from the sixth century until 1868, and reach the cities of Kyoto and Nara, each once the Old Capital of Japan. However, because of modernization pressures in both cities, the face of the pilgrimage routes has changed. Only some parts are still recognizable.

The arrangement of the Wachau Valley towns along the Danube banks reflects the design in the eleventh and twelfth centuries. Although the city of Mautern, a second- to fifth- century Roman city, considered the order of its own modern development, most of the relics in the form of churches (Gothic or Baroque), monasteries, and houses are still well preserved, including the debris of many hilltop castles, which, from a distance, are striking. The railway network, built in 1909, was designed in such a way as not to damage the rural landscape.

This region also witnessed the growth of art in Europe. Since the sixteenth century, thousands of Italian artists have worked in the Wachau. In 1763, at the age of seven-and-a-half, the renowned composer Wolfgang Mozart appeared for the first time at a public concert

Plate 1.9: Pilgrimage route and the Toganoki tea house (photo: Adishakti, 2005)

Plate 1.10: Most of the pilgrimage routes are in hilly sites that pass various temples; bamboo sticks prepared by the local community are freely available (photo: Adishakti, 2005)

in the Wachau region. Many architects, painters, and renowned Austrian sculptors still create works in the valley that is full of charm.

The visual quality and life in the Wachau is a rare example of strong economic development that has not destroyed the very valuable cultural and natural heritage. Moreover, the people are able to preserve the heritage (history, culture, topography, natural space, and ecology) while controlling the industrial growth.

Self-protection of people

Vast areas, ownership of diverse heritage, and improper economic modernization often threaten the sustainable future of the world heritage. Proper management is a must. In Wachau various heritage buildings are professionally protected by the Federal Office of Historic Monuments, located in Vienna, while natural heritage is managed by the Ministry of Nature Protection of Austria.

In the Kii Mountains heritage is protected by an Act of Cultural Property of Japan, which has been regularly revised and reinforced since 1950. The Cultural Office of the Ministry of Education, Culture, Sports, Science and Technology is the authority for the management of world heritage in Japan. In 2005 the legal aspect of heritage became an issue of cultural

Plate 1.11: The pilgrimage routes traverse the hills before arriving in an ancient Kumano street (photo: Adishakti, 2005)

Plate 1.12: Mr. Takafumi Kinoshita, after retirement, dedicated his life as a local storyteller (*Katari Be-san*) in the villages that are passed by the pilgrimage routes; this activity began long before the modern-day inscriptions (photo: Adishakti, 2005)

landscape heritage, while natural heritage is mainly protected under the National Parks Act by the Ministry of Environment.

However, formal efforts alone are not enough. It is necessary that an awareness of heritage protection should also be borne by the local people. Many of the approximately 5000 heritage buildings in the Wachau are privately owned by local residents who have lived there for generations, and vineyards and forests are owned by farmers, farmer associations, or churches. Similarly, along the pilgrimage routes in the area of the Kii Mountains, there is diverse property ownership and management by local residents and local and national governments, while shrines and temples are managed by organizations or individuals. Improvements and management are carried out by them only if required by national governments, which subsidize repairs.

People in both these world cultural landscapes were already likely well informed about the importance of conservation before the UNESCO nomination, as indicated by the condition where the scattered heritage is generally well preserved. Community spirit and the desire of the people in the three provinces in Japan was very strong when they nominated the Kii Mountains as a world heritage cultural landscape, and campaigns were carried out in a stepwise manner.

People spread out various pins, books, and posters in many places to promote their heritage as deserving of world heritage protection. Conservation of the environmental quality and values had been implemented by community efforts before the nomination, and after the listing their role became more and more important, with their prevailing and deep understanding of the values of the cultural landscape.

Lifetime advantages

The future sustainability of heritage will thrive when all parties receive economic, social, and cultural benefits from ongoing conservation – in which case, protection will no longer be a burden. This is the important step to achieve. Heritage conservation not only tells the story of the past, but invites more people's appreciation and/or present and future use of the sites when it functions without negative impact for and by residents and visitors. Heritage is more valuable when it offers a necessary public function.

Conservation of the cultural and natural environments in the Wachau Valley and the Kii Mountains does, indeed, safeguard the living culture. Conservation management has to be handled with care; for example, developing industries should be non-polluting, visual garbage (such as billboards) should be far from the sites, and new buildings should respect the local environment.

Recently, a return to nature has actually invited public interest, especially the fact that modern humans thirst for a healthy living and natural environment. The Wachau Valley claims to offer comfortable and healthy cycling, even across national borders. Bike paths and new dining experiences close to nature are conveniently available. Meanwhile, the Kii Mountains are known for their beautiful pilgrimage routes. On average, they are visited every year by more than fifteen million people, both for hiking and ritual/spiritual purposes, and recently for landscape management also.

Management of *saujana* heritage does not need to be fabricated or exaggerated. It is simply a natural state and a major force. However, it is precisely to maintain quality that decision makers need accurate information, that planners and managers are observant, that residents have a strong sense of heritage, and that visitors appreciate the values.

Rethinking Borobudur as *saujana* heritage

As previously mentioned, *saujana* heritage, or cultural landscape, is the inextricable unity between nature and manmade heritage in space and time or the variety of interactive manifestation between manmade heritage and the natural environment. The interaction of nature and culture has taken on a new perspective in the global discourse of sciences, especially those concerning heritage conservation that started at the end of the 1980s. However, in Indonesian higher education the discourse on cultural landscape has not yet developed despite the fact that Indonesia – from Sabang, off the northern tip of Sumatra, to Merauke, one of the easternmost cities – is a mosaic of one of the world's largest and most diverse cultural landscapes and needs interdisciplinary involvement.

The Borobudur UNESCO Expert Meeting held in July 2003 stated that a study on Borobudur cultural landscape was urgently needed. In 2004 the Indonesian government,

Plate 1.13: Borobudur Temple as a World Heritage Site (photo: Adishakti, 1991)

through the Department of Culture and Tourism, began to prepare the second stage of the Borobudur restoration, which emphasized intangible cultural heritage and community empowerment.

With the implementation of Law No. 26 on Spatial Planning (2007) and Government Regulation No. 26 (2008), concerning the National Spatial Plan, the Government of the Republic of Indonesia has specified the Borobudur cultural heritage area as a National Strategic Area. Based on that legislation, the government has a strong commitment to manage the Borobudur Temple Compounds area (including the Pawon and Mendut temples) and to cushion it from the threat of damage due to improper activity or growth around the temple.

However, the past decade has seen a tremendous movement of local communities that are critically concerned about unbalanced conservation and development on this world cultural heritage site. This concern was observed by the UNESCO–ICOMOS Reactive Monitoring Mission in 2006. Both local and international parties have noticed that the physical condition of this world cultural heritage area is experiencing environmental quality degradation, which has reduced the glory and the grandeur of the image of the temple as the heritage of world civilization.

The rural landscape that characterizes the area, and therefore must be maintained, is under threat due to the changing character and growth of uncontrolled urban economic activity and tourism around the area. Primarily, the threat of this physical character change calls for a strong institution, both at national and local levels, that has the effective capacity to coordinate stakeholders in terms of supervision and control of the development taking place around the Borobudur World Heritage Site.

Brief review of the restoration and management of Borobudur Temple

The first restoration of Borobudur Temple was undertaken between 1907 and 1911, and in 1955 the Indonesian government looked to UNESCO for international help to restore the temple.

Under the initiative of the Indonesian government and with technical assistance from the Japanese government from 1973 to 1979, Borobudur was designated as a national archaeological park. The study by the Japan International Cooperation Agency (JICA) was divided into three stages: a regional master plan study, 1973–74; a project feasibility study, 1975–76; and a review, 1977–79, which examined data and plans from the two earlier stages and undertook a basic socioeconomic survey of the park areas.

In 1979 the JICA Study Team proposed three basic concepts as pillars for further development: the park was to be for the permanent preservation of the monuments, it was to operate as the Center of Archeological Research in Indonesia, and it was to be for all children in the future (JICA Study Team 1979). These concepts were the main goals and characteristics in the restoration of Borobudur, and the team believed that the park could be successful only if all three concepts were integrated.

The project implementation for the restoration ran from 1975 to 1983, and 1983 to 1989 saw the creation of the archeological park, which delineates five management zones:

- Zone I is the monument/sanctuary area (200-meter radius, 44.8 hectares)
- Zone II is the archaeological park area with facilities for visitors, offices, parking, exhibition halls, etc./buffer zone (500-meter radius, 42.3 hectares)
- Zone III is supposed to be controlled to protect the setting of the temple (two-kilometer radius, 932 hectares)
- Zone IV is the Historical Scenery Preservation Zone (five-kilometer radius), which has thirteen archaeological sites
- Zone V is the protected historical district, with twenty-one archeological sites.

Between 1980 and 1983, two villages, Ngaran and Kenayan, were relocated to make way for the second zone (the tourism park). President Soeharto officially reopened the monument to the public in February 1983.

In 1991 Borobudur and Prambanan temples were inscribed in the World Heritage List (numbers 592 and 642) under the cultural criteria that they:

- exhibit unique artistic achievement
- exert great influence
- are directly or tangibly associated with events or ideas or beliefs.

In 1986, 1989 and 1995 restoration work was monitored by UNESCO experts, especially work on the stone work and the stability and drainage of the structure. In 1992 Presidential Decree (*Keputusan Presiden/Keppres*) No. 1/1992 on the Management of Borobudur Temple Tourism Park and Prambanan Temple Tourism Park and environmental control of each was declared.

A celebration marking the twentieth anniversary of the restoration was held in 2003, a year that was also marked by other activities, including:

- the culmination of protests from the local community, as well as from heritage organizations around the world, against the proposal for a large commercial project near Borobudur Temple

- a local community declaration that questioned the management body and its system (Ratu Boko Co. Ltd)
- a reactive UNESCO–ICOMOS Monitoring Mission to the Borobudur Temple Compounds
- the Fourth International Expert Meeting on Borobudur – Prambanan, organized by UNESCO and the Ministry of Culture and Tourism, Republic of Indonesia, in July; this meeting, for routine monitoring, also considered the wider cultural landscape setting of the temple and the tourist impact on the structure itself and the surrounding region, including the role of local communities
- the establishment of the Borobudur Conservation Office in December 2003 by the Ministry of Culture and Tourism; this office has a special task to develop preservation methodology and heritage conservation in Indonesia.

In 2004 the Ministry of Culture and Tourism established the Steering Committee for the Second Stage of Borobudur and Prambanan Restoration focusing on community development.

Brief review on the basic concepts

Before further discussion, a brief review of the basic concepts and the transformation of Borobudur is needed. The three basic concepts for further development concern the main goals and characteristics in the restoration of Borobudur temples (JICA Study Team 1979).

- **Parks for permanent preservation of the monuments:** archeological monuments do not just exist but rather exist under particular historical social and natural conditions, and only on the basis of unified confirmation of them. The monuments need to be preserved for future generations as part of the 'historical climate' in intimate relation with the surrounding natural environment.

  In determining the size of the parks, the main consideration was preservation of the environment of the monuments. In this regard, the securing of space and establishment of a system of preservation for all time for Borobudur as an invaluable legacy of ancient Indonesian culture with universal artistic value was needed. The space arrangement in Borobudur consists of a monument environmental preservation zone covering 39.8 hectares as a circle with a radius of 350 meters from the center of Borobudur Temple; this is a sanctuary (in which no artificial structures are allowed) for the protection of the monuments. In total, 87 hectares (inclusive of the sanctuary area) serve both as a buffer zone around the sanctuary area and as a park facility and service area for visitors.
- **The Center of Archeological Research in Indonesia:** the Borobudur Archeological Conservation Center (BACC) was established in line with the second concept, which concerns archeological research on, and excavation surveys and restoration of, all of the ruins throughout Central Java dating from the Hindu Java period. The main activities of BACC are scholarly research on Borobudur Temple and the monuments in its vicinity, research on restoration techniques, the keeping of records and materials, survey excavation of unexcavated monuments, training young archeologists from various Asian countries under the direction of experts in this field (also from throughout Asia), and hosting international archeological conferences. BACC serves not only as the main center of Indonesian archeological research but also as a center for international exchanges in archeological research.

- **For all children in the future:** the third concept is to serve as places where many visitors can come in contact with the ancient culture of their own country and enhance their interest in and understanding of it. The archeological museums take visitors back in time to the days of ancient Java, and also aim to educate professionals, as well as all children, for future generation.

The abovementioned concepts show that the conservation program does not cover traditional villages nor the mountains and hills around Borobudur. It is limited to the temple and the park, with a clear border and fence. In managing this park, including other parks (Prambanan and Ratu Boko), the government established PT. Taman Wisata Candi Borobudur, Prambanan and Ratu Boko, a limited company owned by the central government. There is no stated concept regarding the role of the local community in managing this heritage environment.

In brief, drawing from these concepts, several issues should be addressed. The large-scale environment of Borobudur Temple (cultural landscape), such as the traditional villages and the mountains, needs to be examined in order to explore its significant values and contributions to the sustainability of the Borobudur Temple conservation, as well as the prosperity of the local community. It is important, in this regard, to note Article 3 of UNESCO's 1991 Universal Declaration on Cultural Diversity about cultural diversity as a factor in development.

Significant research and training on technical aspects have been locally, nationally and internationally conducted by the Center of Archaeological Research. However, there is still limited education for the general public, including the local community and children. The availability and accessibility of detailed information about history, preservation and so on is also limited.

Controversy as 'public education'?

The abovementioned events and controversies attracted public attention. Many local and national newspapers and magazines became the 'Borobudur agents' of information distribution, and international attention came from mass media such as *Time Magazine* (Asia) (see 'Battle of Borobudur' (James 2003)) and the *New York Times* (see 'Borobudur Journal, Buddhist Monument and Mall: Will Twain Meet?' (Perlez 2003)).

In January 2003 ICOMOS Indonesia expressed concerned about:

- a plan to construct a large-scale, dense commercial development and requested a reactive monitoring mission from UNESCO as soon as possible to review the monument
- studies subsequent to the 1991 inscription of Borobudur Temple that suggest that newer borders might be considered for the temple in light of new discoveries about the original site plan of the temple; a mandala-shaped settlement area was 'discovered' and widened the cultural meaning of the temple's environment, which required an immediate study by responsible Indonesian authorities based on these new findings
- a building within the buffer zone, which was planned and built as the archeological study center, which was being used as a commercial hotel facility; the hotel, called the Manohara Hotel, advertised itself as the only hotel in the Borobudur Temple precinct, in direct contradiction to the inscription of the temple as a World Heritage Site.

Many other local and national organizations also expressed concerns about this large-scale commercial development. Among them, Young Indonesian Architects pointed out

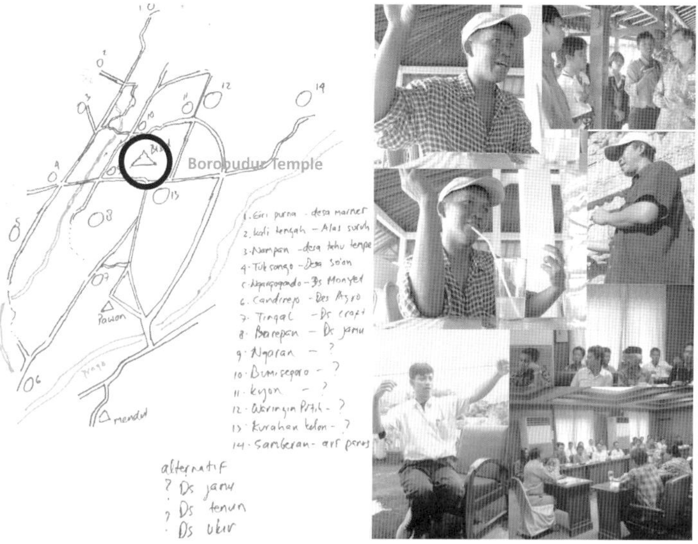

Figure 1.1: Ideas of village development in Borobudur; Jack Priyana (2003) and local people

the inappropriate development concepts and the lack of good and transparent governance in managing this development plan, and the Indonesian Network for Heritage Conservation advertised a statement concerning the development in *Kompas*, the most prominent national newspaper in Indonesia (January, 2003). The statement argued that the controversy was caused by the non-existence of a transparent mechanism for society at large to be informed about and to access the decision-making process. This has become a major barrier for open participation of stakeholders.

Several proposals for development of Borobudur have been prepared by local people and non-government organizations (Figure 1.1) and focus on revitalization of the villages around Borobudur rather than on the centralization of the crafts traders in one huge single building. Although all villages are alike, each village has its own agriculture products and cultural activities. Ideas and discussions are ongoing among the community – locally and internationally – to determine appropriate concepts of conservation and development of Borobudur.

Festivals are another form of education and publicity. Among others, the Borobudur International Festival 2003 commemorated the twentieth anniversary of the Borobudur Temple restoration, and was supported by social events, exhibitions, seminars, and demonstrations and competitions of native games.

The Borobudur Agitatif is an alternative festival that aims to restore the function of Borobudur as a meditation space: 'We want to critically understand the essence of Borobudur', Tanto Mendut, a local prominent artist, explained in 2003. Local people and artists (including world-class painters from Indonesia), as well as concerned communities regionally, nationally, and internationally, use the surrounding area of Borobudur – the settlements, the valleys, and the mountains – as the media for expression of their opinions, thoughts, and ideas towards the future of Borobudur. Protest poetry, open air art exhibitions, theatre, and dramatic design are some forms of such expression.

The Five Mountain Festival is an annual festival during which the five mountain villages overlooking Borobudur celebrate their shared cultural heritage. Each village presents a series of musical and dance performances while villagers parade in their traditional *wayang orang* costumes. This event is supported by a resort in the region.

Beyond the controversies, lessons learned have encouraged many parties to rethink and reexamine the broader dimensions of conservation in Borobudur.

First, the value of the heritage resources and their conservation is not only in temple preservation but also in the conservation of the wider Kedu Plain cultural landscape in which Borobudur lies. As well as the heritage of high culture, such as the temple, valuable but more ordinary heritage, including intangible cultural heritage, is spread across this region. The objective of conservation has moved from mainly isolated objects to the larger scale of the environment and its lively activities.

Second, wider environmental economic development should be provided in parallel with heritage conservation planning, as Borobudur is likely to generate a bigger market and needs to balance its development with the environment as a whole.

Third, the existing heritage management that is based on a centralized system should be examined, and ways must be found to accommodate public opinions into a comprehensive heritage management practice. Since the Indonesia government enacted Act No. 22 on decentralization and Law No. 25 on the financial balance between central and local governments in 1999, the local government has had greater opportunity to manage and utilize the heritage resources in its area. However, as a World Heritage Site, Borobudur stakeholders come from various levels of parties and communities: local, regional, national, and international.

International Field School on Borobudur Cultural Landscape Heritage

In response to various conservation needs – scientific as well as practical – of the Borobudur cultural landscape, since 2004 the International Field School on Borobudur Cultural Landscape Heritage has been organized annually by the Center for Heritage Conservation, Department of Architecture and Planning, Universitas Gadjah Mada, in collaboration with Kanki Laboratory, Department of Environmental System, Wakayama University, Japan, and the Jogja Heritage Society.

Each year the field school has focused on specific implementation techniques of cultural landscape conservation. The first field school focused on enhancing participants' skills in inventory, documentation, and presentation of the unique villages surrounding Borobudur Temple that are ignored in the Borobudur Temple conservation and development plan. The villages are Giritengah, Candirejo, and Wringinputih (Borobudur Sub-district). The second field school focused on similar techniques to prepare design guidelines for Klipoh village (Borobudur Sub-district), a ceramics village, and the third field school continued this work,

Plate 1.14: Punthuk Setumbu, the place to watch the Borobudur sunrise, which is managed by the local communities (photo: Adishakti, 2011)

with an emphasis on generating the design guidelines for Klipoh village.

After three years of concentrating on understanding cultural landscape heritage conservation issues at the micro level, in 2007 the field school focused on the various principles and issues of regional conservation planning for Borobudur. A plan by the UNESCO Office in Jakarta to hold an exhibition in Yogyakarta on the restoration of Borobudur from 20 April to 11 May 2007 encouraged the field school to participate in this important event.

The objectives of the field school program in general are:

- to give participants a comprehension understanding of the conservation and management of the cultural landscape, which includes historical buildings and settings, the cultural system, living culture, and other natural environment components
- to enhance participant skills in implementing concepts, methods, conservation processes, and landscape management in actual field cases
- to enhance participant interest in cultural landscape conservation
- to give participants direct field experience in conducting research on cultural landscape conservation.

Specific objectives emphasize enhancing participant skills in implementing cultural landscape conservation techniques, including inventory, documentation, and presentation, to generate design guidelines in a particular area.

Each program is organized for eight days, beginning with two days in Yogyakarta; the rest of the program is in Borobudur (Menoreh Mountain Range, Magelang Regency, Central Java). During the program participants stay in modest accommodation in Yogyakarta and in homestays in Candirejo village. Learning activities include lectures and international seminars, a Borobudur Heritage Trail and Sunrise Trip, a Kedu Plain trip and field survey, discussions with local communities, presentations, and cultural activities with local communities.

The field school program can learn from the local community movement to understand and formulate action on the conservation and development of *Peraturan Desa* (Village Regulation) for the Borobudur Temple Compounds area. This regulation is an effort to

Plate 1.15: Borobudur Village Tour organized by local communities (photo: Adishakti, 2004)

strengthen village conservation programs in order to solve the imbalance between conservation and development in this area.

Programs that have been successful include the Five Mountain Festival; development of villages as tourist destinations (such as Punthuk Setumbu as the place to watch the Borobudur sunrise (Plate 1.14), Klipoh as a ceramics village, Candirejo village for homestays, and Wanurejo as an arts and culture village); the Borobudur Village Tour, which offers local transportation by horse cart (Plate 1.15); the development and dissemination of the Borobudur Green Map (see Chapter 4); and capacity building for heritage conservation management (with overseas support).

Concluding remarks

Heritage conservation is a cultural movement. The total involvement of the community is an important aspect in resolving conservation through an inclusive bottom-up planning approach and people-centered management. This kind of movement has already been experienced in the Borobudur Temple Compounds. However, greater World Heritage Site conservation management may enhance the response of local communities and enthusiasm towards sustainability. Conservation management by local communities is one of the most important requirements in the management of *saujana* heritage.

2 Evolutive Conservation of Cultural Landscape

Kiyoko Kanki

Introduction

This chapter discusses how cultural landscape can be recognized by those who are involved in the lives and works inevitably related to the conservation and succession of the cultural landscape, not from the viewpoint of installable legal systems but from within inside the landscape. I have been involved with the Borobudur Field School from its inception, and have been a committee member for several conservation areas for cultural landscapes in Japan at the same time. For me, and also for my Borobudur Field School colleagues, the experiences in Borobudur and in several case study areas in Japan have been important – partly similar and partly different – and informative in identifying significant questions such as 'what is cultural landscape from the perspective of the local communities who live and work in or are related to that landscape' and 'how can lives and works coexist with the sustainability of landscapes?' So in this chapter I use several case study areas (Plate 2.1) to highlight discussion points about cultural landscape conservation.

The case study areas are:

1 Borobudur in the Kedu Plain context
2 Sacred Sites and Pilgrimage Routes in the Kii Mountain Range, in Wakayama, Nara, and Mie prefectures in Japan, listed as cultural landscape in the UNESCO World Heritage List in 2004; I was a member of the Wakayama Prefecture committee and undertook several collaborative works with local communities in several villages included in the core and buffer zones
3 Hineno-sho Ogi no Nouson Keikan (Ogi agricultural village landscape in Hineno-sho manor in medieval Japan) in Izumisano City, Osaka Prefecture, Japan, designated as an Important Cultural Landscape (National Designation) by the Ministry of Culture in 2013; I have been a committee member at Izumisano City, as well as a collaborator with local communities, for more than ten years
4 Yusu-Mizugaura no Danbata (Terrace Fields in Yusu-Mizugaura) in Uwajima City, Ehime Prefecture, Japan, designated as an Important Cultural Landscape (National Designation) by the Ministry of Culture in 2007; I have been a committee member at Uwajima City, mainly working as a field surveyor with local communities for the designation.

Plate 2.1: Case study areas for cultural landscapes: (from top row) 1 Borobudur in the Kedu Plain context; 2 Sacred Sites and Pilgrimage Routes in the Kii Mountain Range; 3 Hineno-sho Ogi no Nouson Keikan (Ogi agricultural village landscape in Hineno-sho manor in medieval Japan); 4 Yusu-Mizugaura no Danbata (Terrace Fields in Yusu-Mizugaura)(photos: Kanki)

What is cultural landscape? – from the inside

As often quoted in world heritage operational guidelines, cultural landscape is defined as 'combined works of nature and of man', while the more historic definition in the field of geography and landscape ecology seems to emphasize the ecological viewpoint, closely related to habitat and ecosystem discussions. Additionally, the domestic definition of the term in Japan seems to emphasize local industrial and lifestyle history under the cultural property law. In any case, the definition of cultural landscape is not a simple one because the relation between nature and humans is always diverse and flexible. But such diversity and flexibility is the most important key idea for the realization of a local community's activities towards creative conservation, not towards a freezing protection.

In the focus on nature and humans, cultural landscape cannot be recognized only with these physical components but also requires consideration of the manner of relationships between natural conditions and people. The conservation – or sustainable continuity – of cultural landscape should encompass not only the physical aspects of areas but also the invisible, system-thinking aspects of lives and works.

Plate 2.2 is a snapshot from Chikatsuyu village located in the Kii Mountain Range. It was taken during the new November festival initiated after the registration of the Sacred Sites and Pilgrimage Routes in the Kii Mountain Range as a World Heritage Site. The festival was started by the local community with the collaboration of professional flower arrangement experts. This house is located along the pilgrimage routes and is one of the important old traditional houses in this village. This is a beautiful, old, traditional house with a skillful flower arrangement, which can be evaluated from its physical setting, but the meanings included in this picture are far more diverse and relate to the cultural landscape of the vast area that includes the house. The materials for this flower arrangement come from the forest zones of the village, where local elders are extremely knowledgeable about the flora and fauna in each part of the forest. Flower arrangement experts and local people together create the ideas, and local people advise the type, character, and scent of materials that can be used. So this beautiful scene, with the old house and the flower arrangement, can be understood within the vast scale and recognition of the forest and mountains surrounding this village.

A tradition of this village is that local people have a deep concern for the natural conditions of the forest, and they take care to avoid adverse impacts when gathering materials. Such nature-oriented tradition is also related to this house. In his younger days, the famous painter Nonagase Banka (1889–1964) lived in the house and he was a friend of and had a sympathy for the renowned ecologist and anthropologist Minakata Kumagusu (1867–1941). Nonagase painted several pictures of the village landscape, paintings that remain as evidence of the earlier landscape that is still living and is still managed today. Minakata was one of the first initiators of the nature protection movement in Japan, and he dedicated his days in Wakayama Prefecture to the scientific observation of nature and to deep field study, as well as to detailed and characteristic anthropological studies in the Kii Mountain Range. Minakata's achievements are still highly respected by many local communities, so this house is very important. Besides the interesting features of the traditional house itself – with a well-furnished interior and an interesting plan, yard usage, and micro-environment of the site, and so on – in this one snapshot we should identify the relation among the house, the way of

Plate 2.2: Traditional house and flower arrangement expressing the cultural landscape including various stories of the village area; Chikatsuyu village, Kii Mountain Range (photo: Kanki) (Kanki 2011a)

Plate 2.3: Beautiful villages in the Kedu Plain context of Borobudur – where we should recognize and identify the diverse evaluation (photo: Kanki)

arranging flowers related to local nature, local people's awareness to nature, and the stories as told about Nonagase and Minakata, the small but beautiful festival is successful in visualizing and evaluating this relation, which can be understood by those who know the village well.

Plate 2.3 is a snapshot of hilly village areas in the Kedu Plain context of Borobudur, where we can find the old Hindu temple sites within a short walk. By visiting and experiencing the area and trying to understand what cultural landscape is, here we can not only view the very beautiful scenery but also try to evaluate the meanings that have been produced through the lives and works of the village community and the related human activities. For example, how was the location of the village and the rice paddies settled on this hilltop in the past? How is the diverse vegetation related to the local lives and works suitably in the local climate? Are there any interesting stories about the old Hindu temples that have been told among the local people?

In answer to the question, 'what is cultural landscape?', I propose that cultural landscape is landscape that can be understood with the identification of accumulated diverse evaluations, which is important and sometimes essential to understand the manner of relationships between nature and humankind. It is frequently the case that the landscapes of a certain area are studied by analyzing several physical and spatial data sets via an observational approach, while local communities have advantages in trying to find the various relationships heuristically in their well-acquainted landscape anytime in their daily lives via the approach 'from the inside'.

Value systems with many relationships in cultural landscape

Cultural landscape can be identified with diverse evaluation. It is a rather natural idea, but is important to be noted, especially in dealing with areas with outstanding evaluated heritages. Basically, cultural landscape can be explained from many viewpoints in human and nature systems, such as geological, geomorphological, hydrological, botanical, zoological, architectural, or space-compositional systems, or others with human actions. Human actions are likened to the value settings that can be the motivation for actions and to practicing ways that can be the systems for implementation of the actions (Figure 2.1). For the sustainability of cultural landscape – and the sustainability of relationships, therefore – the objective of conservation is linked to the social/cultural aspects of the relationships.

Value systems – the idea that tries to treat the evaluation of cultural landscape according to the relationships and linkage of physical and social/cultural aspects – can have more than one relationship that can be treated as a value system in a certain area. Among several relationships that can be found in a certain area, some are flexibly substituted in a certain manner, some are strongly continued, and some are newly introduced in a well-examined way – namely every relationship has its own characteristics (Figure 2.2).

Cultural landscape is the outcome of the relationships, not just the assembled physical components. The protection of selected components is not effective enough, not appreciated in some cases, while social and cultural aspects of the relationships are essential. Thus conservation is more likely to be closely related to the initiatives and empowerments of related people, and here it is necessary to be aware of the diverse evaluation of cultural landscape.

In the case of areas with outstanding and important cultural heritages, such as world

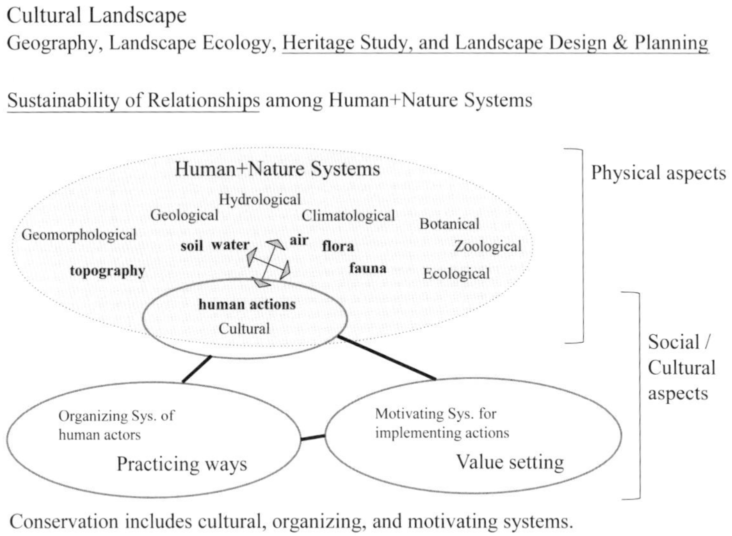

Figure 2.1: Relationships in cultural landscape – physical and social/cultural aspects

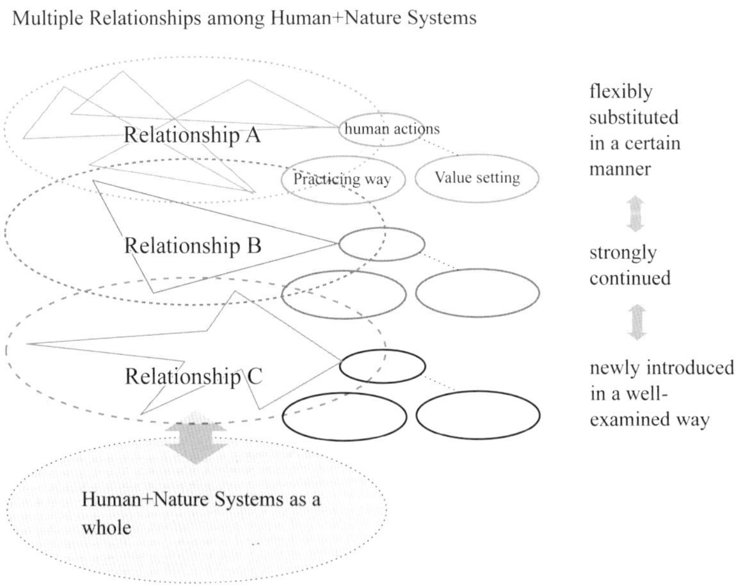

Figure 2.2: Value systems of a certain area with several relationships

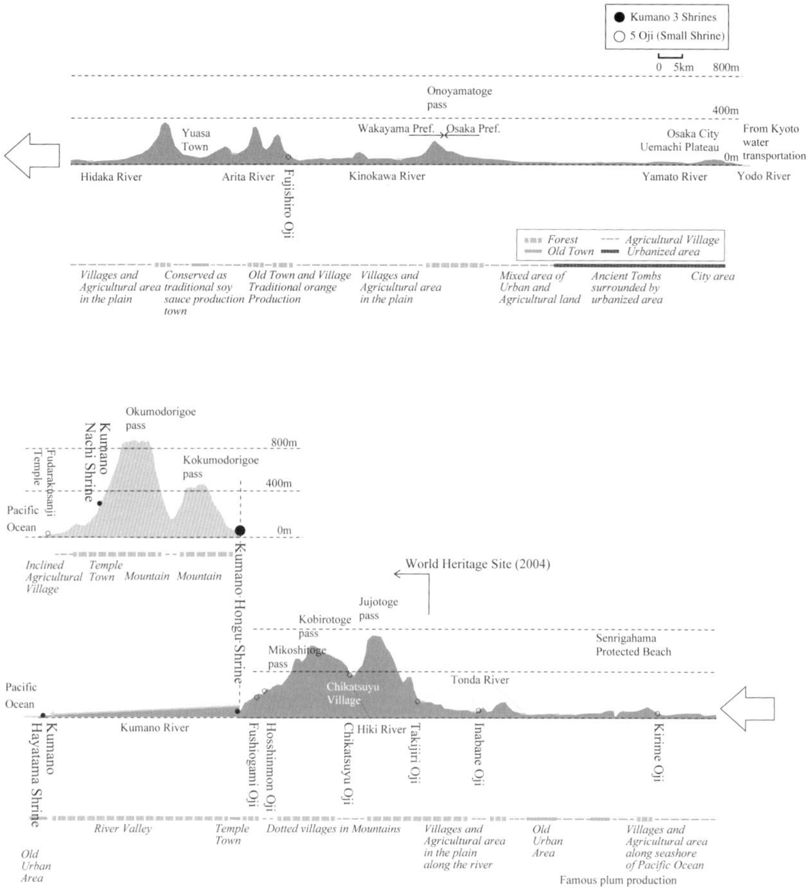

Figure 2.3: Sacred Sites and Pilgrimage Routes in the Kii Mountain Range – topographic features of the pilgrimage routes (Kumano–Nakahechi route) (Kanki, 2011a)

heritage or nationally designated heritage, some relationships are highly evaluated and the documentation for such heritage provides an explanation of the authenticity. In such cases we must be careful to pay attention to other relationships that exist in the same area, since other relationships also provide authenticity.

In the example of the Kii Mountain Range, the world heritage Sacred Sites and Pilgrimage Routes in the Kii Mountain Range comprise several important sacred places, including old shrines and long-distance pilgrimage routes from the city areas to the sacred places. The most important relationship for this cultural landscape heritage is generally regarded as its religious history and historic composition of pilgrimages. The long-distance pilgrimage

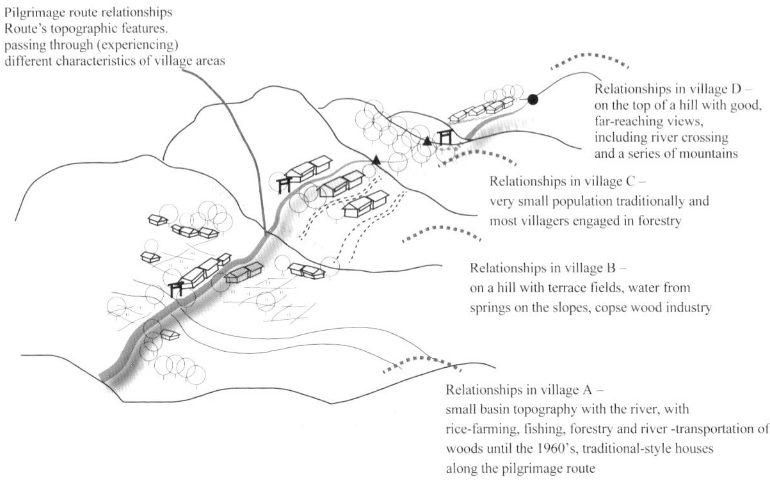

Figure 2.4: Pilgrimage route and village areas – outstanding and locally evaluated relationships (Kanki, 2011a)

routes start from Kyoto, once the capital city, and run through various landscapes – cities, villages, farmland, forestry land, natural forest, rivers, and so on (at present, parts of these pilgrimage routes that retain their good condition are included in the world heritage site). The land use changes from place to place, but the geographic composition of the routes – and the experience of walking long distances with many topographical and urban–rural features, artificial and natural environments, and so on – still remains (Figure 2.3). We can find small shrines like milestones along the routes and every small shrine has kept its name and meaning for the pilgrims. The religious history here combines ideas of animism and Buddhism, which respect the natural phenomena strongly. The climate is warm and precipitation is high, so the forest is vital and water resources are rich, and in the mountainous topography the combined works of humans and nature make it easy for pilgrims – now mostly hikers and walkers – to appreciate that nature might be a great thing to be respected.

However, in the Kii Mountain Range there exist other important relationships to be evaluated nationally, locally, or even individually. For example, each village along the routes holds its own history and environment, where we can find individual characteristics and traditions. Let us see Figure 2.4 which shows a part of the route. One village in a small basin topography with a rather wide river has rice farming, fishing, and forestry, and had river transportation until the 1960s, and has traditional-style houses along the pilgrim routes that were once used as inns for the pilgrims. Another village is located on the terrace topography of a hill, with terrace fields and water from springs; it had a small-scale copse wood industry until the 1950s and has characteristic traditional-style houses that guard against heavy rain. Another village traditionally had a very small population and most of the villagers engaged

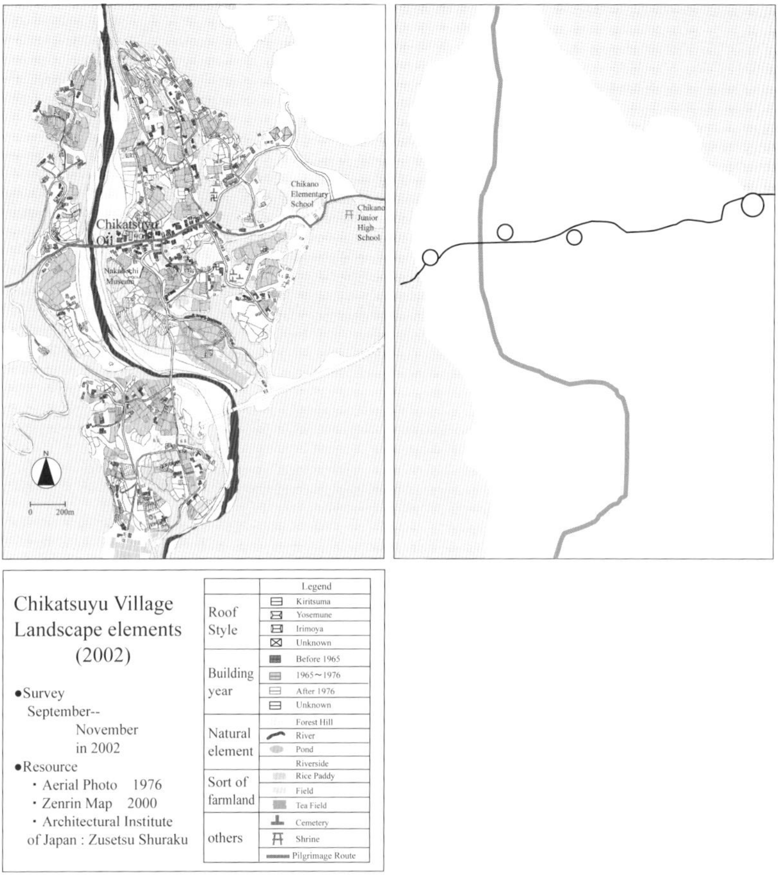

Figure 2.5: Village A: (left) map of landscape composition of land and buildings classified according to use; (right) closely related properties for religious context of the pilgrimage route (Hirata 2003)

in forestry, but around 1970 habitation in the village was halted by a public policy for the restructuring of small villages (the villagers now commute from the new settlement area to the forestry works). Another village on top of a hill has far-reaching views that take in a river crossing and a series of mountains. As such, each village's characteristics and traditions are important, and each village aims to maintain an attractive village landscape and the cultural traditions of local industries and lifestyles. Pilgrimage routes pass through such village areas, so the route is a composition of the different relationships of villages.

From the viewpoint of inhabitants in the village areas, maintaining properties closely related to the pilgrimage routes (Figure 2.5, right) does not always show the conservation

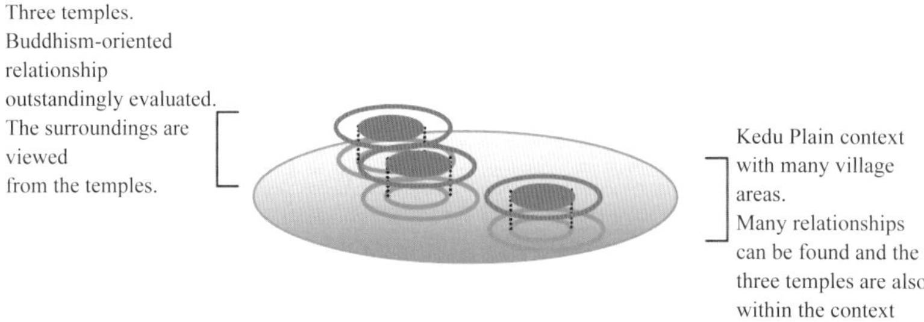

Figure 2.6: Borobudur value system (Kanki, 2012)

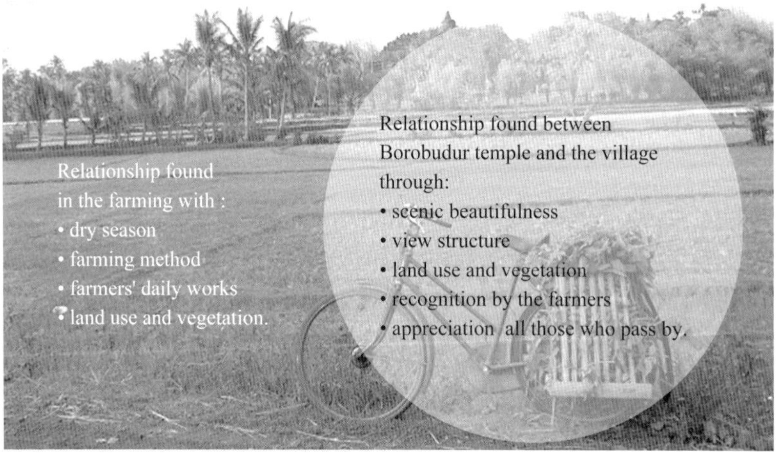

Figure 2.7: Sample of relationships in the Kedu Plain context (photo: Kanki)

policy of the more diverse village area (Figure 2.5, left). It is necessary to consider the many kinds of relationships within the areas that are directly related to daily activities. The village is actually beautiful (Plate 2.1: 2, left) but its characteristics are evaluated locally or nationally, so there are almost no descriptions about them in the documentation for the world heritage nomination. To return to the value system idea (Figure 2.2), from the viewpoint of the inhabitants in the village areas, the value system is composed of the outstanding religious-

Plate 2.4: Ogi village – river terrace topography and land use distribution (photo: Kanki)

Plate 2.5: Ogi village – traditional houses constructed in modern and contemporary times (photo: Kanki)

oriented relationship of the pilgrimage route, as well as locally important relationships in villages. In total, this value system with many relationships is meaningful to maintain the attractive village areas of the pilgrimage route, and to maintain the cultural landscape of the pilgrimage route.

In the case of Borobudur within the Kedu Plain context, the three main Buddhist temples and the buffer zone are listed on the World Heritage List as the Borobudur Temple Compounds. The vast Kedu Plain context area within a basin topography is surrounded by mountains and hills. When we view Borobudur within the Kedu Plain context as cultural landscape, we need to know and study the relationships in the vast area related to the three temples. Here we can well understand the meaningfulness of the activities of the village communities for the identification of its attractiveness, of the green map activities by non-profit organizations, and of the Borobudur Field School activities (Figures 2.6 and 2.7).

Accumulation by time – time axis layers

Another discussion point is the time axis layers of cultural landscape. A cultural landscape is formulated over a long time through history. In some cases of cultural landscape, a certain historic focus point is regarded as important. But, as above, the value system of a cultural landscape includes several relationships to be evaluated, so the long time history should be examined along with the value system idea.

Hineno-sho Ogi no Nouson Keikan (Ogi agricultural village landscape in Hineno-sho manor in medieval Japan) was designated as an Important Cultural Landscape (National Designation) by the Ministry of Culture, with an evaluation as an evolved landscape from the medieval time. Hineno-sho is the old name of the large region in the southern part of Osaka Prefecture that was settled in medieval times, and several original documents and paintings about this region still survive, so we can identify present situations as similar to the medieval times by such evidence. There are several archeologically important sites in

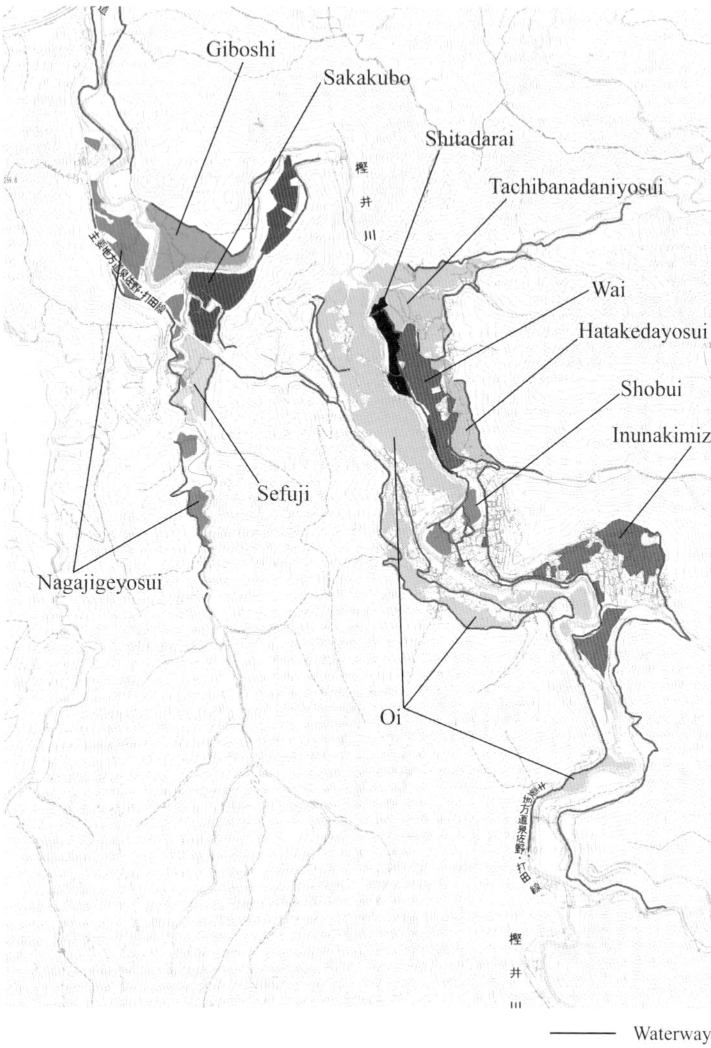

Figure 2.8: Locations of irrigation waterways and irrigated fields since medieval times (Kanki, 2011b, Izumisano City Board of Education, 2008)

the region and some were designated in a different category as cultural property before the Important Cultural Landscape designation.

My colleagues and I began preparatory surveys to identify the cultural landscape of Ogi village. Ogi village is in a valley topography within a hilly district, and retains an agricultural land use and large open spaces located outside the urbanized area of Izumisano City. The

Plate 2.6: The material and structure of the waterways – not the structure itself but the three-dimensional location of the waterways – are significant and originated in medieval times (photo: Kanki) (Kanki, 2011b)

outlook of Ogi village is traditional, but closer inspection shows that most of the traditional houses and temple buildings were constructed after the modern time (the oldest in the latter half of the pre-modern era). Of course, we can find many newly constructed or transformed structures in the village, but while the total impression of the village is well harmonized, it is not straightly original from the medieval time.

Plate 2.4 shows the valley topography and terrace land form, and Plate 2.5 shows houses of different ages in a harmonized group. Specifically, we can confirm that the houses and buildings in Ogi village are built in a traditional style but the outlook of the village is far more recent than medieval times. The medieval time is ancient compared with the visible components.

So, we started considering the time axis idea in this village to identify the medieval time-related relationships in this cultural landscape. We examined the formulation time lines of many parts of this village.

The southern part of Osaka Prefecture including Ogi village is known for its irrigation systems, which comprise small rivers, many ponds, and long waterways. In Ogi village the basic topography comprises the valley and the river at the bottom of the valley. There was a relative shortage of irrigation water from the small rivers, so the village had to be constructed as a series of terraces and irrigation water was drawn from the upper stream of the river. This topographic setting, the distribution of the waterways, and the location of irrigated fields near each waterway have not been readily changed in this special location because the slightest

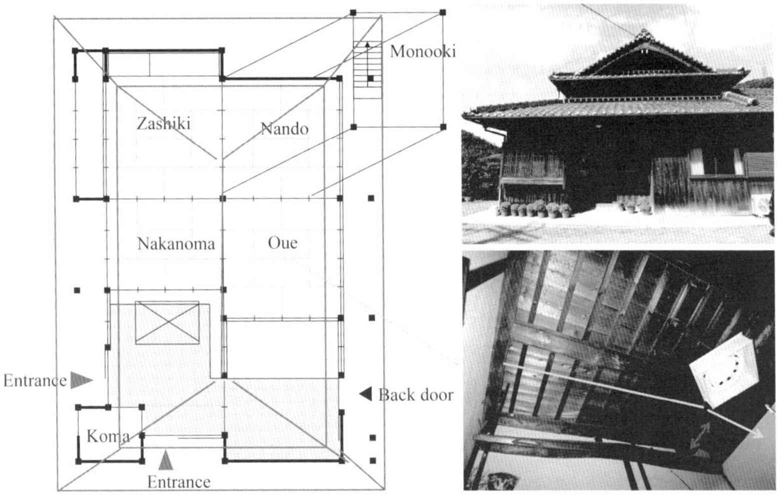

Notes: Zashiki, the Japanese-style room traditionally formed and furnished for greeting guests and for family ceremonies, usually located facing the front garden and with a good environment; this name is generally used all over Japan. Nakanoma, the neighboring room to zashiki (naka means 'the middle' and seems to indicate the room's location between zashiki and the entrance); this name is a rather locally used one but not rare. Oue, the family living room (ue means 'on the floor' and this name seems to indicate one step higher than the entrance space which has no floor); this name is locally used in this region. Nando, the storeroom; generally used all over Japan. Koma, the small room; this small room at the entrance is a special style of the traditional house in this region, so the name is locally used (ko means 'small' and ma means 'room'). Monooki, another name for storeroom; generally used all over Japan.

Figure 2.9: Typical plan of traditional houses until around 1960 (Izumisano City Board of Education, 2008)

change can result in a change of water levels and failure to distribute water to the fields. The name of each waterway remains the same as the name that can be found in the original documents from medieval times. The materials and structure of the waterways are very sound, and are fabricated with contemporary open pipes with reinforced concrete. So we did not evaluate the structure itself, but we did evaluate the special, three-dimensional shape of the topography and waterways, and identified the locations as succeeding and originated from medieval times (Figure 2.8).

Through surveys of traditional houses, it became clear that houses constructed until around 1960 had a common floor plan (Figure 2.9), while the structures are classified in three types (Plate 2.7). Today, the contemporary type with two stories prevails but we can still see common characteristics, mainly in the roofs, so the total outlook has a certain harmony. Therefore, we can evaluate the houses as part of the village landscape and as having a certain

Plate 2.7: Types of traditional houses and common characteristics: (top row from left) oldest type till around 1910, typical half two-story till 1960, typical flat till 1960; (bottom row from left) contemporary type with two stories, common characteristics from oldest type till contemporary times
(Izumisano City Board of Education, 2008)

relationship, but they are not from medieval times.

So we determined the time axis layer idea for this cultural landscape.

The basic valley topography, including irrigation waterways and the land use and form of agricultural fields, is highly evaluated as originating from medieval times and is identified in its designation as an Important Cultural Landscape. Ogi village has three neighborhood, each with its own temple, which is also used as the meeting room. The temple locations originate from the medieval temple locations, as proved by an archeological study. In this way, the three-dimensional special composition of the village forms a cultural landscape with relation to the medieval time, which, with enough attention, we can recognize and experience. At the same time, the traditional houses and the types of products from the fields are characteristic but relatively new and transformable compared to the topographic system. So we identify the new and transformable parts separately and set such relationships to be managed through the communities' activities and initiatives (Figure 2.10).

Thus, a cultural landscape can be recognized as the accumulation of time through a long history (Figure 2.11). In the case of Ogi village, the medieval time layer is special and can be examined by several kinds of evidence under rather strict regulation as cultural landscape, but, at the same time, modern and contemporary time layers are also characteristic and transformable, and are managed by the community. Here I would like to emphasize that meaningful time axis layers can be drawn for any cultural landscape, and if part of the layers are especially important we can set different policies for the different time layers.

In the case of Borobudur within the Kedu Plain context, the time layers can be adapted

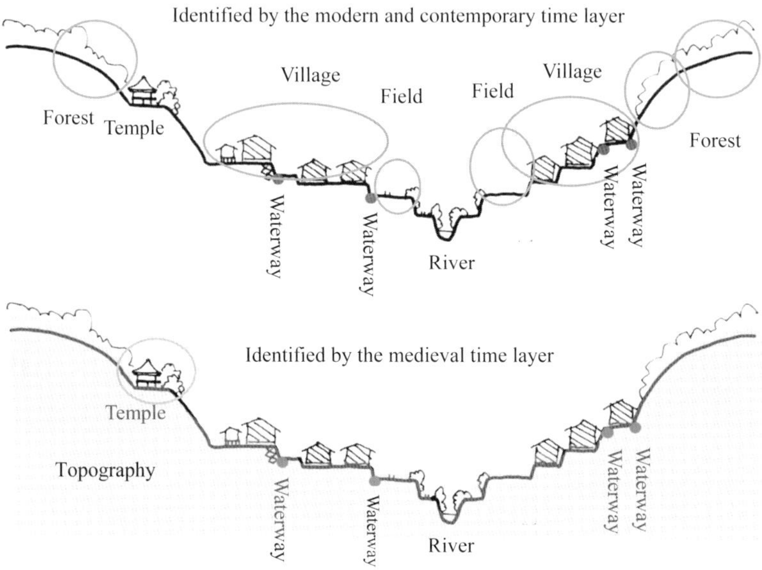

Figure 2.10: Cultural landscape with two different time axis systems (Izumisano City Board of Education, 2008) (Kanki, 2011b)

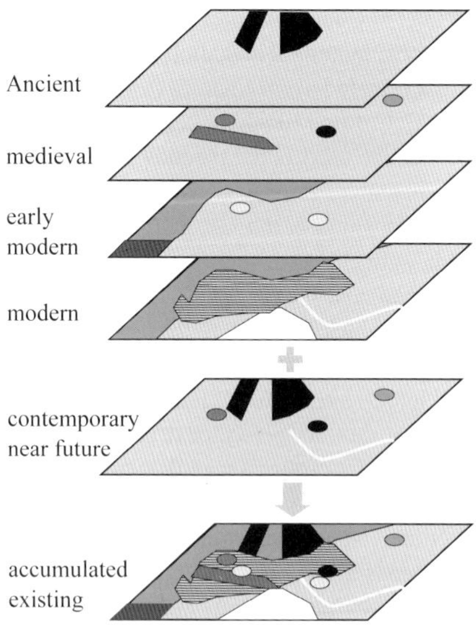

Figure 2.11: Cultural landscape formulation through accumulation of time

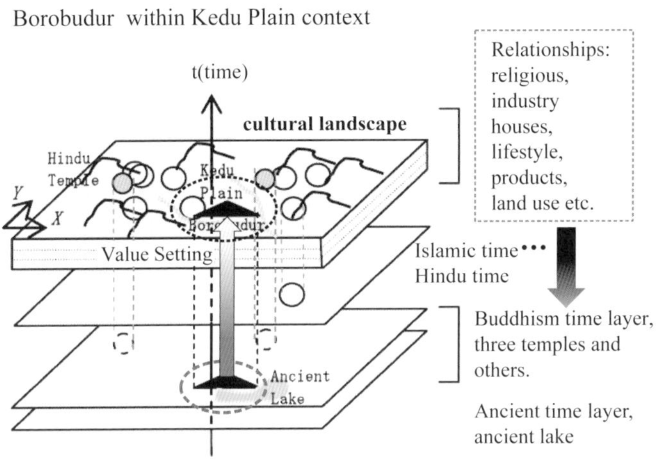

Figure 2.12: Borobudur within the Kedu Plain context time layers (Kanki, 2012)

in thinking about cultural landscape recognition. The Borobudur Temple Compounds are especially evaluated in the Buddhism era. At the same time, we can identify many relationships in the contemporary time layer, and geological aspects, such as through ancient lake research, can be identified within the ancient time layer. By picking up relationships and ordering them through the time layers, we can identify the Borobudur temples in the Buddhism time layers; namely, we can relativize the Borobudur temples inside the cultural landscape of the Kedu Plain context (Figure 2.12).

Evolutive conservation – dynamic authenticity with value system

Having recognized the cultural landscape with a value system and time layers, we have to find a way for conservation. From the value system idea, conservation is not the freezing protection of a landscape's physical components but the continuing relationships that comprise the value system. This means that according to the relationships, conservation sometimes includes certain transformations. Here I would like to introduce the idea of evolutive conservation (first introduced by the Architectural Institute of Japan Sub-committee for Rural Cultural Landscape), whose meaning is the conservation of cultural landscape, but including certain transformations while being sustainable as a total value system. Figure 2.13 shows the scheme of evolutive conservation. There are several relationships in a cultural landscape, and some are likely to be flexible while some are likely to be stable. If relationship A changed in a certain way and had some impact on the other relationships, we should examine the change with reference to the affected relationships.

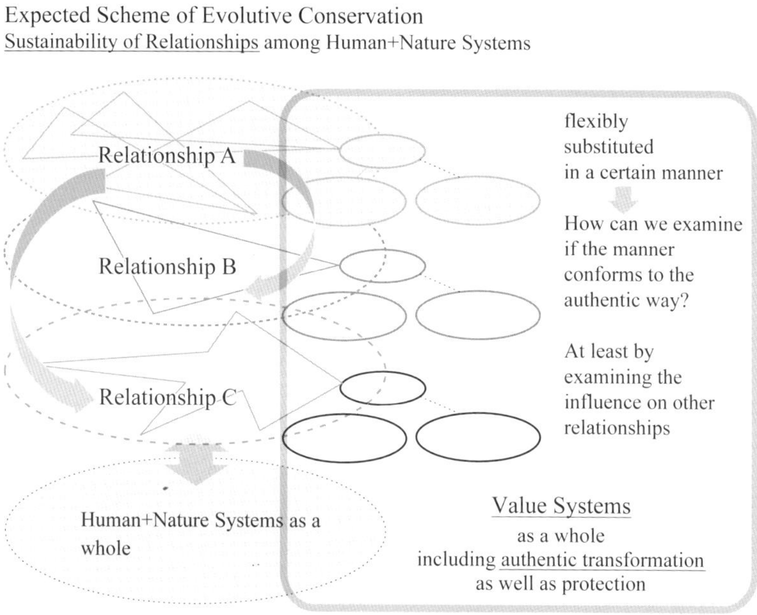

Figure 2.13: Value system and evolutive conservation – examining the change of relationship A with reference to other relationships

Yusu-Mizugaura no Danbata (Terrace Fields in Yusu-Mizugaura) in Uwajima City, designated as an Important Cultural Landscape (National Designation) by the Ministry of Culture in 2007, might be one good example of evolutive conservation. The cultural landscape here can be recognized with several relationships related to agriculture, fisheries, raw silk production in the past, the small food industry, and so on. The special terrace fields are constructed on steep land with stone walls that have many small voids (Plate 2.8). This structure works well in the early spring, with the sun warming the soil, and the dry conditions (watering is difficult) and sea wind support the present production of potatoes. To maintain the steep terraces, farmers must repair the walls frequently and remove the grass that grows in the voids of the walls. Such frequent and heavy maintenance work by the farmers is an essential relationship for the terrace field cultivation, and this relationship is most important in Yusu-Mizugaura as a cultural landscape.

Potato production is not very traditional here, and sweet potato used to be more common until recently. Hence, potato production is a drastic transformation of the relationship for the terrace fields, and might be an example of evolutive conservation. The present potato production is successful, very tasty, and of high quality and is very popular with consumers, although the quantity of production is limited by the fields' small area. In the relationship to the local industry, it is often the case that agricultural evolution might be expected and is

Plate 2.8: Terrace fields of Yusu-Mizugaura, and stone wall with small voids that require frequent maintenance (photos: Kanki)

suitable to the cultural landscape – it is transformable but meaningful.

The success of this case can be examined through the impact of the transformation of production to the relationships. Introducing the potato in early spring is more suitable to the structure of the terrace fields than traditional sweet potato. The decrease of sweet potato resulted in the decrease of a certain food culture, a kind of sweet potato cake, but the impact is more positive that simply the income from the terrace fields because farmers have been motivated to cultivate the fields despite the heavy maintenance work. This potato production is limited only to the early spring harvest and, in this manner, soil degradation does not occur and the harvest continues every year. Since the designation as an Important Cultural Landscape, some villagers now engage in new potato product development, such as potato-distilled spirits, and some are searching for other successful products suitable to the structural characteristics of the terrace fields.

In this case, the authenticity of cultural landscape is not limited to the sorts of products, but is more related to the structural and conditional character under local environment. When the farmers repair the stone walls, it is often the case that they use and add any type of stone and blocks, but the meaningful character of the stone walls is in the specific high heat, the voids, the steepness, and the maintenance works. The voids are probably necessary to absorb the tiny slides of the very steep terraces. In this way, authenticity sometimes depends on the relationships themselves to support the value system. Here I would like to introduce the idea of dynamic authenticity as relationship–conservation oriented. In this case the dynamic authenticity involves most of the structural and conditional characters of the terrace fields, not

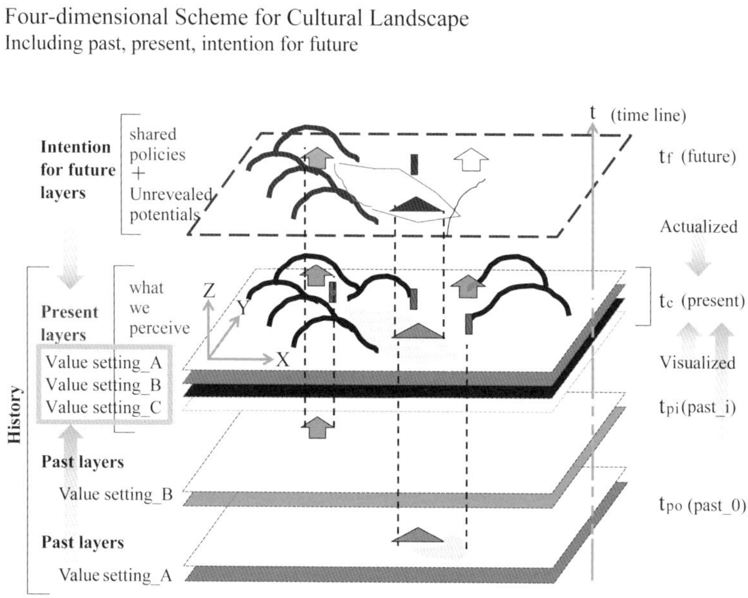

Figure 2.14: Four-dimensional scheme for cultural landscape as a whole

the type of product.

The evolutive conservation idea includes future intentions – what the inhabitants should do for the next time layer (Figure 2.14).

Figure 2.14 illustrates the time layers, including relationships (value settings), and introduces the future time layer. The future time layer is the intention of the inhabitants and related players, and expects some relationships will be changed or kept, or a brand new relationship will be introduced. In this scheme, in which the intention can be examined, the future agenda might be more evolutive.

Cultural landscape field school as a methodology for the actualization of evolutive conservation

The Architectural Institute of Japan Sub-committee for Rural Cultural Landscape has held a Cultural Landscape Field School three times since 2010. This is a compact, customized application of the Borobudur Field School. The first school was held in the Kii Mountain Range to support the inhabitants to repair quickly important traditional house and to improve

Lecturers: K. Suginaka (Historian), S. Yamamoto (Museum Curator), S. Yamamoto (Pref. Gov.), H. Koura (Planning/Univ.), T. Sakamoto (Local Expert), K. Tane (Local Community), K. Kanki (Planning/Univ.)

Preparation of wood

Professional carpenter's school

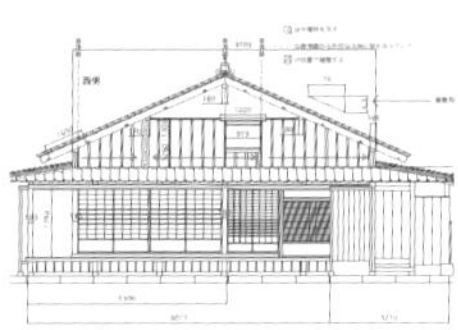

West elevation to be repaired (Akashi Tech HighSchool/ Kudoh Labo.)

Tools, materials, and styles and methods are original in this village

Emergent repair of the aging mud wall, Measurement practice, Surveying history from old material, Field survey

Figure 2.15: Cultural Landscape Field School in Kii Mountain Range, 2010 (Kanki, 2011a)

the recognition of the cultural landscape value system (Figure 2.15). The school is mainly for students more than twenty years old and has several instructors and support from the local community. It includes a field survey program, landscape management experience, and lectures plus dialogues. Repair work is instructed by professional carpenters. Local community members are invited as lecturers and experts on cultural landscape, as well as professional planners and landscape designers.

The carpentry work, lectures, field surveys, accommodation in the village, consumption of local food, and dialogue with the local community intuitively enhance the understanding of cultural landscape as a whole and the understanding of relationships evaluated in cultural landscape.

Those programs – lectures from the different academic active research fields, contents of works and surveys, and cooperative preparations of the related settings – had played the roles of introduction to the participants as well as local community what sorts of relationships can be found in the village landscapes. To prepare, operate, and collaborate on the programs are a certain step for the evolutive conservation by understanding a certain part of the value systems including the relationships and time layers of the area through the experiences of human interactions.

Evolutive conservation involves understanding the value system with relationships and time layers and the intended future time layers by examining each relationship. The field school is a tentative, trial event, but such program can be treated as the first practicing way for thinking about suitable evolutive conservation for the cultural landscape.

By recognizing more and more relationships, we are able to perceive the landscape as an integrated unity of diversity. Such perception will help us to consider if our new action might be meaningful to the landscape. Cultural landscape will be kept dynamically authentic in such active ways.

3 The Cultural Landscape of Borobudur

Borobudur villages – continuity and change

Dwita Hadi Rahmi

Introduction

Exploring the area of Borobudur is interesting. From the viewpoint of cultural landscape, Borobudur is the expression of the evolution of human cultural values, norms, and attitudes towards the land. This area has strong historic values, archaeological sources, special geographical conditions, natural systems, and changing landscape and sociocultural processes which are still ongoing. Geographically, the Borobudur area is a plains area located in the Kedu basin among several volcanoes (Mount Merapi, Mount Merbabu, Mount Sumbing) and mountains (Mount Tidar, Mount Telomoyo, Mount Andong), and the Menoreh Mountain Range. A compound of three Buddhist temples, Borobudur Temple, Mendut Temple, and Pawon Temple, inscribed by UNESCO as a World Cultural Heritage Site in 1991 (UNESCO World Heritage 2003), is in the middle of the area and is the center of the cultural landscape.

The Borobudur area itself is a fertile area with beautiful views from its villages and rice fields. Besides Borobudur, Mendut, and Pawon temples, this area is also rich in archaeological assets from the Hindu period, including Selogriyo Temple, Ngawen Temple, and Asu Temple. The Progo River, Elo River, and other small rivers flow through the area. Village people in the Borobudur area have a unique social and cultural life, including their traditions, beliefs, way of life, and arts. Many local cultures indirectly reflect the relation between nature and humans, such as the belief in a mountain's soul. The biodiversity of the area is essential to the life of the local community and contains ecological values. The relation between natural and village cultural potencies creates a unique and qualified cultural landscape between the villages and all the Borobudur area. The Javanese philosophy of the local community, which believes in a balanced and harmonious life with nature, is the base of the village cultural landscape form. Subconsciously, by that life philosophy, the village communities maintain the cultural landscape.

With population growth, development pressures, and modernity, changes to the physical and sociocultural quality of life have been experienced in the Borobudur villages. The absence of the concept of Borobudur cultural landscape, combined with a lack of policy or clear plan regarding development of the area, has increased pressure on environmental and cultural changes. These weaknesses result from a lack of understanding by the community and the government about the valuable assets of Borobudur, and those assets tend to be forgotten. Attention by the government, and also by the community, focuses only on the temples and the surrounding area, and not on other assets of the Borobudur area, such as its natural beauty, villages and their life, and small temples (Soeroso 2007; Adishakti 2008).

This chapter is based on research on Borobudur cultural landscape heritage and describes the cultural landscape of villages in the Borobudur area. Data and information for this research were compiled from in-depth interviews with the local community, field observation, and secondary data in the form of maps, Borobudur history, pictures, and related literatures. Two approach methods were used – historic interpretation of the Borobudur area and qualitative research that focused on contemporary phenomenon. It is hoped that this chapter can provide an understanding of the high value of the cultural landscape of Borobudur villages.

The history of Borobudur villages

Borobudur has a long history of settlement. The history of the settlements began with the Old Mataram Kingdom in Central Java between 732–929 AD. This kingdom had two religions, Hindu and Buddhist Mahayana, as documented in archaeological remains, which include 112 inscriptions and thousands of old buildings, such as temples and places of worship (Darmosoetopo 1998). In the Kedu basin, where Borobudur is located, four inscriptions have been found. The oldest one, Tuk Mas, was inscribed by the Kalingga Kingdom in 500 AD, and the three other inscriptions – Canggal or Gunung Pring (732 AD), Poh (905 AD), and Mantyasih (907 AD) – were inscribed during the period of the Old Mataram Kingdom. Tuk Mas tells about a fertile plain area located between two holy rivers and surrounded by holy mountains. The assumption was that there were settlements in the Kedu area before the inscription was written, and it is also known that those settlements were located in the plains area around the rivers (Progo River and Elo River), with mountains as the holy places. This inscription also leads to the assumption that there were human settlements in the Kedu area with rice paddy plantations and activities of worship. It was believed that mountains were considered as holy places, and plains areas near rivers were chosen for settlements because rivers were considered as a source of life (Moehkardi 2008).

The other three inscriptions tell about settlements (villages), places of worship, mountains, farms, and rivers. The Poh inscription tells of settlements in Kedu, the Rumasan and Nyu hamlets in Poh village, which was located in the Kiniwang area, whereas the Mantyasih inscription tells about Kuning village. These two inscriptions also tell about two holy rivers and mountains in the Kedu area. Again, the assumption is that there were settlements in the Kedu area before the inscriptions were written, and that those settlements were located in the plains area around the rivers, with Mount Merapi as the holy place (Moehkardi 2008). Before the Poh and Mantyasih inscriptions, the Canggal inscription from the Old Mataram Kingdom told about 'rice paddy' and 'worship places' in the Kedu area. This inscription leads to the assumption that there were human settlements in the Kedu area with rice paddy plantation and activities of worship.

The history of the Borobudur villages can also be traced from the origins of their names (toponyms). A village toponym can provide meanings about the physical condition of the area at that time or the time before the occurrence of the villages. Names of villages in Borobudur were in Javanese. From an old map, this research tried to interpret the meaning of village names around Borobudur Temple, for example:

- Giritengah – *giri* means mountain
- Pragawati – *praga* means river
- Kaliduren – *kali* means river
- Bumisegoro – *segoro* means sea; *bumi* means earth
- Sabrangrowo – *sabrang* means cross over; *rowo* means swamp
- Tanjungsari – *tanjung* means peninsula
- Barabudur – *barabudur* means Borobudur
- Candirejo – *candi* means temple; *rejo* means wealthy
- Gopalan – *gopala* is a name of a giant stone statue as a gate guard.

Village toponyms in the Borobudur area indicate four areas of settlement locations: (1) mountain slope areas, (2) river edge areas, (3) extinct ancient lake areas, and (4) areas around Borobudur Temple.

Another way to trace the existence of Borobudur settlements is from the history of the construction of temples, especially Borobudur Temple. In the study area, there are a number of archaeological remains in the form of temples and red brick buildings that may have been places of worship. Today, three temples still exist – Borobudur Temple in Borobudur village, Pawon Temple in Wanurejo village, and Mendut Temple in Mendut village. Indications show that community settlements occurred and developed before the temples were erected between the seventh to eighth centuries, because temples and buildings for worship were built for community religious activities. It can be imagined that the buildings were an important part of the life of the village community and the authority of the kingdom.

In the past, it seemed that the construction of temples by a kingdom was perfectly designed. Temples were built close to the settlements because of the need for a lot of construction labor. So, at the time when Borobudur Temple was erected in the ninth century, areas around it had already been inhabited. During the construction, several hamlets were used for construction activities; for example, a hamlet for collecting stones from the river; a place for the artists to carve the temple reliefs and ornaments; a place to create holy Buddha statues and conduct spiritual activities; a place for the stone-carving artists to live; and public kitchens for the preparation of food for the laborers. The use of hamlets in the Borobudur Temple construction means that community settlements had previously existed. Archaeological remains, particularly Hindu and Buddhist temples, show the high culture of the community at that time, such as the high quality of art and design of the temples; the ability to use the simple construction technology; and the philosophy of those temples. The use of the villages around the temples for construction processes shows the command of the kingdom authority.

The existence and development of settlements were also influenced by the fertile plains area around Borobudur. The fertile lands are the result of the soil type from Mount Merapi, Mount Sumbing, and Mount Tidar and a number of rivers that flow through the area, as well as soil from an ancient lake. The fertile Borobudur land was used by the community as agricultural land in the form of *sawah* (paddy fields). In the Kedu area, where Borobudur is located, agricultural activity has long been conducted. In the Hindu era, from the beginning of the tenth century until the sixteenth century, *sawah* was dominated by various types of plants (polyculture) to maintain the natural tropical environment and an ecosystem with plant diversity. This polycultural system ended in the eighteenth century when the Dutch colonial rulers adopted a monoculture system with only one type of plant (paddy) in *sawah* at one time.

Plate 3.1: (left) a farmer uses cows to plow the soil; (right) a corn field and some people serving food (Krom 1927)

Agriculture activity in Borobudur is depicted in temple reliefs. A Karmawibangga relief (panel number I Ba., Number 336, in Krom 1927) shows a farmer using two cows to plow the soil (Plate 3.1, left), indicating that the community knew techniques of soil preparation. Another Karmawibangga relief (panel number O.122 in Krom 1927) shows a corn field and some people serving food (Plate 3.1, right).

The agricultural activity of old Java, including in Borobudur, has continued since the Hindu Mataram Kingdom, or possibly before that era, through the Dutch colonial era, and until today. The type of land use, traditional farming techniques, and seasonal dependency have been much the same. Based on the existence of the Borobudur Temple and the flow of events in Borobudur, the history of the development of the Borobudur settlements and agricultural activity can be divided into four periods (Rahmi 2012): (1) before the construction of Borobudur Temple, (2) at the time of the construction of Borobudur Temple, (3) after the construction of Borobudur Temple until the second restoration (1973–79), and (4) after the second restoration (after 1979) until now (Table 3.1).

Cultural landscape of Borobudur villages

As mentioned in many books on cultural landscape, the terms 'culture' and 'landscape' carry many meanings, explanations, and understandings and create many possibilities. Two perspectives may suit the study of cultural landscape of Borobudur villages:

> Cultural landscape has both a physical dimension – traces of human activity in the landscape as humans have influenced and modified 'nature' through time; and a cognitive dimension – the cultural meanings that humans attach to their physical surroundings, both natural components and human components... The way in which the physical surroundings, whether of natural or human provenance, are structured and shaped in people's minds begins with the naming of landscape features and places, itself a very culture-specific practice. Hence cultural landscape is more a perspective than a 'thing'. (Jones 2003:32)

Table 3.1: Four periods of the development of Borobudur settlements and agriculture activity (Rahmi 2012)

Historical components	Before the construction of Borobudur Temple	At the time of the construction of Borobudur Temple	After the construction of Borobudur Temple until second restoration (1973–79)	After second restoration (after 1979) until now
Settlements (villages)	a. Settlements have existed, spreading from the Borobudur area. An inscription dated 500 AD states the existence of settlements	a. A number of settlements in the form of hamlets. b. The location of villages tends to be around water sources and in fertile land. c. Several hamlets are used for Borobudur Temple construction. d. The life of the traditional village community is depicted in temple reliefs.	a. The number of settlements increases. Many hamlets merge into villages with clear administrative borders. b. In the seventeenth century the Kedu area becomes a warehouse of rice to provide food for soldiers.	a. Two villages (Kenayan and Ngaran) are moved and the land reused as a park surrounding Borobudur Temple. b. More tourism facilities (hotels, restaurants, art shops) are built in the Borobudur Temple area. c. At present, villages are more densely concentrated and the village scape has change a lot, especially villages adjacent to Borobudur Temple
Agricultural activities	a. Traditional farming activities are conducted by the community. They open forests for farmlands b. Types of farming systems are *sawah*, *gaga* (dry farmland), plantation. c. Agriculture land is dominated by various kinds of vegetation, including trees.	a. Traditional farming activities are the main occupation of the village community. b. More land is used as agricultural land. c. Types of farming systems are *sawah*, *gaga*, plantation. d. Various kinds of vegetation are planted in the agricultural land. e. Farmers depend on seasons.	a. Traditional farming activities are the main occupation of the village community. b. Types of farming systems are *sawah*, *gaga*, plantation. c. Since seventeenth century *sawah* is cultivated with one type of plant (paddy). d. Agricultural land is increasingly widespread. e. Traditional farming techniques are still practiced, although there are irrigation systems. f. Farmers still depend on seasons.	a. Traditional farming activities remain the main occupation of the village community until today. b. Types of farming systems are *sawah*, *gaga*, plantation. c. Traditional farming techniques are still practiced, although irrigation systems are also used. d. Farmers still depended on seasons. e. Agricultural land is decreasing, caused by changing function.

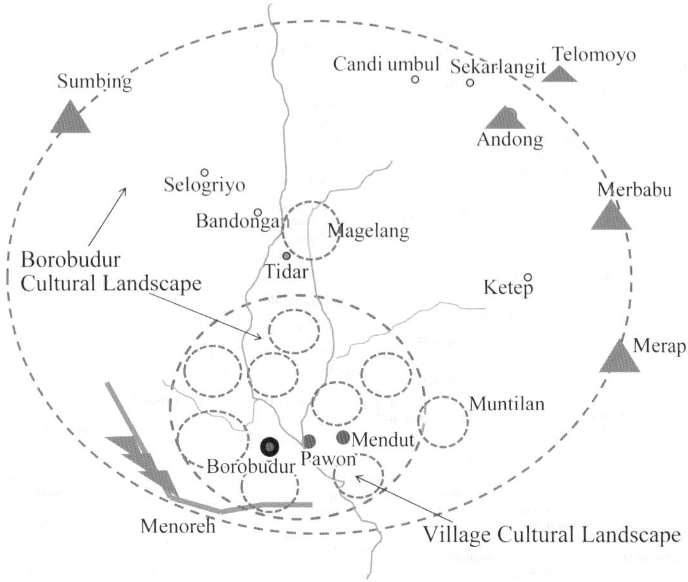

Figure 3.1: Borobudur area with villages as cultural landscapes (Rahmi 2012)

> Cultural landscape is the mirror of the society reflecting all the attributes, features and characteristics of our existence by means of spaces created based on the knowledge acquired in time. (Calcatinge 2012:76).

Thus a cultural landscape can be seen as a long history of human interaction with nature that relates to tangible and intangible dimensions. According to Taylor (2003), the form of cultural landscape tells us the achievements of our ancestors, and informs us about values at present and in the future. A cultural landscape is a window that shows our past time, our culture (Taylor 2003), so to understand the form of the village cultural landscape also means to understand the history and present time of the village. The Borobudur villages are the product of such interaction. Each village in Borobudur is a cultural landscape. The combination of villages surrounding the Borobudur Temple creates a cultural landscape on a larger scale (Figure 3.1). The form of a cultural landscape is the product of the integration of cultural landscape elements, which are physical elements (landscape) and community culture, including tangible and intangible culture, and which form a harmonious balance between nature and humans.

From the cultural point of view, Lewis (1979:19) argued that all landscapes have cultural meaning. He claimed that there is no such thing as uninteresting landscape from the cultural viewpoint, irrespective of how ordinary it may be: 'all human landscape has cultural meaning, no matter how ordinary that landscape may be...No matter how ordinary it may seem, there's no such thing as a culturally uninteresting landscape.'

Plate 3.2: (a) Terraced *sawah*; (b) tobacco plantation (photo: Rahmi, 2012)

Thus in studying a cultural landscape, the unique elements of the landscape must be looked upon, but so must the plain, ordinary ones, which tend to be neglected during the process of identifying and investigating the cultural landscape, precisely because of the simplicity and habitualness they represent. In line with Lewis's argument, Farina (1998), Vink (1983), and the Cultural Properties Department (2003) explain that the forms of a cultural landscape in a rural area are reflected in its ordinary landscape and culture, which are land utilization, architecture, community life pattern (way of life), and natural features. According to research by Rahmi (2012), these forms, which are described below, are also found in the cultural landscape of Borobudur villages.

Land utilization

Landscape conditions in the tropical climate and highly fertile land enable people to use the land for wet agriculture or *sawah* (rice fields), which dominates land use in Borobudur (Plate 3.2a). This type of irrigated and non-irrigated *sawah* with paddy is still the main type of land utilization in the villages. Besides *sawah*, the land is also used for dry field production, settlement, and plantations. Mostly, chili, tobacco, and cassava are planted in the dry fields (Plate 3.2b), whereas plantations are mostly papaya, rambutan, and various productive trees. In several villages, paddy can only be planted once a year because of the poor irrigation. Only villages that have irrigation from springs with high water availability are able to utilize the *sawah* for paddy two to three times a year. An example of a twice-yearly plantation is paddy – paddy – vegetable, which means that paddy is planted twice, particularly in the rainy season, and then various vegetables are planted, such as cucumbers, eggplants, tomatoes, peanuts, and soybeans. These vegetables fertilize the soil, so that in the next period the soil can be used again for paddy. For the *sawah* that can be used only once a year for paddy, the pattern is paddy – vegetable, which means that paddy is planted once in the rainy season and is followed by vegetables. Agricultural land use that depends solely on rain water (without irrigation) is called *gaga*, where paddy is planted once a year in the rainy season and is followed by plants that do not need much water, such as cassava and peanuts.

Agricultural land cultivation in Borobudur has used traditional technology from

Plate 3.3: (a) Traditional technique to plow the soil with buffalo; (b) using *ani-ani* during harvest time (photo: Rahmi, 2011)

generation to generation, from cultivating land with animals to planting, watering, and harvesting manually. An inherited technology is the wooden plow, used with buffalos (in Javanese, *ngluku lan nggaru*), to stir and turn the soil so that fertile soil is moved to the surface and water can easily be absorbed (Plate 3.3a). During harvest, a traditional technique is still used by the village people, who hit bundles of paddy on top of a bamboo tool to separate grains from the stalks (Plate 3.3b).

Land in Borobudur is also used for dry agriculture (unirrigated farms), and the most common use is *tumpangsari*, a traditional planting of various kinds of vegetation in one area (polyculture), including big trees and scrub. As an example, in one area there are jackfruit, *sengon* (hardwood), and mango trees, and under those trees are cassava, yam, ginger, turmeric, peanuts, and spinach. Several villages, such as Karanganyar and Wanurejo, produce tobacco in the dry season. In the yards or gardens of houses, various plants can be found, such as papaya, *salak* (a fruit), cassava, and peanuts, and trees such as teak, coconut, and rambutan. House yards are also used to keep livestock, such as goats, cows, and chickens. Settlements also dominate the land use, particularly for villages close to Borobudur Temple. The use of land for settlement always maintains harmony with nature. Settlements usually cluster close to the rice fields and dry farms. Roads connect the clusters of settlements and villages.

Way of life of the community

As a cultural landscape form, community life patterns encompass all types of community activities, traditions, and beliefs without written regulations that have become community customs or part of daily culture. The village community has had a socio-life system since long ago. The local knowledge of many traditions and customs is inherited and continues today. In the Borobudur villages, farming is the main community activity. As an agrarian community,

Table 3.2: Types of craft and home industry (Rahmi 2012)

Handicrafts	Home industry
Wood crafts, wooden furniture, gypsum casts, coconut shells, fiberglass casts, resin prints, bamboo carvings, bamboo furniture, bamboo baskets, stone casts, stone carvings, children's toys, cooking grates, pottery.	Tofu, rice crackers, cassava crackers, *tempe* (soy product), brown sugar, vermicelli, *batik*.

Plate 3.4: Handicraft products: (a) bamboo baskets, (b) gypsum casts, (c) bamboo carving, (d) stone carving, (e) pottery, and (f) vermicelli making (photo: Rahmi, 2012)

farming, religion, and Javanese beliefs – the daily customs and traditions – have influenced the whole life of the community. Besides farming, many village people are also crafters and have small-scale home industries, which, for some people, form their main income. Some people also work in tourism; for example, as hotel and restaurant owners, vendors, souvenir makers, and so on. Many kinds of crafts and home industries can be found in Borobudur villages, as seen in Table 3.2 and Plate 3.4.

Of all the handicrafts, the traditional clay pottery from Klipoh village is the oldest and has been practiced from generation to generation. The use of clay pottery for eating and drinking equipment is even depicted in carved Borobudur Temple reliefs, and it is assumed that the pottery came from the same source. Home industries have been operated by people since long ago, and they use raw materials from surrounding villages, such as wood, stone, bamboo, cassava, and coconut. The continued use of natural materials indicates that the village community participates in conserving the environment. New craft products are influenced by the tourism activity in Borobudur Temple.

Borobudur village communities still live in a traditional way. They have social systems, social customs, and local knowledge, which are still practiced in their daily lives. These

Table 3.3: Village traditions that still exist (Rahmi 2012)

Type of tradition	Description	
Traditions that relate to agriculture	*Wiwitan*	A ceremony before planting and harvesting to make an offering to maintain a life balance and harmony with nature
	Tumpengan	A ceremony to maintain sustainability of farming activity
Traditions in neighborhood relationships	*Gotong royong*	Mutual cooperation among the community
	Kerja bakti	Working together to clean the village environment
	Tepo-seliro	Tolerance in neighborhood relationships
	Arisan	Collect money, exchange knowledge, etc. – usually done by housewives once per month
Traditions that relate to birth and death	*Selapanan*	Ceremony for 35-day-old baby
	Khitanan	Circumcision ceremony for boys
	Nyadran	Praying in family cemetery before fasting period
	Selamatan kematian	A ceremony, praying together at 3, 7, 40, 100 and 1000 days after a death in the family
Traditions influenced by Islamic religion and Javanese beliefs	*Rejeban*	Ceremony in Rejeb (one of the Javanese months)
	Ruwahan	Ceremony in Ruwah (one of the Javanese months) before fasting period
	Syawalan	Celebration after fasting (Idul Fitri)
Tradition that relates to Islamic religion	*Pengajian*	Reading the Qur'an routinely by men, women, and children
Tradition that relates to village development	*Rembug desa*	Routine discussion about village problems, usually by men

Table 3.4: Traditional arts of the village community that still exist (Rahmi 2012)

Type of art	Form
Kuda lumping	Dance
Warok	Dance
Ketoprak	Drama, music
Pitutur	Speech
Rebana	Music
Berjanji	Speech
Jathilan	Dance
Shadow puppet	Drama, music
Gejog lesung	Music
Kubro siswo	Dance
Arumba (bamboo orchestra)	Music
Dayakan (*topeng ireng*)	Dance
Orkes keroncong	Music
Gendhing Jawa (*karawitan*)	Music

Plate 3.5: *Dayakan* dance (photo: Rahmi, 2012)

traditions are mostly influenced by their agriculture activity, religion, and Javanese beliefs. Although in some villages some traditions are no longer practiced, a number of traditions still exist and give the rural life its character. Table 3.3 shows traditions that are still practiced today.

Traditional arts or folk arts, which have belonged to the community for a long time, are an important part of village community life. These folk arts follow local traditions; for example, in the *wiwitan* ceremony, traditional Javanese dances and songs are performed. In wedding and circumcision ceremonies, shadow puppets are used to perform related stories. Various traditional arts still exist and are performed today in Borobudur villages (Table 3.4).

Traditional arts that are still often performed by the Borobudur village communities are *jathilan*, *kubro siswo*, and *dayakan* dances, and Javanese *gamelan* music. Every village, particularly villages around Borobudur Temple, has a traditional art group that practices routinely and has a chance to perform in the Borobudur Tourism Park. Plate 3.5 shows *dayakan* (*topeng ireng*, means black mask) dance.

Architectural expression

Rural architecture is one physical element of cultural landscape that can clearly be seen. Unique rural architectural features mirror the way of life of the community, so that architecture cannot be separated from the local culture. As more generally in Javanese rural architecture, the character of Borobudur architecture is simple in design and is in harmony with nature, so that natural exploitation is minimal. Unique characteristics of traditional Borobudur rural architecture are the setting or environment, the housing layout, and vegetation layout in the yard and village area. On a macro scale, the Borobudur landscape has a unique character with its integration among mountains, rivers, villages, agricultural land, and the temples that enhance the area. The integration among these landscape elements creates a harmonious environment. The rich abiotic and biotic environment, the culture of the village community, and the Borobudur, Pawon, and Mendut temples as world masterpieces make Borobudur a

Plate 3.6: Traditional architecture of the village environment (photo: Rahmi, 2012)

special cultural landscape. On the village scale, the integration among the elements of the village design of traditional houses, agricultural land, roads, rivers, trees, and open spaces creates a harmonious village atmosphere (Plate 3.6). Usually, the village houses have large yards. A house is built in the center of the yard, which has many kinds of local trees and shrubs – usually fruit trees such as jack fruit, guava, mango, rambutan, and coconut, and hardwood trees such as *sengon* and teak. People who have livestock, such as cows and goats, put the stalls at the sides or behind the houses. Wells are close to the houses.

Three strengths or values of Borobudur rural architecture flow from these unique characteristics.

1 Integration between design and nature: the architecture of the traditional houses is inherited from ancestors, and the design is influenced by the tropical climate; for example, the use of local materials (bamboo, wood) that are light and enable the flow of air; the slope of the roof to allow the flow of rainwater; and a veranda that acts as a foyer before entering the house. Many kinds of trees in the yard benefit the household needs and provide a natural and shady environment.

2 The design of the houses and environment to suit the dweller's needs: traditional houses are not only for living but also provide a place to work. In a farmer's house there is a room for the farming equipment; in a sugar-maker's house there is a large kitchen to cook the brown sugar; and in a pottery crafter's house there is a room for making pottery. A house yard also has multiple functions, such as paddy drying, pottery firing, tobacco drying, corn and cassava drying, and so on.

3 Design that has simplicity and harmony with the values of nature: the traditional

Plate 3.7: (top left) Mount Merapi; (top right) Elo River; (bottom left) Menoreh Mountain Range; (bottom right) steep riverbanks (photos: Rahmi, 2012)

architecture of the houses and the village environment shows the simplicity of the life of the dwellers, in which nature has a strong influence. The environment is in a simple unity, because no houses dominate or exist differently from others. The influence of *urban* architectural design has an impact on rural architecture and can change the existing village environment and destroy the soul of its simplicity.

Natural features

Natural features found in the Borobudur area – rivers, steep river slopes, volcanic rocks, and distant mountains (Plate 3.7) – form the physical elements of the village cultural landscape. In the early settlements rivers were the most important requirement in deciding the location of a settlement, because rivers were considered a token of land fertility. Today, almost all villages in the Borobudur area are bordered by rivers. Borobudur rivers – Progo, Elo, Tangsi, Sileng, and Pabelan – are wide and have steep, sloping riverbanks. These rivers are mostly used by the village communities for irrigation, with only a few used for domestic supply.

The natural steep, sloping riverbanks are geologically special. The slopes have soil layers that can be seen clearly from the river. The soil layers explain the types of rock and soil, and the age of the layers. According to Murwanto and Sutarto (2008), the layers and the condition of stones in the rivers show that in the past a paleolake environment existed in Borobudur, and the present river flows have different directions than the ancient rivers. Thus rivers, river slopes, and volcanic stones in Borobudur are part of the geomorphological history of Borobudur.

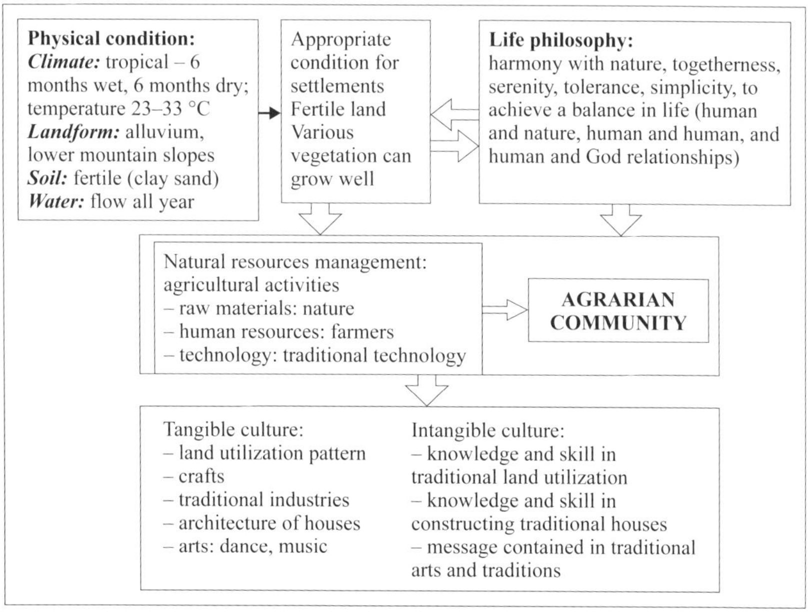

Figure 3.2: The integration between landscape and culture (Rahmi 2012)

Other natural features that influence the village cultural landscape are the volcanoes and mountain range that surround the Borobudur area – Mount Merapi, Mount Merbabu, Mount Sumbing, Mount Andong, and the Menoreh Mountain Range. Although the distance between Borobudur village and those mountains is quite far, their existence is integrated in harmony with the life of the community. Village people believe that a mountain is holy and they pay respect to it. People believe that a mountain brings wealth to the community in the form of fertile land, good water quality and quantity, and good weather, and it seems that the existence of the volcanoes and mountains were a consideration in deciding the location to build Borobudur Temple and other temples. The natural features are part of the life of the Borobudur village community, so people feel that they have a responsibility to conserve them. The natural condition of these features indicates continuity and the participation of the community in conservation.

Looking at the four forms of the cultural landscape of Borobudur villages, the good physical condition of the area (the tropical climate, the plains, fertile land, and good water condition), as well as the life philosophy of the local communities, has created communities with unique social and cultural lives, including their traditions, beliefs, their ways of life, and their arts. The communities use land for their settlements and plant various vegetation, so that an agrarian community has developed. Land utilization based on life philosophy and adaptation to the environment over a long time has created a community culture. The integration between nature (landscape) and the community culture of Borobudur is illustrated in Figure 3.2.

The four forms of the cultural landscape of Borobudur villages are interrelated and are based on the Javanese life philosophy to achieve a balance in life and harmony with nature. These forms also show the rich potency of the landscape and community culture. The integration between them gives the Borobudur villages their unique cultural landscape quality, which differs from the village cultural landscape in other places. The uniqueness of the village cultural landscape is extraordinary and contributes authenticity and high integrity values to the villages. The uniqueness is in the integrity between nature and community culture, which has existed continuously since the foundation of the villages. Three unique qualities arise from the four forms of the cultural landscape of Borobudur villages.

1 The continuity of local community culture in agriculture activities: farming has been the main community activity since the emergence of settlement in Borobudur and remains the main activity today. The continuity of agriculture activity is also seen in farming techniques, which still use traditional techniques for plowing, paddy planting, harvesting, and rice processing. Agricultural knowledge is the intangible culture of the village community, and includes knowledge on the planting season, types of plants, and soil and water quality.

2 The uniqueness of land use patterns that continue today: village settlements, with their unique way of life, have existed for a long time and have indirectly influenced unplanned land use patterns. Generally, the pattern of village land use includes land for agriculture and land for settlements around the agriculture land. The landform of the Borobudur area includes plains and mountain slopes that have led to the terracing of agricultural land based on the land contour. This unique environment, with volcanoes and mountains, creates beautiful natural views of the village areas.

  Related to the life philosophy of achieving a balance in life, the existence of agricultural land shows the relationship between the community and nature as a life resource; the settlements show social relationships among the communities; and the landscape as a whole, with the volcanoes and mountains in the background, shows the relationship between humans and God. This philosophy allows for the continuity of the land use, because the community participates to conserve the environment.

3 The rich tangible and intangible local culture constitutes the community response to the natural condition and their life philosophy: tangible culture includes land use patterns, village architecture, traditional architecture of houses, traditional craft products, and traditional food products. Intangible culture includes traditional farming activity (knowledge and skill in farming), skill in making traditional crafts and foods, traditional music and dance, and traditional rituals and beliefs. These tangible and intangible cultures are influenced very much by the physical conditions in which the communities live, and by the philosophy that life must be in balance. These two cultures are rich in local values and are deeply rooted in the lives of the people who are born and grow up in the villages.

Threats to the continuity of the cultural landscape

As mentioned by Ndubisi (in Thompson and Steiner 1997), cultural landscape is naturally dynamic because it is in a dynamic environment that always changes with time. Landscape and culture always change, increasing or decreasing with the quality of the landscape and the life of the people. Likewise in the Borobudur area, many changes have been experienced in the village cultural landscape since the foundation of the villages.

Development always impacts and changes the environment (Rahmi and Setiawan 1999), and this has happened in Borobudur (Rahmi 2012). Since the construction of the Borobudur Temple until today, the cultural landscape of Borobudur villages has experienced many changes caused by the slow shift of the culture. Physical changes and cultural shifts have been ongoing in Borobudur and have changed the interaction between the community and the environment. The growth of the tourism industry in Borobudur has indirectly influenced the local culture – that is, Javanese traditional agrarian culture. However, it is important to note that the forms and elements of the cultural landscape of Borobudur villages have remained the same, and some cultural landscape elements have changed, while others have not. Thus, it can be said that there are changes and continuity at the same time. The cultural landscape of Borobudur villages, which has existed since hundreds of years ago, in fact, continues today and its elements remain the same. From field observations, secondary data, and interviews, the elements of the cultural landscape of Borobudur villages that have changed and continue can be concluded (Table 3.5).

Table 3.5 shows that cultural landscape elements – traditional agriculture (village and buildings), land utilization, religion, beliefs, and traditions – are the same as they were hundreds of years ago, and the beautiful panorama of the landscape can still be enjoyed. This continuity is influenced by several factors:

- inherited culture that becomes a part of the community life so that it cannot easily be changed
- traditional culture with a Javanese life philosophy is still strongly applied by the community in their everyday lives
- interaction between nature and community culture is ongoing and in harmony so that, indirectly, the community has participated in the conservation of nature and culture.

The cultural landscape of Borobudur villages has faced threats to its continuity. It has experienced many changes, both in landscape and culture, particularly after the last reconstruction of Borobudur Temple and the development of tourism in the 1980s. Table 3.5 shows that changes in Borobudur are dominated by changes in land use, particularly the conversion of agricultural land for buildings. These changes have created visual pollution with the impact of large-scale building developments and modern architecture; for example, art shops, restaurants, hotels, Buddhist *vihara* (monasteries), billboards, houses, and offices are physically not in harmony with the environment. Changes in community culture are evident in several villages where some traditions are no longer practiced, and in the changing occupations of a number of community members from farmers to vendors or providers of other tourism activities. The number of traditional houses is decreasing due to new buildings with modern architecture that are not in harmony with the environment, and there is no cultural relationship between the village community and Borobudur Temple, which is a

Table 3.5: Changes and continuity of cultural landscape elements of Borobudur villages (Rahmi 2012)

Cultural landscape element	Continuing elements	Changing elements
Land utilization		
Land use	Land use pattern: agricultural landscape with groups of housing, river flows, and local roads have existed until today	*Period of construction of temples (c. 800s – c. 900s) until reconstruction of temples* People have been doing farming activities. Agricultural land and settlements have increased. The utilization of land for the construction of temples and other archaeological sites. The building of connecting roads. Replacement plant type for *sawah* (eighteenth century) in the Dutch colonial era. Different types of plants grown in *sawah* (polyculture) changed to the use of one type of plant (monoculture), which is paddy. *Period of reconstruction of temples and construction of park (1973–84)* Two villages (Ngaran and Kenayan) in the Borobudur Temple area were moved for the park construction. There were new settlements for these people. Agricultural land and settlements have increased. *Period since 1980s until today* Settlements have increased. Various types of tourism facilities have been built (hotels, restaurants, shops) by converting agricultural land, including the construction of 159 new buildings during the eight years since 2000.
Types of agricultural land	*Sawah*, dry farmlands, and plantations continue to be cultivated	In several villages there have been some changes to the type of land use, from irrigation *sawah* to rain-only *sawah*.
Agricultural techniques	Land cultivation, planting, and harvesting continue to use traditional techniques	Some modern farming techniques are used, such as chemical fertilizers and transporting the harvest with motorized vehicles.
Way of life		
Occupations	Farming continues as the main occupation of the village communities	A small number of village people have changed their occupations, from farmers to vendors and souvenir makers.
Crafts	Craft making with traditional techniques and local natural materials continue to be practiced	Some new crafts use non-local materials.
Traditions	Some traditions related to agriculture, religion, and beliefs continue to be practiced Traditional culture in the daily life of the community still exists	In some villages, some traditions, especially those related to agriculture and beliefs, are no longer practiced; for example, *wiwitan* (ceremony before harvesting) and *merti desa* (ceremony for village safety). Many modern cultural advancements affect daily activities; for example, the use of motorized vehicles, communication equipment, and electronic goods. Since the restoration of Borobudur Temple and the limited access of the local community to the temple, cultural ties between the village community and the temple have disappeared.
Arts	Several traditional dances continue to be practiced	New types of dances and music with traditional style are occurring.
Architecture		
Village architecture	The Javanese traditional architecture can still be seen.	The architectural quality of areas around Borobudur Temple has declined as a result of the construction of modern buildings.
Building architecture	Houses with Javanese traditional architecture have been maintained	New private houses with modern architecture have been built.
Panorama	The beauty of the panoramic views of the landscapes can still be seen from various viewpoints	The building of the tower base 5 transmitter station (BTS) is too close to the temple and has disrupted the panorama. The construction of 159 new buildings with modern architecture is not in harmony with the environment.

Plate 3.8: (top left and bottom right) Houses with modern architecture; (top right) restaurant; (bottom left) Buddhist *vihara* (photos: Rahmi, 2012)

result of the difficult access for the community to the temple. In some villages, the impact of the development of tourism has resulted in a number of dry farms being converted to building sites, especially in the area close to Borobudur Temple, such as Wanurejo village. These farms are now the site of hotels, restaurants, souvenir shops, and private houses. In Wringinputih village, many parcels of land are now sold to people from outside Borobudur for teak plantations that can be harvested several years later. In Karanganyar village, several dry farms with good views have been bought by foreigners and may be developed for buildings or housing. Agricultural land conversion continues, especially along the road to the Borobudur Temple. This land is converted into buildings, especially for tourism facilities (Plate 3.8).

The changes that have occurred in landscape and culture have been influenced by several factors:

- population increase, which causes higher use of land and natural resources
- urbanization, which is caused by the close proximity of towns (Magelang and Muntilan)
- development of tourism activity in Borobudur Temple, which provides opportunities for village people to benefit economically
- improper environmental management, including lack of development controls, guidelines, and land conversion policy
- lack of understanding of village potencies (landscape and culture) by the government and community, which can actually be developed to improve the economic conditions of the village communities.

Changes will be ongoing, influencing the existence of the Borobudur cultural landscape.

This study concludes that although many changes have occurred, they have not impacted on the continuity of the cultural landscape. It is presumed that the changes are the result of the dynamic of ongoing development and cannot be avoided, but most of the cultural landscape elements still exist alongside the pressures of change. Nevertheless, all changes threaten the cultural landscape and the sustainability of Borobudur villages. If those conditions are neglected and changes continue to happen, the quality of the cultural landscape will decrease and the uniqueness and identity of the area will be gone.

The cultural landscape of Borobudur villages has experienced change and continuity throughout history, and this will continue into the future. To achieve sustainability a balance between change and continuity is needed. Bimbaum and Peters (1996) stated that a cultural landscape needs a balance between change and continuity for all the landscape and cultural resources. Adishakti (1999) also mentioned that sustainability of a cultural landscape – with its history, landscape, and culture – is its ability to face changes and development to both maintain continuity of the old assets and meet the present and future needs. For that purpose, it is expected that the form of cultural landscape of Borobudur villages has continued under the increasing pressures of physical and cultural changes. If there is no proper management of Borobudur, those changes will threaten the sustainability of its cultural landscape. Suwarsono and So (1991) stress that pressures on the environment can result in a change or loss of valuable local culture, which will eliminate the identity or the uniqueness of the community. Adishakti (1999) also said that changes should not be drastic, but natural and selected. The cultural landscape of Borobudur villages will surely undergo changes, but these changes should not be imposed but be in harmony – and should even support the identity of the area as a cultural landscape. There is a need to study which parts of the cultural landscape elements can be altered and the extent of the changes, as well as which parts need to be maintained.

Conclusion

The cultural landscape of the Borobudur villages represents a continuing relationship between landscape and community culture that spans many generations. The rich potencies of the landscape and culture of the Borobudur villages, and their strong unity, create these villages as unique cultural landscapes, which is not a quality that other places have. The forms and unique values of the cultural landscapes of Borobudur villages show the high heritage value of the area, which becomes the community's collective identity. As such, Borobudur villages are considered as a cultural landscape heritage with exceptional values.

The forms and uniqueness of the village cultural landscapes have continued until today in the midst of ongoing changes to the landscape and the community culture. Until now, changes have been caused mostly by tourism activity and development and have threatened the forms and unique values of the cultural landscape of Borobudur villages. Although this study shows that not all those changes have impacted the continuity of the cultural landscape, it can be said that the cultural landscape of Borobudur villages presently is in a dangerous situation. Improper management has become a constraint in achieving a balance between cultural landscape changes and continuity. Responsive management is needed in managing all changes for the sustainability of the cultural landscape of Borobudur villages.

Biogeographical structure of the Borobudur basin

Amiluhur Soeroso

Introduction

The Borobudur Temple Compounds are reference number 592 on the UNESCO World Heritage List. The three Buddhist temples in the complex are the Borobudur Temple, Mendut Temple, and Pawon Temple. W. O. J Nieuwenkamp (1933), a Dutch artist, interprets the Borobudur Temple as a lotus flower floating on a lake, as the epitome of supreme embodiment – a symbol of purity, cleanliness, integrity, spiritual progress, and religious enlightenment. He also said that the Buddhists believe that Borobudur is the birthplace of the next Buddha, Maitreya. The region where the temples stand is known as the Kedu Plain but we also commonly refer to the area as the Borobudur basin. This plain is located in the southern part of the province of Central Java.

The Borobudur Temple Compounds were built by the Sailendra Dynasty, which ruled Java from around the fifth century until the tenth century. The three monuments are connected by an imaginary axis in the form of a straight line, which seems to be the epicenter of the environment around them. The name 'Sailendra' (Sanskrit: शैलेन्द्र) means 'lord of the mountains' (NWE 2013; Zakharov 2012), which is consistent with the ecology of the Kedu basin, where the temples are surrounded by eight mountains – Menoreh, Sindoro, Sumbing, Tidar, Telomoyo, Andong, Merapi, and Merbabu. Mounts Sindoro, Sumbing, Merapi, and Merbabu are still active volcanoes. The Borobudur Temple itself stands as the midpoint of the mountains that surround it, and can be personified as the ninth mountain. Figure 3.3 shows the ecology boundary of the Borobudur basin.

UNESCO inscribed the temples as World Heritage in 1991 according to three of the ten criteria of outstanding universal value. The Borobudur Temple Compounds reflect the beauty of the buildings and the surrounding environment (criterion i) 'with its stepped, unroofed pyramid consisting of ten superimposing terraces, crowned by a large bell-shaped dome [which] is a harmonious marriage of stupas, temple and mountain that is a masterpiece of Buddhist architecture and monumental arts' (UNESCO 2013).

The constellation of the landscape of Borobudur is like a mighty stage of performances, with Borobudur rising on its top, making it memorable and creating a deep curiosity. The overall composition of the natural landscape is an outdoor museum space with melodramatic and vast beauty, a reflection of the surrounding volcanic hills. The shape of Borobudur itself reflects the mountaintop, so the appearance of the temple in its natural landscape provides an awe-inspiring sight (Taylor 2003). Soeroso (2007) said that the natural landscape and the

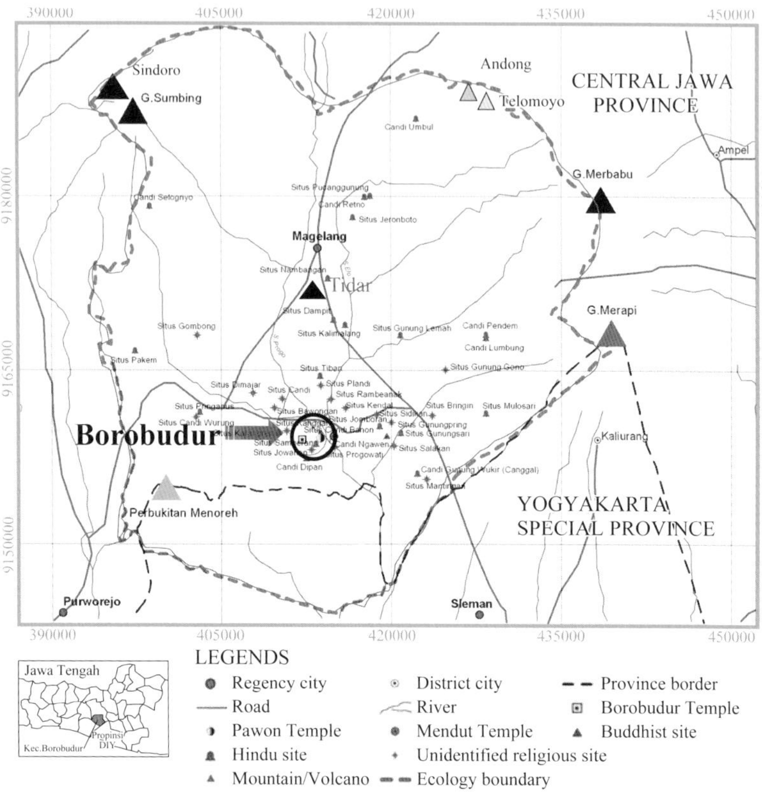

Figure 3.3: Ecology boundary of the Borobudur basin (Soeroso 2007)

communal vitality of Borobudur are resources that provide economic and cultural values. Their combination forms an important cultural landscape as the basic capital in the development of Indonesian society in the future.

Since the completion of the restoration of the Borobudur Temple Compounds in 1981, this area has grown relatively rapidly. The temples are currently used as a tourist attraction and by Buddhists for the Vesak (Buddha Day) ceremony. Approximately two million tourists visit per year, and almost all want to climb to the top of Borobudur Temple. Of course, such activity eventually threatens the preservation of the temple.

The numerous tourists also keep investors interested in building tourism facilities, such as hotels or inns, restaurants, and spas. In addition, the nuanced serenity and sanctity of Borobudur invites the community to build housing, offices (even political party offices), boarding schools, meditation houses, monasteries, and so on. The buildings seem to swarm and to press on Borobudur from all directions. Ironically, modern telephone towers to support ICT (information, communication, and technology) infrastructure and billboards or advertisement boards, placed regardless of the condition of the biogeographic regions, impact the beautiful Borobudur scenery with visual pollution.

The impact of uncontrolled development in the area of Borobudur has changed the atmosphere of rural areas with urban characteristics; the concentration of mixed garden vegetation, which characterizes rural areas, began to disappear and to be replaced by massive buildings. Unfortunately, the biogeographical conditions in this region and their significance for the benefit of the communities who live there are scarcely known. Therefore, here I provide an overview of the biogeography of the Borobudur area.

The landscape ecology

Landform

The landform of the Borobudur basin consists of undulating plains, hills, and volcanoes. This area is a valley that is surrounded by the foot of the volcanic Mount Sumbing (3135 meters (m)) to the north-west, the plains of Mount Tidar (505 m) to the north, the lower slope of the Mount Merbabu (3142 m) volcano on the east, and the slopes of the Mount Merapi (2911 m) volcano to the south-east. On the western side are denuded hills and in the south are the denuded forms of the Menoreh hills (Figure 3.4).

The area of the Borobudur basin is formed by seven lithologies: (1) andesite breccia unit – old andesite formation, the Upper Oligocene age; (2) sandstones – old andesite formation unit, the Upper Oligocene age; (3) andesite intrusion – old andesite formation, the Upper Oligocene age; (4) breccia unit of Sumbing volcano, the old Pleistocene age; (5) claystone unit, the Pleistocene age; (6) sandstone unit of Merapi volcano, the Pleistocene to Holocene age; and (7) alluvial deposition unit, the Holocene age.

Furthermore, in geomorphology, Borobudur basin is divided into four units of the origin of rock formations: (1) structural formation with geomorphic subunits of the structural mountains; (2) denudation with subunits of isolated hills; (3) volcanic formation with subunits of fluvial plains; and (4) fluvial formation with subunits of the river body and alluvial plain (Figure 3.5).

According to the Directorate of Geology (1975), the four volcanoes (i.e. Sindoro, Sumbing, and Merbabu in the north-west/north-east and Merapi in the east/south-east), along with twenty-two derivative volcanoes with average heights of between 208 and 1378 meters above sea level, have dominant affects towards the Borobudur basin ecosystem. Those volcanoes play a crucial role in geological and human history (Soeroso 2007). In other words, the dynamics of paleo-geomorphology in the Borobudur area is influenced by volcanic activity.

Rein Van Bemmelen (1952), a geologist, said that, based on the Calcutta Stone inscription made in the days of King Airlangga in Syaka 928 (1006 AD), a Merapi volcanic eruption was the most terrifying ever experienced and caused a catastrophic *Mahapralaya* (apocalypse). The result was that the central Hindu Kingdom of Mataram moved from Central Java to near the mouth of the Brantas River in East Java. Changes in the morphology of the land are commonly caused by the deaths of ancient rivers and the material released by volcanoes, both of which caused the drying out of the Borobudur paleolake.

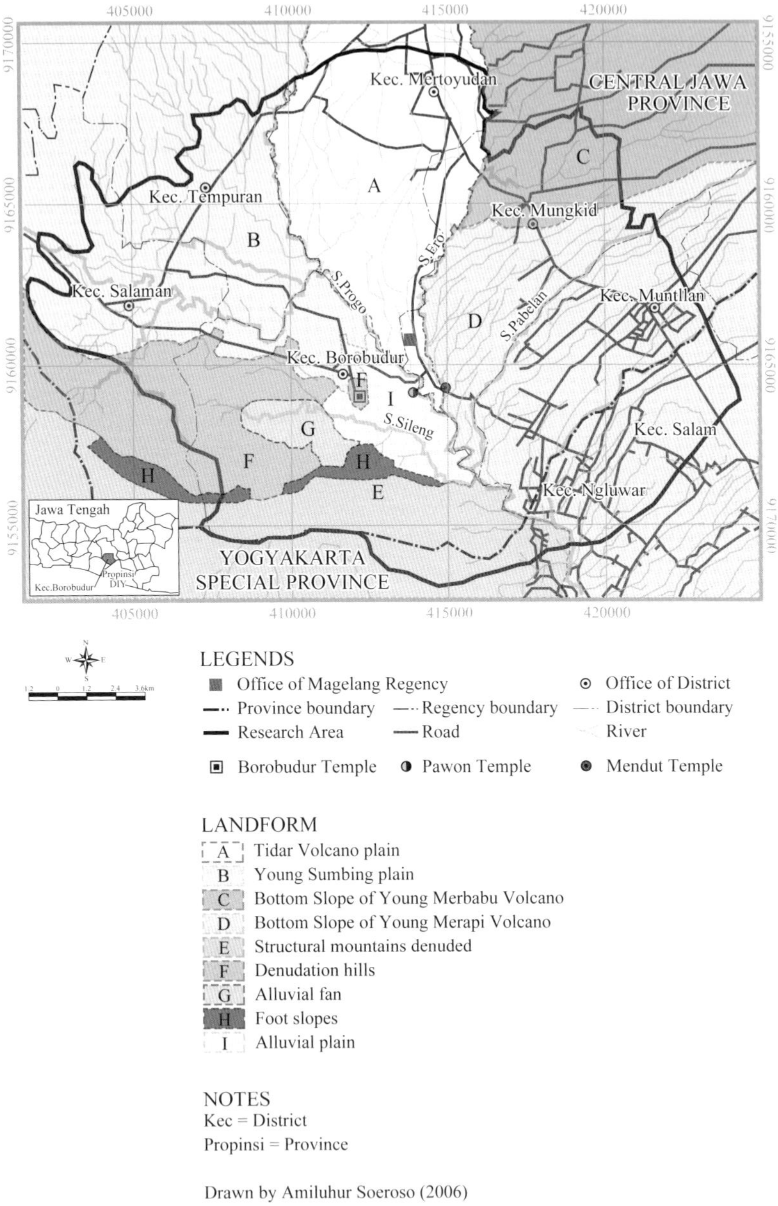

Figure 3.4: Landform map of the Borobudur basin (Bakosurtanal 2001; Geomorphology of the Borobudur Basin 2003)

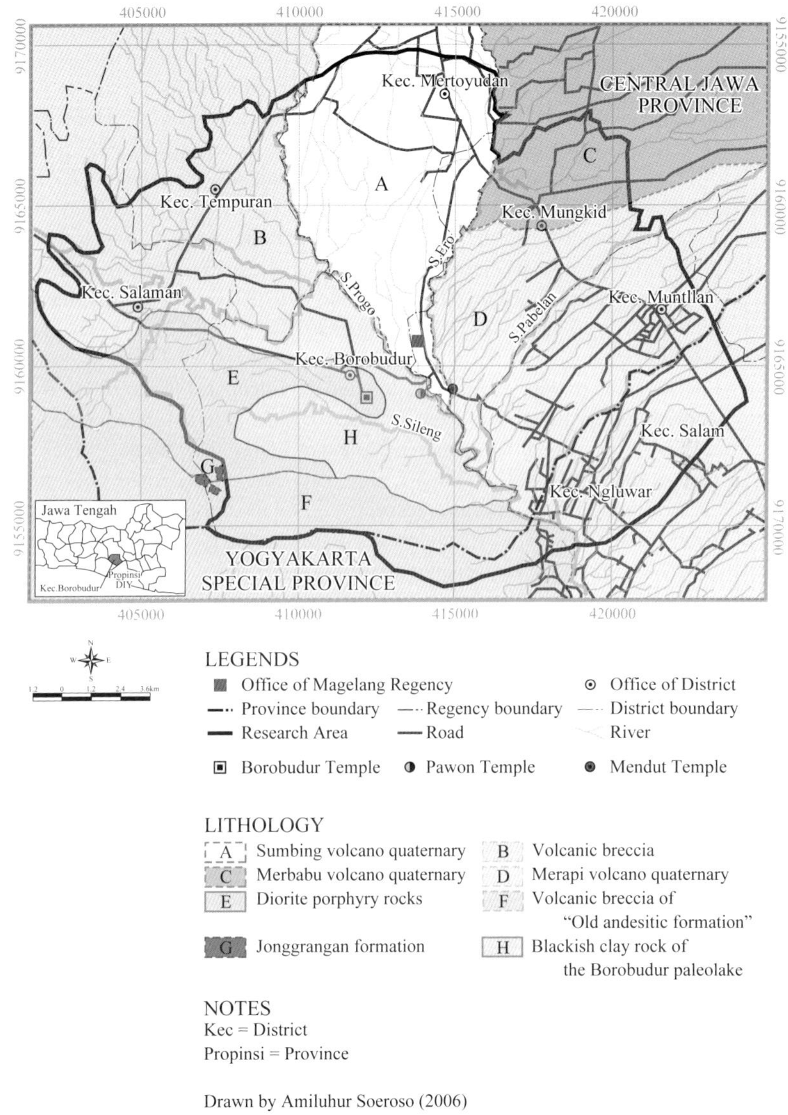

Figure 3.5: Lithology map of the Borobudur basin (Bakosurtanal 2001; Geomorphology of the Borobudur Basin 2003)

Recently, in October and November 2010, Mount Merapi erupted explosively again. Volcanic eruptions affected the Borobudur basin, and the volcanic ash from Mount Merapi fell on the temple compounds, which are approximately 28 kilometers (17 miles) west-south-west of the crater. Antara News (2010) reported that Borobudur Temple was covered in volcanic ash as thick as 0.5–1 centimeter (cm) after the Mount Merapi eruption on 26 October, and that eruptions between 3–5 November 2010 caused the temple to be covered in a 1–2.5 cm layer of ash. Nearby vegetation was uprooted and leaves, grass, and beautiful plants in the gardens withered beneath the covering of volcanic ash and sand (Tribun News 2010). The acidic properties of the volcanic ash had the potential to damage the stones of which the temple was made. Mount Merapi unleashed nearly fifty million cubic meters of gas, rocks, and ash, its most powerful eruption in a century (Jakarta Globe 2010). The temple authorities closed the Borobudur Temple to visitors from 5–9 November 2010 to clean up the ash (Jakarta Globe 2010; Tribun News 2010).

Alluvial plains in the middle of the valley, around the Sileng and Progo rivers, comprise loose gray, blackish-brown material from the eruptions of Mount Merapi and Mount Sumbing, and the frozen andesitic rocks of the Menoreh Mountain Range. The lithology (rock) of the Borobudur area at the north-west, north-east, and south-east is Quaternary rock from the Sumbing, Merbabu, and Merapi volcanoes respectively; on the northern side is the volcanic breccia of Mount Tidar. On the west side, there are diorite porphyry rocks and in the south is the volcanic breccia of old andesitic formation. Murwanto (1996) said that in the middle area, on the surrounding Borobudur hills, are clay sand materials, gray-blackish in color, formed by the Borobudur paleolake, which is covered by a pyroclastic layer of recent age from the Merapi volcano.

The sandy mudstones found in this area are lacustrine sediments, loaded with pollen from the plants of swamp habitats deposited in the Borobudur basin until the end of the thirteenth century. The sediments are exposed at the lower valleys of the Progo, Elo, and Sileng rivers. On top of the sandy mudstone are deposited brownish-gray lapilli tuffs containing fragments of porous, compact pumice with a thickness of more than ten meters, due to Quaternary volcanic activity in the north (Murwanto 1996).

The ecosystem of the area is also affected by the mount of 'Menoreh', from an old Javanese word meaning 'tower' (Soekmono 1976), part of the formation of the Kulon Progo mountains, an area that provides water to the Kedu Plain. Menoreh hill is a Tertiary-age volcanic formation. The Menoreh hill soils are prone to land movement and landslides, especially in areas that are relatively steep, because they are composed of thick clay mixed with sandstone and weathering andesite breccia. In the dry season, the hill soils are porous and easily cracked. Moderate-intensity rainfall for two hours is enough to trigger landslides on the Menoreh hill.

Elevated land in the Borobudur area reaches an altitude of approximately 200–350 meters above sea level. Figure 3.6 shows that the majority of land is relatively flat, with an undulating slope up to 0–7°. The steep areas with gradients of 25–40° are mostly located in the Menoreh Mountains.

The geomorphology of the Borobudur area, according to Van Bemmelen (1970), was formed by the tectonic processes of plio-pleistocene orogenesis in the late Tertiary period, around one to two million years ago. As a result of the ongoing process from the beginning

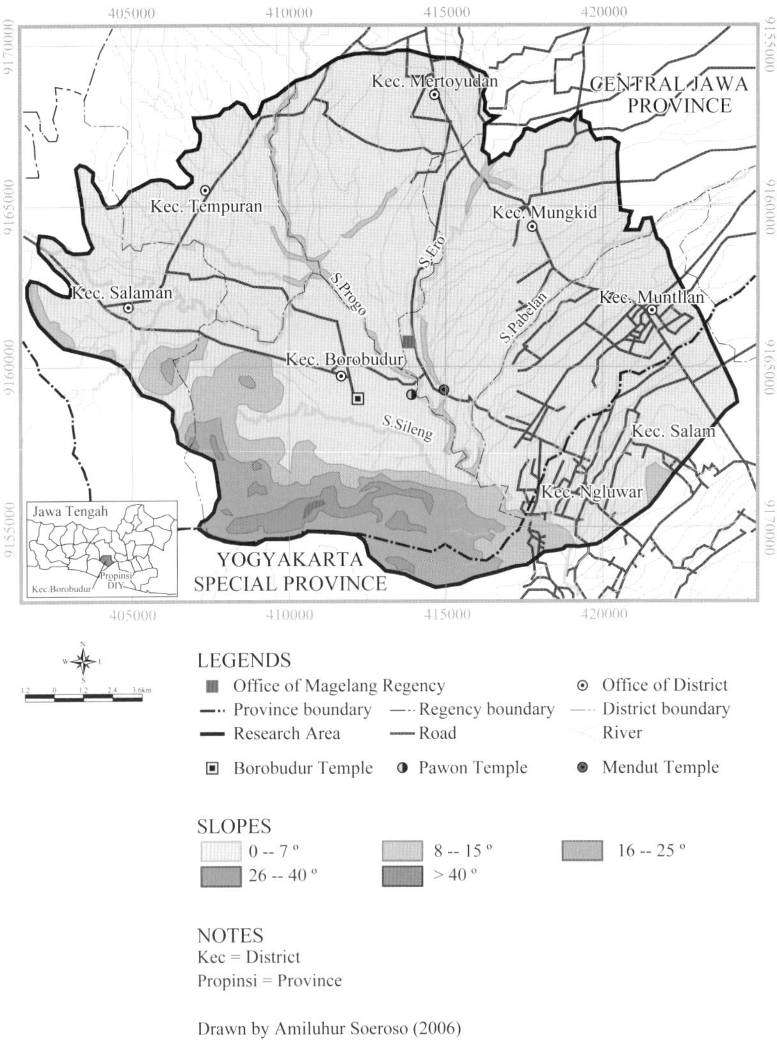

Figure 3.6: Slopes map of the Borobudur area (Bakosurtanal 2001; Geomorphology of the Borobudur Basin 2003)

until now, the Tertiary sedimentary basins of Kulon Progo folded, lifted, and faulted, forming the dome of Kulon Progo. On the northern side, the Kulon Progo dome structure is interrupted by multilevel normal faults and forms the canyon and cliff of the Menoreh Mountain, which extends east to west for nearly twenty kilometers. The fault of the northern part of the Kulon Progo dome block is immersed below sea level, while some of its top rises up, creating a row of isolated hills (i.e. the hills of Gendol, Sari, Pring, Borobudur, Dagi, and Mijil). The immersed areas in the Quaternary age developed further to be sedimentary basins of the Quaternary Borobudur.

At that time, the Borobudur basin both connected to the Indian Ocean through the crevice of Bantul Graben in the south and to the Java Sea in the north. The presence of salty water in the villages of Candirejo, Sigug, and Ngasinan (*asin* means salty), and also in the Karst of Menoreh, is evidence that the Borobudur area was once below sea level.

Close to the end of the plio-pleistocene orogenesis, magmatic activity began to appear on the north side of the Borobudur basin, forming a series of young volcanoes in the Quaternary period such as Sumbing, Sindoro, Tidar, Merbabu, and also Merapi. Even now, Merapi is the most active volcano in the world. Since then, the Borobudur basins gradually changed from the marine environment into lagoons. Along with the development of the growing volcanoes, which became higher and larger, the basins were entirely isolated from the Indian Ocean and the Java Sea. Eventually, the basin of the Borobudur Inter Mountain was formed. It was surrounded by rows of young volcanoes and Menoreh mount on the south side. The basin is closed and is called an isolated basin (Sutikno et al. 2006). Furthermore, this area is suspected to have once been a lake. The sediments of the paleolake are closely related to the environment that formed the salt water contained in the black clay rocks from the sediments in the middle beneath the lake. The evidence of drilling results during the Borobudur restoration project in 1973 supports this. In the plane of the former lake there was salt water at depths of more than forty-five meters, which was allegedly formation water.

Soil

The type of soil in the Borobudur area is generally the result of weathering or the debris of volcanic or sedimentary rocks; the wet climate, main rocks, topography, vegetation distribution, and human activities affect its formation. The wet climatic conditions, deforestation, and conversion of forests for agriculture use cause the weathering of the main rock and the soil to erode quickly.

According to the geological conditions, some rocks in the region formed in the Quaternary–Tertiary age, such as breccia, tuff, and the lava of volcanic sediment. The alluvial soil in the Borobudur basin was formed by new and youngish volcanic deposits at the foot of the volcanic plains of Merapi and Sumbing. The main material is volcanic pyroclastic rock, which is of relatively recent–subrecent age. Other soil types are Regosol, Litosol complex, and Latosol (Figure 3.7). The Litosol soil is generally shallow and is located on the main hard rock with a depth of less than 30 cm (11.8 inches), usually on steep slope areas with a high risk of erosion. The volcanic ash, with continued weathering, forms the Latosol soil.

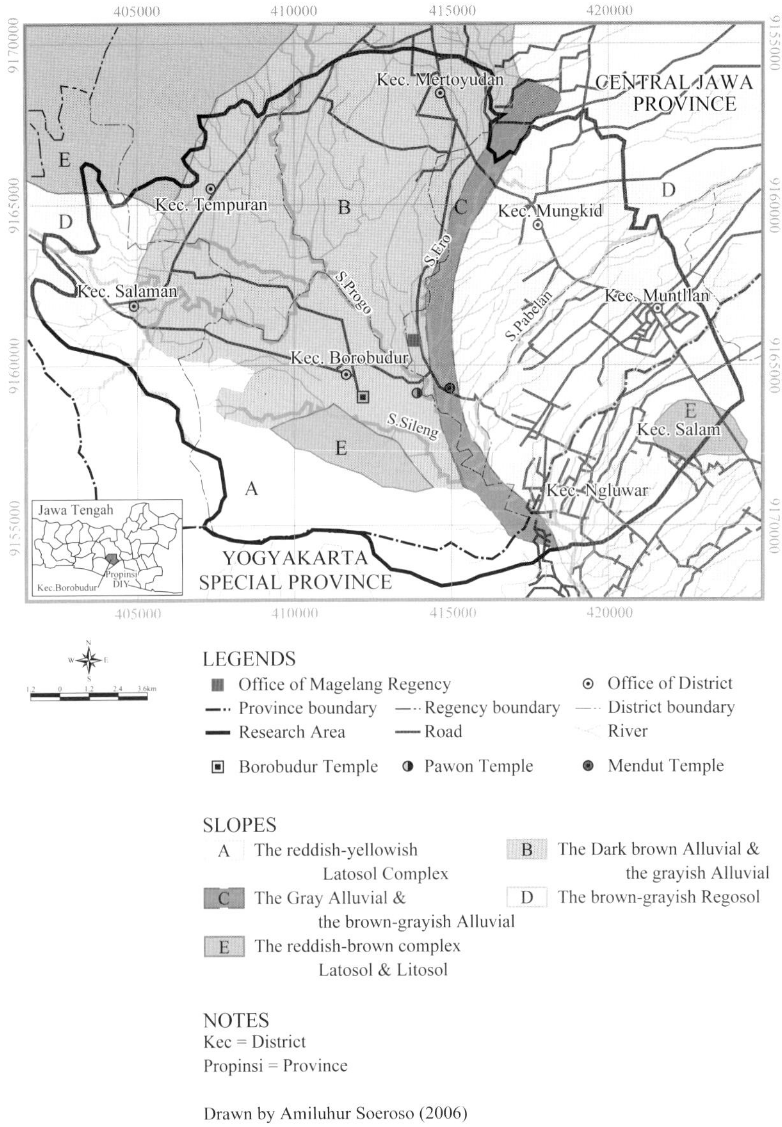

Figure 3.7: Soil map of the Borobudur basin (Bakosurtanal 2001; Geomorphology of the Borobudur Basin 2003)

Table 3.6: The demand for water in the Borobudur area (Soeroso 2007)

Items	Westside	Eastside
	of Progo River	
Total population (people)	173,326.68	213,908.97
Population concentration		
Urban area		
a. Percentage (%)	13.87%	35.50%
b. Population (people)	24,034.63	75,937.69
Rural area		
a. Percentage (%)	86.13%	64.50%
b. Population (people)	149,292.04	137,971.29
Water consumption		
Urban area (liters per person per day)	130.00	130.00
Rural area (liters per person per day)	100.00	100.00
Water demand		
Urban area, coverage 90% (liters per second)	32.55	102.83
Rural area, coverage 50% (liters per second)	86.40	79.84
Total domestic demand	118.94	182.68
Non-domestic water demand (industrial, etc.), assuming 10% of the total demand (liters per second)	11.89	18.27
Total water demand (liters per second)	130.84	200.94
Water loss (assuming 30% of total demand)	39.25	60.28
Raw water demand	170.09	261.23
Raw water available in the spring	206.00	3,472.50
Water conservation demand 20% (liters per second)	41.20	694.50
Remaining raw water (liters per second)	–5.29	2,516.77

Hydrology

According to the classification of Schmidt and Ferguson (1951), the Borobudur basin has a C-climate type with annual rainfall of about 2701 millimeters (mm). The number of wet months with rainfall of more than 100 mm per month ranges between eight to ten months; the dry months occur in June to August. The mean temperature is 25.82 °C, with relative humidity in the rainy season of 85–90% and in the dry season of 70–80% (CBS of Central Java Province 2013).

The pattern of stream flow in morphological units of the Borobudur area is parallel, subparallel, and radial, with the rivers freely supplied by the natural groundwater. The drainage terrain of the region is the Progo River, with several tributaries such as the Elo and

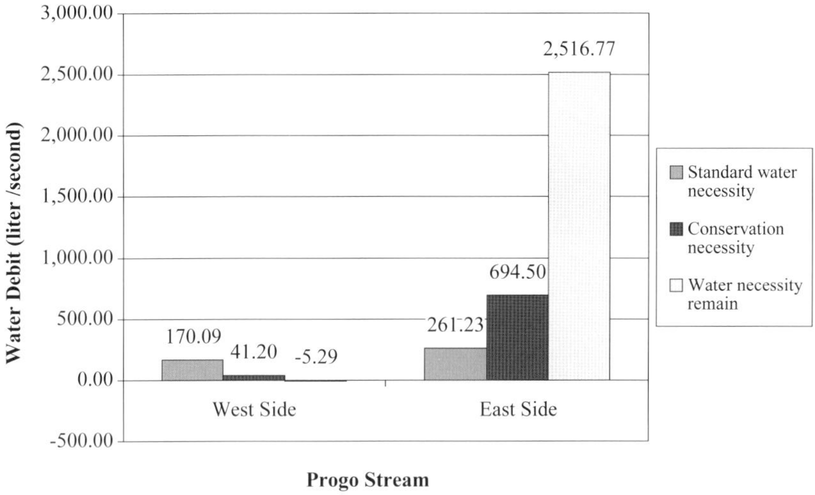

Figure 3.8: Water balance of the Borobudur basin (Soeroso 2007)

Sileng. 'Progo', according to Monier-Williams et al. (1979), is derived from a Sanskrit word, *pragma*, meaning 'reach to or go to the future'.

Based on the records of the Regional Water Company 'Tirta Dharma' of Magelang Regency (2005), the location of water sources is in the contact springs and the fracture springs. Other water sources are supplied mostly from surface water (i.e. the rivers originating from the springs on the slopes), with relatively large fluctuations of flow, and are affected by rainfall; the water enters the streams along the Progo watershed. There is also groundwater from precipitation (rain) and surface water that is drawn down into the soil through the flow system of the ground and rocks and cracked rocks due to gravity. Until now, the Regional Water Company only uses 42.5 liters per second from springs in the Borobudur area; the rest of the 150 liters per second is allocated from the water industry.

To determine the availability of fresh water in the Borobudur area, an analysis was carried out assuming (1) the population as the basis of calculation according to the 2004 report of the Central Bureau of Statistics of Magelang Regency; (2) there is a difference in the water needs of urban and rural areas and that the concentration of population in each region needs to be taken into account; (3) the water consumption for urban and rural areas is 130 and 100 liters per person per day respectively; (4) the urban and rural residents who are the consumers of the clean water from springs are 90% and 50%, while the rest use water from wells or other sources; (5) the water needs of non-domestic users is 20% of the total demand (domestic plus non-domestic); and (6) the loss of water in the supply systems reaches 30% (Government of Magelang Regency 2000).

The calculation results of water demand are shown in Table 3.6. The western part of Progo River has a shortage of 5.29 liters per second of raw water, besides the fresh water.

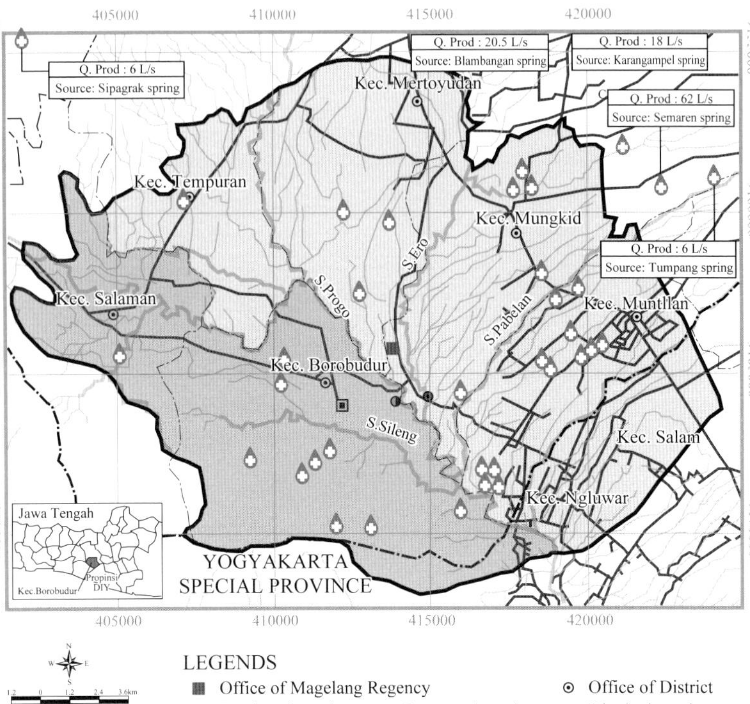

LEGENDS

Office of Magelang Regency
Office of District
Province boundary
Regency boundary
District boundary
Research Area
Road
River
Borobudur Temple
Pawon Temple
Mendut Temple
Spring water

WATER CONSUMPTION LEVELS

Water Crisis
Water Surplus

WEST SIDE OF PROGO RIVER
Water demand = 170 l/s
Debit = 206 l/s
EAST SIDE OF PROGO RIVER
Water demand = 261 l/s
Debit = 2516/77 l/s

NOTES
Kec = District
Propinsi = Province

Drawn by Amiluhur Soeroso (2006)

Figure 3.9: Water consumption levels of the Borobudur basin (Soeroso 2007)

The demand of the area for raw water reaches 206 liters per second, and the demand of water conservation is 41.20 liters per second, but the unused raw water is not sufficient. Conversely, the eastside of the Progo River has a relatively high surplus of raw water (2516.77 liters per second). Therefore, the westside of the Progo River should get supplies from other regions with surplus water availability (Soeroso 2007).

The analysis graph of the water balance is shown in Figure 3.8, while the level of water consumption, both in the westside and the eastside of Progo River, is presented in Figure 3.9.

The bioecology

Vegetation

Karmawibhangga reliefs carved at the foot of Borobudur Temple show the varieties of plants in the region during the seventh century, and include a depiction of the tree of life, which is often referred to as the *Kalpataru* (*Kalpa* means 'the time of the world', or a long time period, while *taru* is tree; as an example of 'a long time' in Hindu cosmology, the time in the world from the periods of Krita, Treta, and Dvāpara until Kali Yuga is 4.32 billion years (NARC 1986)). At Borobudur Temple the Kalpataru character is used to mark the beginning and the end of a puppetry story. Whitten et al. (1996) and Sumukti (2005) said that the Kalpataru is like the *Gunungan* (mountain; also often called *Kayon*), which is personified as a cosmic ecosystem in the universe of Javanese puppetry. In a broader wisdom, Kalpataru reflects the environment, which is harmonious and balanced, so it reflects a desire for order and symbolizes the forest, soil, water, air, and living organisms.

Reliefs of Borobudur Temple (Figure 3.10), referred to by Sarwono (1988), also document many stories about plants that lived in the past; for example, amethyst (*Datura metel*), areca nut (*Areca catechu*), banana (*Musa* sp.), breadfruit (*Artocarpus communis*), coconut (*Cocos nucifera*), durian (*Durio zibethinus*), hibiscus (*Hibiscus tiliaceus*), guava rose (or, as local people know it, *Klampok arum*) (*Syzygium jambos/Eugenia jambos*), jackfruit (*Artocarpus heterophyllus*), langsep (*Lansium domesticum*), mango (*Mangifera indica*), mangosteen (*Garcinia mangostana*), millet (*Setaria italica*), papyrus (*Borassus flabellifer*), sugarcane (*saccharum officinarum*), and taro (*Colocasia esculenta*).

Another important tree, the Bodhi (*Ficus religiosa*), which is referred to as a sacred tree for Buddhists, was planted around the Borobudur basin. *Bodhi* is both a Sanskrit and Pali word that is traditionally translated as 'enlightenment' but often, and more accurately, as 'awakening' or 'to know' (TAS 2013). This tree is viewed as a symbol of strength, warnings, inspiration, and peace, and plays an important role in Buddhist tradition, where it became a symbol of enlightenment. However, today some plants such as the guava rose, millet, and papyrus are no longer seen to grow in this area, while the Bodhi tree grows around only a few temples and government offices.

Vegetation is also considered important for imagining the villages, so the toponyms of hamlets around the Borobudur basin are often associated with the presence of plants that once grew there. For example, Kali Duren (Durian Stream) is associated with the durian tree (Javanese: *Duren*) because durian trees once grew in this area, and in Gunung Pring (Bamboo Hill) the hills were once widely covered in bamboo trees (Javanese: *Pring*) (see Soeroso

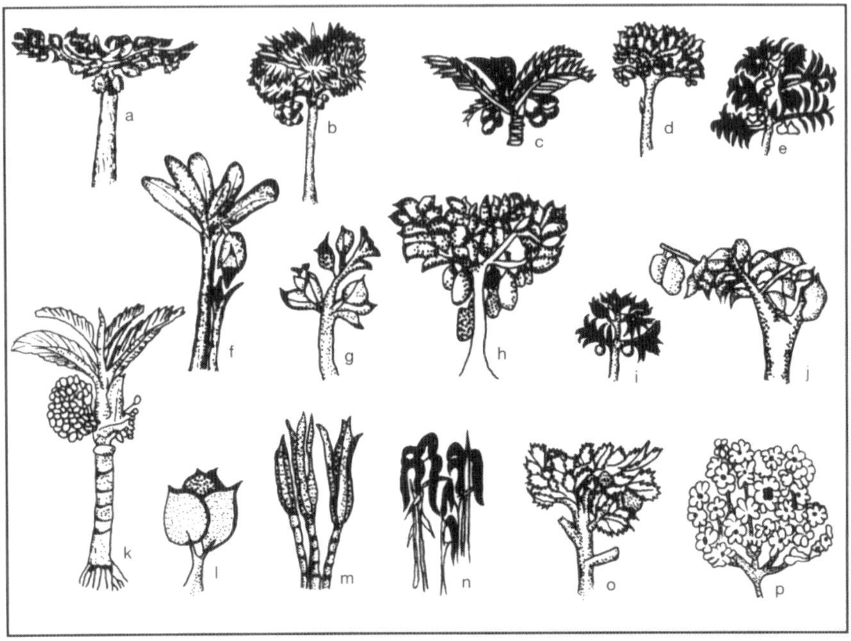

Figure 3.10: The ancient vegetation in Borobudur area (Whitten et al. 1996) (Notes: (a) durian, (b) papyrus, (c) coconut, (d) langsep, (e) guava rose or *Klampok arum*, (f) banana, (g) amethyst, (h) jackfruit, (i) mangosteen, (j) mango, (k) areca nut, (l) taro, (m) sugarcane, (n) millet, (o) bread fruit, and (p) hibiscus)

(2007) for other examples).

Plants are important elements of biodiversity in the Borobudur area. Vegetation from ancient times that is still recognizable in the villages includes coconut, corn, rice, breadfruit, and others, and is the mainstay of the food security buffer. The vegetation cultivated by the Borobudur communities includes fruits and plantation crops, while others grow wild. Plants such as breadfruit, gayam (*Inocarpus edulis*), kedondong (*Spondias pinnata*), maja (*Aegle marmelos*), and sugar palm (*Arenga pinnata*), and bamboo all grow naturally. Breadfruit is rich in carbohydrates, so it can be a substitute for rice. In Brojonalan village, a Borobudur sub-district, there is a small forest on the banks of the Progo River where the bamboo is interspersed with sugar palm trees. The bamboo, besides its use for construction materials and furniture, is used for crafts, rayon, animal feed, paper, food, and cordwood.

The pattern of planting in some areas of Borobudur, especially on the westside of the Progo stream, is unique because it is conducted as polyculture (intercropping) of three to five different species consisting of annual and seasonal plants (the people of Central Java usually

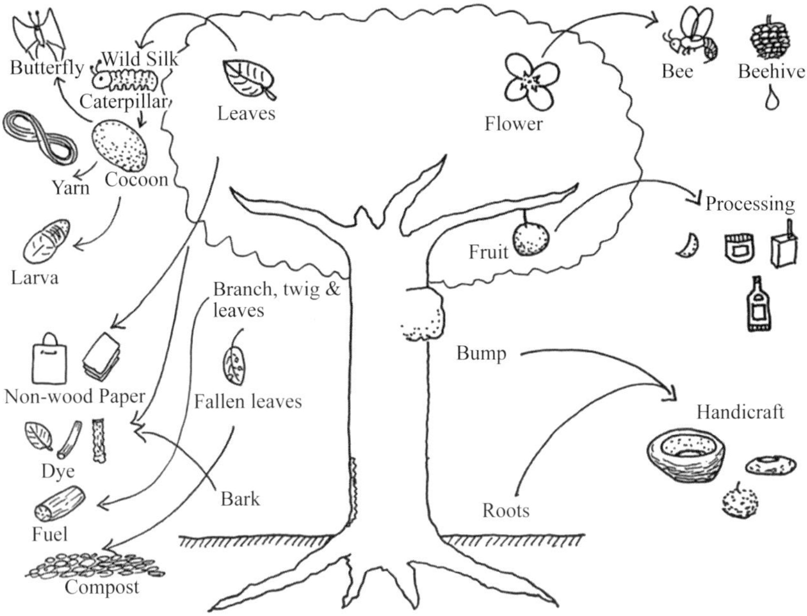

Figure 3.11: The use of vegetation for various economic purposes (Kuroda 2004)

practice polyculture with only two types of plants). The combination of polyculture is citrus (*Citrus* sp.) or mango with cassava (*Manihot utilissima*), chili (*Capsicum annum*), chili sauce (*Capsicum frustescens*), peanut (*Arachis hypogaea*), spinach (*Amaranthus tricolor*), or sweet potato (*Ipomoea batatas* L.).

In the dry season there is often no water supply in the area, so there is no crop planting. During droughts, the farmers work over the land and allow the soil to rest to restore its natural nutrients. The planting of peanuts (the roots of which can bind nitrogen in the soil) at the beginning of the planting season provides the necessary nutrients for other plants.

Various kinds of plant remains such as twigs and branches, stems, leaves, and flowers are usually discarded – such as those of bananas, jackfruit, kapok (*Ceiba pentandra*), larasetu (*Vetiveria zizanioides*), peanuts, pineapple (*Ananas comosus*), and taro (*Caladium* sp.) – but they can be used as the raw materials of environmentally friendly products ranging from perfumes, candles, cooking oils, and soaps to wine and tea liquors and jams. Fruit trees provide the fresh fruit that we can consume immediately, but fruit can also be processed into jam, wine, and fertilizer. Meanwhile, the other materials, like the twigs, branches, leaves, and roots, can be made into new value-added products. Charcoal, compost, and pulp can be made from the leaves, and dye from the bark. Trees also have the potential to support the production of other materials, such as honey and royal jelly (which are produced by bees), propolis stucco or red plombir (which bees collect from the tops of plants and which is useful in strengthening the body's cells), and butterfly cocoons, which can be processed into silk thread, cosmetics, and medicines. Butterfly larvae can also be processed into food (Figure 3.11). Such products are environmentally friendly and can increase local people's incomes. Another potential of the existing plants in the Borobudur basin is as raw material for medicines (Soeroso 2007).

Fauna

According to Almo Farina (in Von Droste et al. 1995), heterogeneity is an important character of the cultural landscape. The components of landscape, such as its shape and size, can affect animal distribution, abundance, behavior, movements, and preferences. Fauna are fragile organisms that need large areas to live and to reproduce. The disruption of the landscape threatens their lives and ultimately affects human beings. The natural fauna at Borobudur is diverse, ranging from mammals to insects. In pristine places where human disturbance is rare, such as forests, steep cliffs, and the riverbanks, small animals still live and wild birds, lizards (*Varanus nebulosus*), and local fish survive in their natural habitats.

The Menoreh Mountain Range has bats of the order *Chiroptera* and flying foxes (*Pteropus vampyrus*), which help to naturally eradicate pests and maintain the continuity of certain plants through pollination and by spreading seeds. Local people living around the Menoreh highlands often still breed and keep deer as livestock. In addition, storks (*Leptoptilos javanicus*), herons (*Egretta garzetta*), grouse (*Dendrocygna javanica*), and many other birds settle in rice fields, looking for food such as frogs (*Fejervarya cancrivora*), paddy snake (*Python reticulatus*), and small fish. These animals are now rarely found in the wild, due to their diminished habitat and human hunting.

The national park of the Merapi–Merbabu mountains, on the east boundary of the Borobudur basin, comprises naturally mountainous tropical forests affected by volcanic activity. The forests have many birds and animals, such as the Javan hawk-eagle (*Spizaetus bartelsi*), black eagle (*Ictinaetus malayensis*), kestrel (*Falco moluccensis*), eagle-snake 'Bido' (*Spilornis cheela*), partridge (*Gallus varius*), turtledove (*Streptopelia chinensis*), wren (*Parus major*), deer (*Muntiacus muntjak*), hedgehog (*Hystrix javanica*), mongoose (*Paradoxurus hermaphroditus*), long-tailed monkeys (*Macaca fascicularis*), leopards (*Panthera pardus*), and others (Wikipedia 2013b, 2013c).

The Javan hawk-eagle is endemic to the island of Java. The bird is a predator and occupies the top spot in the food chain hierarchy. It controls animal populations and maintains the natural balance. The absence of these predators would disrupt the ecosystem and increase the number of pests on agricultural land. For example, if eagles became extinct, the population of sparrows and other similar birds would become uncontrollable as rice crop pests. In the end, disturbances in the animal food chain can disrupt the human food system. Thus efforts to conserve wildlife such as the Javan hawk-eagle are essential for human survival.

Post-independence in 1945, the Javan hawk-eagle (often called *Garuda* in Indonesian) serves as a symbol of the Republic of Indonesia. It has been designated as the endangered species mascot of Indonesia since 1992 (Wikipedia 2013a).

Discussion

The Borobudur cultural landscape, if we refer to the UNESCO (2012:14) definition, has cultural properties and represents the 'combined works of nature and of man', as designated in Article 1 of the Convention Concerning the Protection of the World Cultural and Natural Heritage. The Borobudur area is a place of interaction between the power of the natural environment and the strength of social, economic, and cultural arts over a long time.

Yet based on the facts that have been revealed, the cultural landscape of Borobudur can be also referred to as a bioregion. According to a NSW Government (2011) definition, a bioregion is a relatively large geographical area characterized by broad, landscape-scale natural features and environmental processes that influence the functions of entire ecosystems. The Borobudur basin covers large-scale bio-geophysical patterns across two provinces, the Central Java Province and Yogyakarta Special Province. The Borobudur area as a bioregion, described in terms of its unique pattern combinations of landscape, is linked to geology, climate, plants, water sources, wildlife, and also to the living culture of humans (Ask 2013; Sustainability-now 2013). Thus natural forms and living local communities in the Borobudur area become the extraordinary features of the bioregion.

However, the Borobudur basin consists of two conditions that are mutually opposite. On the eastside of the Progo River, a stretch of land is a relatively flat and fertile plain because of the influence of the Merapi and Merbabu volcanoes. Water supply in the area – from the springs and rivers that flow – must meet the demands of households, irrigators, and others so that this area can be planted with rice throughout the year. The supply is technical because the irrigated paddy fields are in the plains of fluvio-volcanic bottomland, the river valley, where the river meanders and flows.

Conversely, on the westside of Progo River, the land is mountainous and hilly and was once also an ancient swamp. The land is infertile due to lack of water and agriculture relies on rain-fed irrigation. Dry land such as fields, mixed farms, plantations, and settlements are found on the flat land but have no access to irrigation. Rice farming is highly dependent on the rainy season, so farmers intercrop and plant alternately or in rotation with rice and secondary crops such as cassava and peanuts.

The land use of the Borobudur area is shown in Figure 3.12. Currently, housing and residential developments, offices, hotels, recreation facilities, and all forms of commercial business and infrastructure are being built on the westside of the Progo River due to the magnetic and attractive economy, namely the Borobudur Temple. The result is a change in the spatial structure of the Borobudur area. Paddy field land use has seen an accelerated decline of 0.54% per year, while the state forests and plantations are decreasing at 0.35–0.74% per year. The amount of rural land remaining is only 44.34%, indicating that rural areas of the Borobudur basin are now becoming urban areas. The area of rice fields is smaller than the area of settlement; in some areas there is even critical land (Soeroso 2007).

Furthermore, local people who have usually made a living from the land are changing jobs; for example, by becoming traders (even though they lack product knowledge or knowledge of the twists and turns of the trade itself). Most eventually become hawkers, who sell goods like T-shirts, pictures, and books around Borobudur Temple. Goods offered by vendors are not unique and the quality is mediocre. Worse yet, of the 170 kinds of souvenirs offered

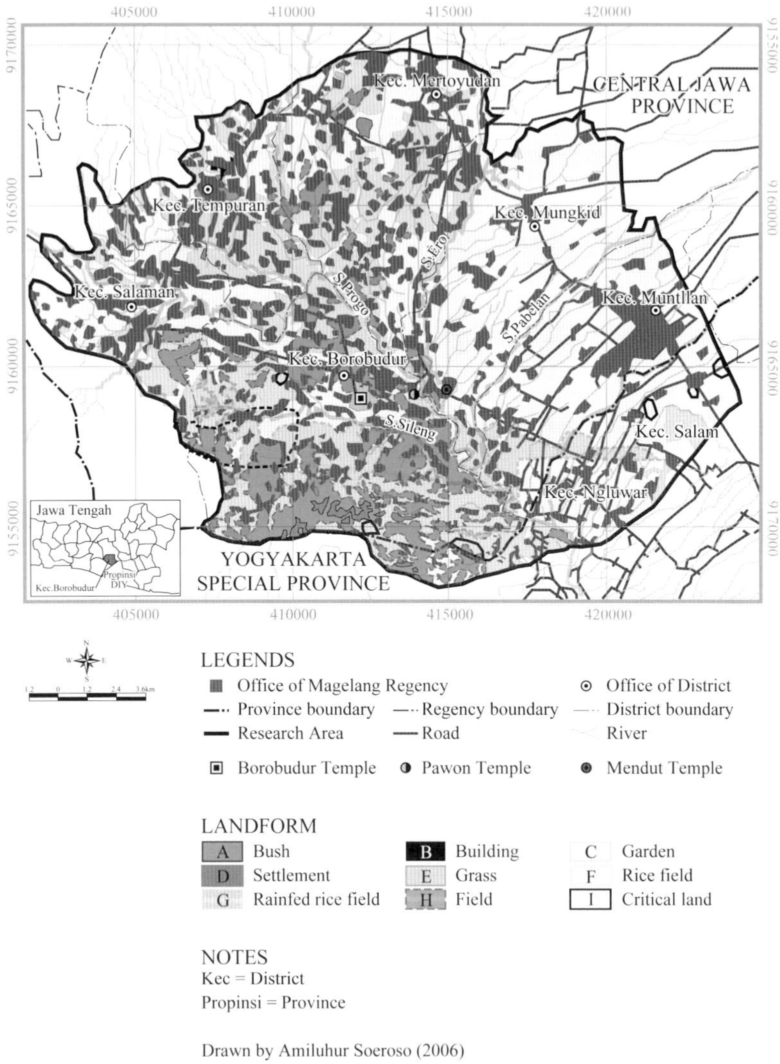

Figure 3.12: Land use of the Borobudur basin (Soeroso 2007)

by hawkers, only seven items come from local production (BTSS 2005). Meanwhile, the farmland they once worked now lies fallow. Rice production per year, which is not great since the land relies on rain-fed irrigation, has progressively decreased. The net result is precisely that the economy of the local community has worsened. Although in 2011 the sub-district of Borobudur, as the closest region to Borobudur Temple, has relatively moderate to fast economic growth (4.51%), its 6098 people still live in poverty (CBS of Magelang Regency 2013).

Conclusion

The cultural landscape of the Borobudur basin has beautiful scenic views, and there seems to be a real fusion between the natural landscape and local culture. The cultural landscape of Borobudur consists of mountains and hills combined with temples, flora and fauna, and human activity. But, regardless of its attractiveness and beauty, as an inseparable biogeographic area, the Borobudur valley also keeps records that need to be considered. Any development of the Borobudur area must be environmentally friendly.

Nevertheless, many investors are still racing to hunt for land in the hills around Mount Menoreh, on isolated hills (like Punthuk Setumbu, Dagi, and so on), or on land that was once the paleolake to become the site of the next hotel, inn, or attraction because it offers panoramic views towards Borobudur Temple. They do not consider that the land in that area is prone to landslides, is arid, or has hard water. Although we can reduce the risk of landslides in bioengineering by creating terraces planted or cultivated with grasses or herbage (*Gramineae* and *Caliandra callotrisus*), and can also reforest the public forests, the westside of the Progo River is former swampland and thus has less fresh water and is also a difficult area to absorb hotel wastewater. Hence, the Borobudur area is actually a fragile land, particularly the westside of the Progo River. The area is not suitable for large and massive buildings, so development should be limited.

Meanwhile, on the eastside of the Progo River, although the land is relatively better than the westside in terms of flatness, irrigation, and soil fertility, it also is not feasible for massive building because this area provides the water source and houses the barns for food sources. Permission to construct buildings should be selective and should consider the condition of the surrounding landscape. Therefore, so as not to interfere with the aura and nuance of Borobudur, development should be directed to Mertoyudan City and Muntilan City, about ten kilometers from the Borobudur Temple Compounds. Both these cities have been growing since the Dutch colonial era, bypassed by the main road that connects the city of Yogyakarta and Semarang.

In the infertile land of the Borobudur basin, especially on the westside of the Progo River, community food security can be improved by enriching the food diversity. The residents' daily staple food can be expanded. The provision of carbohydrates, satisfied only by consuming rice, in the future should be enriched with a variety of other foodstuffs (e.g. cassava, sweet potato, breadfruit, and so on).

The description of the land, flora, and fauna of the Borobudur basin shows the interaction between biological diversity and cultural diversity that proves the true variation of human life, reflecting the relationship between humans and the natural environment. Hence the areas from the south-west to the north-west side of the Borobudur basin, along the Menoreh hills to Mount Sumbing and ranging south-east to north-east, surrounding Mount Merapi and Mount Merbabu, should be designated as a sub-bioregion. The purpose of the determination of this sub-bioregion is as a place of conservation, both for water resources and endangered wild animals. Society should be actively involved in the preservation of endangered species in the Borobudur area.

If an eco-friendly development program is successful, one day the Borobudur basin will become a more attractive tourist destination, especially in terms of bird-watching, trekking, biking, mountaineering, rafting, photography, sightseeing, and so on. As a further expectation in the future, not all the tourists who visit Borobudur Temple will have to climb to the top of the temple, which was originally treated as a sanctuary. By doing so, the expansion of tourism in the Borobudur area will help local residents to improve their welfare.

Borobudur ancient lake site

Helmy Murwanto and Ananta Purwoarminta

Introduction

A hypothesis about the existence of a Borobudur lake was first introduced by Nieuwenkamp (1933). He speculated about the relationship of Borobudur Temple with the surrounding lakes. Borobudur temple, where Buddhist embodiment is born into this world, is a large building, which Nieuwenkamp described as a lotus flower floating in the middle of a lake. The hypothesis was fantastic but had opposition, as well as support, from experts. One opponent was Van Erp, who, from 1907 until 1911, led the restoration of Borobudur Temple. The hypothesis was considered not to have strong supporting evidence (Soekmono 1976), but in *De Geschiedenis Van Geologiche Indonesie*, Van Bemmelen (1952) explains that the Nieuwenkamp hypothesis makes sense because the southern part of the Magelang area had once formed a quite extensive lake environment. The environment of the lake was disrupted by a strong eruption of the Merapi volcano, which resulted in a peak that slumped to the south-west, stemmed the flow of the Progo River, and formed a large lake in those areas.

Geology of the Borobudur area

Based on the physiographic zones of Central Java described by Van Bemmelen (1949), the Borobudur area is located in a central depression zone between the Menoreh Mountain Range on the south side and a Quaternary volcanic zone on the north side. The Borobudur terrain has an elevation of 225 to 240 meters above sea level.

Borobudur Temple stands on top of an isolated hill in the middle of the landform plains (Plate 3.9). On the south side the plain is bounded by the Menoreh Mountains, steep cliffs that extend east–west with a height of 500 to nearly 1000 meters (Figure 3.13).

A chain of Quaternary volcanic mountains – Mount Sumbing (3135 m), Mount Sindoro (2271 m), Mount Tidar (505 m), Mount Merbabu (3142 m), and Mount Merapi (2911 m) – limits the Borobudur plains to the west, north, and east. The Borobudur plain is eroded by rivers and streams that flow from the volcanic slopes and cliffs, including the Menoreh Mountains, among others: Progo River, Elo River, Pabelan River, Tangsi River, and Sileng River. The rivers flow across the Borobudur plain and join with the Progo River; after arriving on the south side of the plain, the flow is blocked by the Menoreh Mountains and turns to the south-east, flowing out into the ocean.

Plate 3.9: The appearance of a former lake plains landform in South Borobudur (photo: Murwanto)

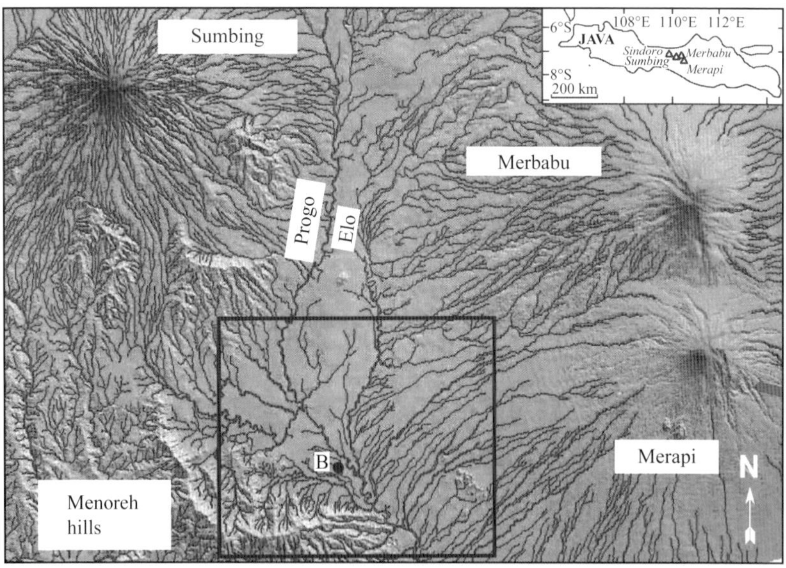

Figure 3.13: Digital relief map of Borobudur and the surrounding plains (B: Borobudur Temple) (Source: Murwanto et al., 2001)

Figure 3.14: Last puddle of the Borobudur lake trail that has undergone the process of drying (Source: Google Earth, modified by authors)

Traces of the ancient river

Observations indicate the direction of rivers on the Borobudur plains derived from Mount Merapi; Pabelan River, Keji River, Lamat River, and Blongkeng River initially flowed to the south-west, towards the lowlands around Borobudur. These river flows changed direction to the south to become one with the Progo River, which flows into the ocean. Flow changes also occurred in rivers originating from the eastern slopes of Mount Sumbing; namely Tangsi River and Merawu River, which initially flowed eastwards towards the Borobudur plain. Now both rivers, before reaching the Borobudur plain, change direction west of Wringinputih village to the north and flow into the Progo River.

The rivers originating from the northern slopes of Mount Sumbing and the western slopes of Mount Merbabu, namely the Progo and Elo rivers, flow to the Borobudur plain. Neither river shows any change in the direction of flow, but indicates geomorphic processes and the formation of river terraces.

Field data show that rivers flowed towards the lowlands in the vicinity of Borobudur (Borobudur lake). Now the flow of these rivers has been partially changed, as shown in the distortion of the flow direction, which tends to avoid the Borobudur plain; only Sileng River, which springs from the Menoreh Mountains, on the south side of the Borobudur plain, joins the Progo River and flows into the ocean.

In physiography, Central Java is located in the south of a depression zone among the Kulon Progo mountains on the south side and a Quaternary volcanic arc on the north side. Based on the results of geological study, the Borobudur plain is a former swamp or lake (Murwanto 1996). Establishment of the lake environment occurred before the Holocene epoch or more than 10,000 years ago. Borobudur lake environment has the lowest topography in the Magelang Plain region, and on the south side is bounded by a fault scarp (the Menoreh

Plate 3.10: Borobudur lake sediment outcrop at Sileng River, Soropadan village (photo: Murwanto)

Mountains), along more than 20 km, with an altitude of 500 to nearly 1000 m above sea level; in the west-north-east the area is bounded by the slopes of Mount Sumbing, Mount Sindoro, Mount Tidar, Mount Merbabu, and Mount Merapi. Consequently, all the rivers that originate from the slopes of the volcanos and the Menoreh Mountains converged into the Borobudur lake. The Borobudur lake environment acts as base level temporary erosion before the flow reaches the ocean.

Lake sediment

In the Borobudur area and surrounds, most of the rock is composed of black clay with silts, sandstone, and gravel. Units are covered by young volcanic sediments in the east, north, and west, and by Tertiary volcanic deposits in the south. Tertiary volcanic rocks are exposed in several places among black clay units (Plate 3.10). In general, black clay cut by a conglomerate of sandstone sediments forms 'scour and fill' gravel sedimentary structures.

Sandy clay, according Murwanto (1996), is lacustrine sediment that contains a lot of pollen that comes from marsh plants sedimented in the Borobudur basin. Lacustrine sediment is exposed on the valley of the Progo River, Elo River, and Sileng River, over sandy clays sedimented with brownish-gray lapilli tuffs, many containing fragments of pumice. The layer is compact, with a thickness of more than ten meters from the proceeds of young volcanic eruptions in the north.

Regional stratigraphic studies

The research area encompasses the plains around the Kulon Progo dome in a Quaternary volcanic complex. Borobudur basin stratigraphy based on field observations shows the Old

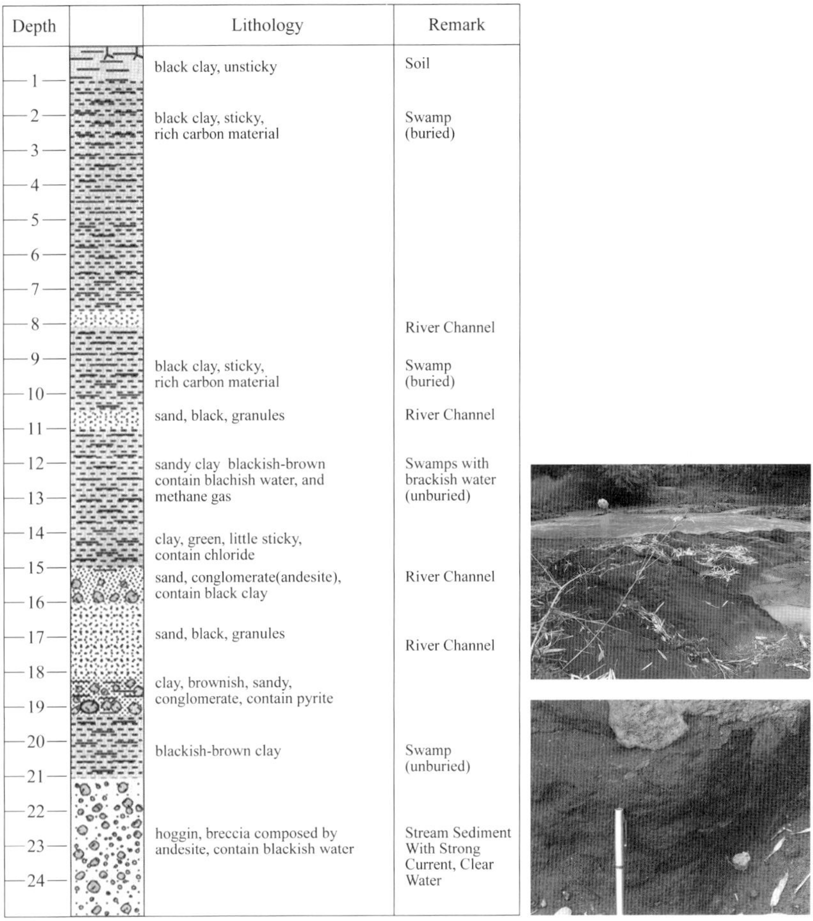

Figure 3.15: Lithology log of drilling in Sileng River showing the dominance of black clay sediments with volcanic sandstone insertion and conglomeratic sandstones (Murwanto et al., 2001)

Andesite Formation as a base (bedrock); this rock is composed of volcanic breccia and diorite porphyry igneous rocks, with the rocks exposed in several places to form isolated hills surrounded by a sediment quarter. The andesite formation is covered by sandy black clay rich in organic matter and containing fossil plants, and is brittle with low porosity (Figure 3.15)

The second type of rock is sandy clay sediments with lacustrine sediments, which contains a lot of pollen (from the marsh plant communities) that was sedimented in the Borobudur basin until the end of the thirteenth century. The sediments exposed in the Progo River valley,

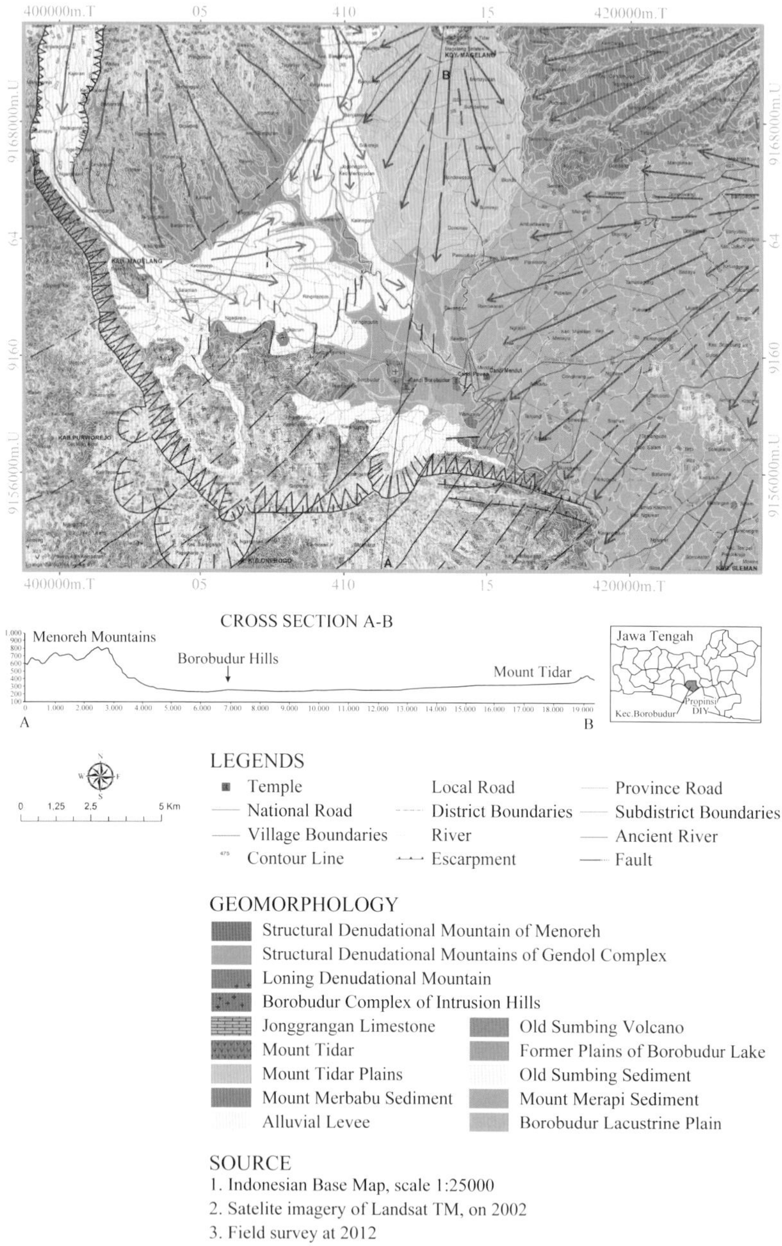

Figure 3.16: Geomorphological map of Borobudur

Pollen Analysis

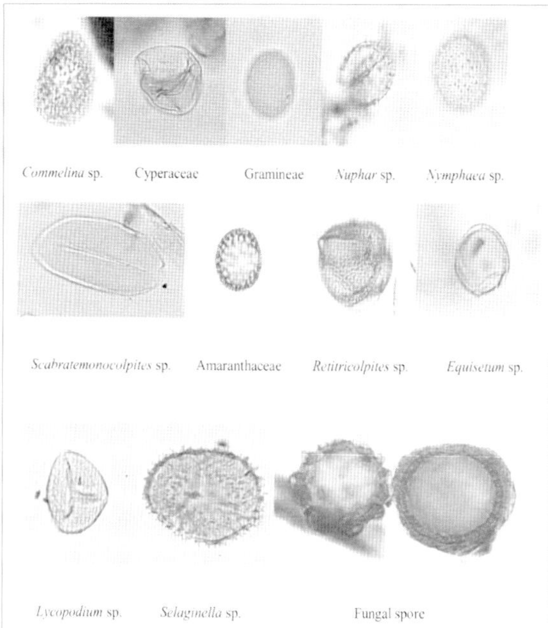

Figure 3.17: The appearance of the pollen photo as lake environment pointer, taken in black claystone samples in Progo river

the Sileng River and the Elo River, above sandy clay sediment of brownish-gray lapilli tuffs, contain fragments of pumice: the layer is compact, with a thickness of more than ten meters as a result of the volcanic eruptions.

Deposition environment

Evidence from the lake environment found pollen, which indicates the environment that previously existed. Results of analysis of pollen and spores contained in the upper black clay sediments show several types of pollen derived from plants such as *Commelina*, *Cyperaceae*, *Eleocharis*, *Nymphaea stellata*, *Polygonum berbatum*, and *Ranunculus blumei* (Backer and Bakhuizen van Den Brink 1963).

Figure 3.17 shows images of pollen taken from the lake. Many are types of Pteridophyta spores largely thought to have come from upstream in the surrounding area (upland), from where they were carried by the wind or rivers that flow towards the Borobudur lake and were sedimented together with black clay.

The above results prove that in the past the plains of Borobudur once formed a lake environment, while the environment around the lake was open. The open environment around the lake can be interpreted from the pollen type; the determination of treeless vegetation ('un aboreal') was much greater than the percentage of the pollen types of fringe vegetation ('aboreal') (Murwanto et al., 2001). The open condition of the lake was most likely influenced by Quaternary volcanic eruptions. The effect is reflected in the magnitude of volcanic materials that sedimented together with black clay in the form of lahar deposition. Young volcanic activity resulted in changes in the lake environment and gradually the lake became more shallow and narrow.

Geological structure

The geological structure of the study area is strongly influenced by the orogenesa Plio-Pleistocene age, and is characterized by folds and fault structures. With aerial photography these structures are very clearly detected; a fault escarpment alignment with rows of triangular facets, shift off set, and straight river flow patterns that developed in the zone structure. Direct observation in the field found the data structures in the form of drag faults, fault scraps, and fault breccia. Fault planes filled by ore minerals and salt water springs and swamp gas pass through the fault plane. The fold structure that developed in the study area resulted in the Old Andesite Formation. The layering of rock formations is sloped in the same direction, with the same relative slope in the range of 23° to 27° tilted towards the south.

Borobudur lake history

An overview of the geological formation of the Borobudur basin shows a close relation with tectonic plate processes, with the Indo-Australian plate moving towards the north at a speed of ± 7 cm per year, and infiltrating beneath the continental crust of south-east Asian 'Sunda land' (Simanjuntak and Barber 1996 in Murwanto et al., 2001). The process of plate collision resulted in the formation of the volcanic arc and arc trench as the oceanic plates and arc basin sedimentation formed in the front and rear of the volcanic arc. The initial plate collision in Java produced old Tertiary or Oligo-Miocene (18–27 million years) volcanoes known as the Old Andesite Formation (Bemmelen 1949). A sedimentation basin, namely the Kendeng basin or Serayu basin in Central Java, formed at that time, behind the arc of volcanoes. When the Miocene volcanic complexes were inactive, a coral reef grew on top of a volcano located in shallow waters, while in deeper seas sand-sized clastic limestone alternating with clay marl was deposited, forming the Jonggrangan Formation (early Miocene) and the younger Sentolo Formation (early Miocene epoch to late Miocene (Dolinger and Ruiter 1975 in Murwanto et al., 2001)).

The collision process of the tectonic plates is ongoing, resulting in a gradual increase in the compression force and changing the Kulon Progo volcanic complex, along with marine sediments (namely Jonggrangan and Sentolo formations). Magmatic rock activity intruded upon the older formations, such as the Old Andesite Formation, the Jonggrangan Formation, and the Sentolo Formation.

Borobudur basin

Based on Murwanto et al.(2001), the peak compression forces of the tectonic plate processes in the early Quaternary age resulted in structures such as shear faults, reverse faults, and shear zones that formed in the process of release of the compression. As a result, the force of gravity became more involved, resulting in the formation of graben structures and normal faults. In

Central Java this occurred at the northern tip of the Kulon Progo dome, where the block in the northern part of the dome underwent a process of sinking to a block in the south, forming steep walls extending east to west ± 20 km. The northern block was partially submerged beneath sea level, while the top part of the block appears above sea level, forming isolated hills such as Gendol, Sari, Pring, and Borobudur hills. The drowning process of the northern part of the Kulon Progo dome structure of the Menoreh Mountains, in the late Pleistocene epoch, was the beginning of the Borobudur Quaternary basin formation events.

A sinking process also occurred on the east side of the Menoreh Mountains, as well as the west side of the southern mountains. The process formed the Bantul Graben structure, which separates the south mountains of the Menoreh Mountains. On the eastern side the Menoreh Mountains are bounded by the major Progo and Serang faults: the west side of the south mountains is bounded by the Opak and Oyo faults.

In the middle of the Pleistocene epoch, Bantul Graben (in the south of the Borobudur basin) was the entrance for sea water from the Indian Ocean to the Banyuasin and Borobudur basins. Then, in the north of the Borobudur basin, volcanoes such as Sindoro, Sumbing, and Merbabu appeared. So, in some places, volcanoes and hills blocked the Borobudur basin from the Java Sea.

In the middle quarter age, the connection of the Borobudur basin with the Java Sea to the north was totally blocked due to the Kendeng basin and North Serayu basin experiencing a multiplicity of folding, uplifting, and scarp formation following magmatic activity. The orogenesa process is still ongoing, forming the lines of the Kendeng Mountains and North Serayu Mountains. Magmatic activity began with the formation of Mount Tidar, the Puser hill north of Secang, Windusari hill, and Mount Bibi in Boyolali, followed by the emergence of the volcanoes of Mount Andong, Mount Telomoyo, and Mount Gilipetung.

In the late Quaternary periods (from the late Pleistocene until recent times) large new strato volcanoes were created, such as Mount Merbabu, Mount Sumbing, Mount Merapi, and Mount Sindoro. Along with the growth of the young volcanoes, the Borobudur basin became increasingly narrow and shallow. This is evidenced by ancient Mount Merapi activity, which left a trail 40,000–20,000 years ago in Plawangan and Turgo (Berthommier 1990), where the eruption products were largely deposited on the southern and south-western slopes. Eruption products during this period were carried away by the flow of the rivers, as well as fluvio volcanic material, and then sedimented in any part of the basin south-east of Borobudur. There is also a very thick sediment covering of Bantul Graben.

Merapi volcanic eruptions early in the period 40,000–20,000 years ago resulted in the closure of the connection between the Indian Ocean and the Borobudur basin, resulting in changes in the environment in the Borobudur basin from a lagoon environment to a lake environment (in the late Pleistocene epoch, ± 22,000 years ago (Murwanto et al. 2001)). The lake environment left a trail of brownish-black clay sediments containing high organic carbon. The black claystone contains pollen from the water plant community.

The very beautiful landscape of the lakes and natural surroundings led to the choice of Borobudur hill as the location for the construction of the largest Buddhist temple in the world around the year 800 AD (Soekmono 1986). The beauty supported by the quiet natural setting made Borobudur Temple an ideal place to study the Buddhist teachings.

However, the calm atmosphere and the beauty of nature around Borobudur Temple was

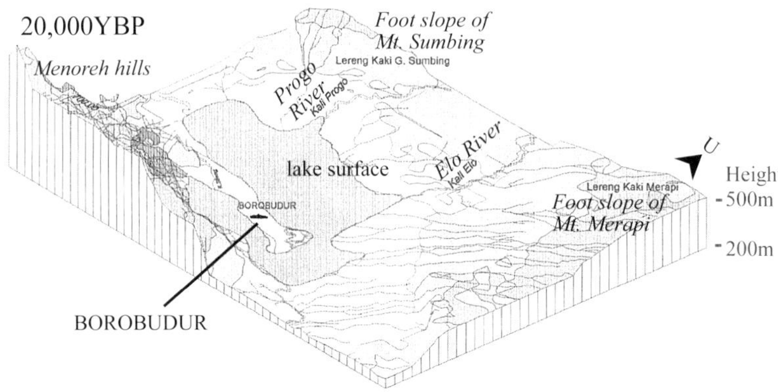

Figure 3.18: Block diagram of the surface reconstruction of Borobudur lake at 20,000 YBP (Murwanto et al., 2001)

enjoyed for only two to three centuries before a geological disaster occurred. The disaster took the form of a volcanic eruption around the basin. Strong indications proceeded the eruption in the form of a powerful earthquake that triggered eruptions from the Sumbing, Sindoro, and Merapi volcanoes. Most of the material results of the eruptions, both in primary forms like ash-lapilli, as well as the secondary form of lahar floods, sedimented in the Borobudur basin. As a result of the disaster, the lake environment in the Borobudur basin gradually became dry because the material from the volcanic eruptions reached a thickness of more than ten meters. From the eleventh century until the thirteenth century, the events of the devastating earthquake and volcanic eruptions changed the Borobudur basin into a plains landform called the plain of south Kedu.

Borobudur lake dynamics

Lakes or marshes around Borobudur have certainly existed for more than 22,000 years, aside from the Nieuwenkamp (1933) hypothesis and support from van Bemmelen (1952), and the existence of the lake is strongly supported by this study. Black clay sediments outcrops along the Sileng River and in the Elo River north-west of the Mendut Temple to near its mouth in the Progo River, and a few outcrops in the Progo River (east of Pawon Temple and the north of Teluk village), suggest that the Borobudur lake was vast. Variations in sediment, soil chemistry, pollen, and spore content on the surface are very supportive of the lake environment.

The development of the lake area and palaeogeographic evidence around the Borobudur Temple area are strongly influenced by sediment results of volcanic activity of Mount Merbabu, Mount Sumbing, Mount Merapi, and the Menoreh Mountains. The data above and age of black clay or pollen are presented in a palaeogeographic reconstruction, especially with respect to the development of the lake area, assuming that all levels are deemed to be in a horizontal position. Figures 3.18 to 3.20 show the development of the lake area from

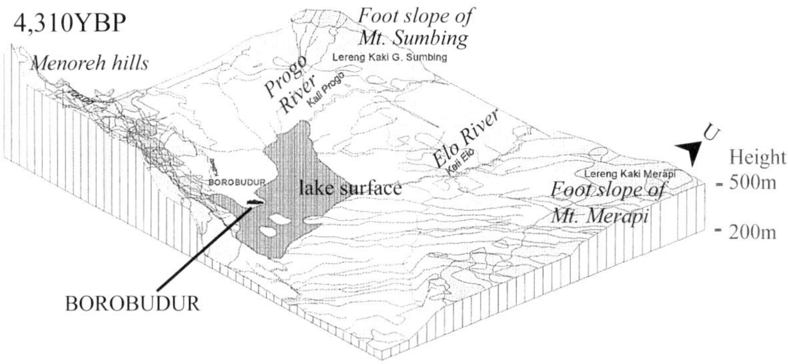

Figure 3.19: Block diagram of the surface reconstruction of Borobudur lake in 4310 YBP (Murwanto et al., 2001)

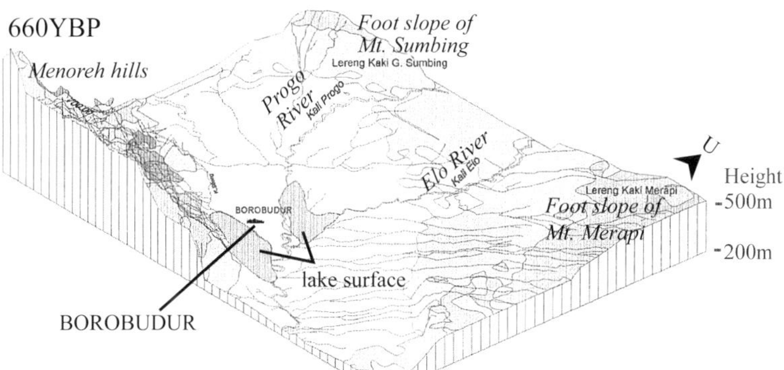

Figure 3.20: Block diagram of the surface reconstruction of Borobudur lake at 660 YBP (Murwanto et al., 2001)

22,000–19,000 year before present (YBP), at 4310 YBP, and at 660 YBP.

At 22,000–19,000 YBP the lake extends further north and west, while in the east the spread of the lake is not very far. This suggests that the formation of the lake has been affected by volcanic activity. The southern part of the lake is bounded by hills occupied by the Old Andesite Formation. This formation exposes the Progo River (east of Pawon Temple) and a horst (eastern Borobudur hills).

Table 3.7: Toponyms of Borobudur plains

Toponym	Meaning
Sabrangrawa	Across the swamp
Tanjung	Peninsula
Bumi Segara	*Bumi*: land
	Segara: sea
Gopalan	*Nggo*: use
	Kapalan: ship (boat)
Tanjung Sari	headlands
Kedungombo	wide river
Segaran	sea
Teluk	gulf
Wanurejo (Banyurejo atau Ranurejo)	plenty of water/large lake

In the north the Borobudur Temple environment frequently changed; sometimes it was land and sometimes it was inundated. This is evidenced by ancient soil layers in drilling result data at the Elo River. At the Sileng River the swamp environment/lake remained closed. At 4310 YBP the lake spread was narrower than before. The lake was elongated north-west–south-east and there were small islands from east of Borobudur Temple.

At 660 YBP the lake environment was divided in two. The Sileng River remained as a marsh/closed lake, while Elo River surroundings frequently changed the environment to marshes.

Influence of the Borobudur lake on human activity

The past existence of the Borobudur lake can still be observed today. In the past the lake served as a source of livelihood for people living around the lake. People preferred to live around the lake because it was easy to fulfill their daily needs. The past existence of the lake still influences present-day human activities and is evidenced by toponyms that refer to the physical condition of the environment. The existence of lake ecosystems also affects the livelihood of local communities for agriculture and tourism.

Toponyms

In toponyms around Borobudur Temple, village names are associated with water. Although these places are now dry, it can be presumed that in the past they hosted lakes or at least swamps, (Daldjoeni 1984). Some toponyms used in the ancient Borobudur lake area are shown in Table 3.7.

Based on the various toponyms in the Borobudur area, it can be concluded that toponyms are closely linked to environmental conditions. This is also in accordance with interviews

Plate 3.11: The utilization of former lake plains for agriculture and fisheries (photos: Murwanto)

Plate 3.12: Rafting at Elo River, in which part of Borobudur lake ecosystem (photos: Murwanto)

with people who live in the Sabrangrawa hamlet. Based on interview results, the role of Borobudur lake toponyms can be seen.

Agriculture and fisheries

Traces of the lake are still clearly visible, with the area usually having clay and mud materials and many wet areas. This region has a low topography and features such as streams (Plate 3.11) and is used by people for farming and fishing activities. Almost the whole valley is used for farming because the area has fertile land and abundant water.

Tourism

The existence of the lake affected river development in the Borobudur area. The Elo River has a stable water flow which originates from Mount Merbabu and joins the Progo River in the Borobudur plains. Some rivers disgorge from Mount Merapi; Mangu River, Gung River, Kunjang River, and Keprekan River flow wildly. The ancient lahar flows from Mount Merapi filled the Elo River and consequently these materials now form rapids, so the river is used for rafting tourism. This tourism is much in demand by the public, so this special interest tourism benefits the surrounding community.

Conclusion

Evidence of the lake environment that formed around Borobudur Temple is found in sandy siltstone and brown-black clay sediments, which contains pollen of marsh plant communities, fossils, and swamp gas. The lake was very large but has now dried as a result of landform changes caused by volcanic eruptions and tectonic activity. The existence of the Borobudur lake in the past is still evident in toponyms and in community livelihoods. The site of the Borobudur lake must be conserved for an understanding of the geological environment around Borobudur Temple.

Saujana heritage planning and the role of community

Punto Wijayanto

Background

With Borobudur as world heritage, it is mandatory for the government of Indonesia to have a management plan. Until now, there has been no official UNESCO model for a management plan. The technical principles of a management plan are based on the World Heritage Convention and other international conventions. It is the significance of a site that forms the basis for its management.

A narrative was used to identify the significance of Borobudur when it was listed as World Cultural Heritage in 1991. It meets two World Heritage List criteria: as an outstanding example of Indonesia's art and architecture (criterion ii) and as a reflection of a blending of the very central idea of indigenous worship and the Buddhist concept of attaining Nirvana (criterion vi). Borobudur Temple is a world heritage monument situated in the fertile Kedu Plain, bounded by Mount Menoreh in the south, Mount Merapi and Mount Merbabu in the east, Mount Sumbing and Mount Sindoro in the west to north-west, and Mount Tidar, Mount Andong, and Mount Telomoyo in the north to north-east. According to Nieuwenkamp's (1933) perception, Borobudur Temple was like a lotus floating on the water, but the lake had grown smaller and was eventually lost due to volcanic eruptions (Murwanto et al. 2004). Sukmono (1976) suspected that there had been a grand design to include various monuments such as Borobudur Temple, Mendut Temple, and Pawon Temple in a single system. It is a challenge for the Borobudur management plan and also for planning processes to accommodate such diversity.

Constructing Borobudur management zones

The UNESCO world heritage listing of the Borobudur Temple Compounds comprises Borobudur, Mendut, and Pawon temples. The epicenter of the management should be the imaginary line between the three temples. For this reason, in 1979 JICA proposed that the management of the Borobudur area should be distributed into five zones.

Zone I, with a radius of 200 meters around Borobudur Temple, was designated as a preservation zone. It is organized and managed by the Balai Studi dan Konservasi Borobudur (The Agency for the Restoration of Borobudur Temple/Borobudur Conservation Heritage), an institution under the Ministry of Culture and Tourism. Zone II, with a 500-meter radius,

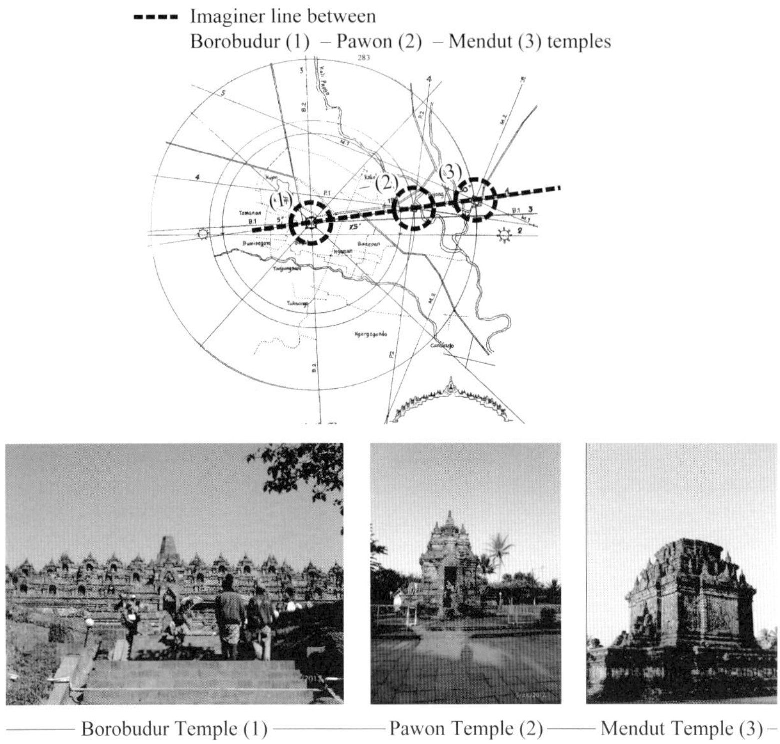

Figure 3.21: Borobudur conservation zoning system based on JICA Master Plan, 1979

is designated as an archaeological park, which is equipped with a museum and office area, parking spaces, and commercial strips. This zone is managed by a state-owned company, PT. Taman Wisata Candi Borobudur, Prambanan and Ratu (TWCB).

Zone III is an area set aside for limited residential land use and agriculture, and as a green belt area for rice fields. It includes villages and the sites of Mendut and Pawon temples. The aim is to maintain the atmosphere of the monuments. Zone III is managed by the Government of Magelang Regency.

Furthermore, zone IV has a five-kilometer radius projected as a place to enjoy the panoramic views and to protect historical Borobudur landscapes. Zone V, with a sixteen-kilometer radius, is a national archaeological park for monument protection. Zones IV and V are important elements in the context of cultural landscape because they are part of the concept of creating a large outdoor museum. Three zones – zones I, II, and III – were adopted by Presidential Decree No. 1/1992 (Figure 3.21).

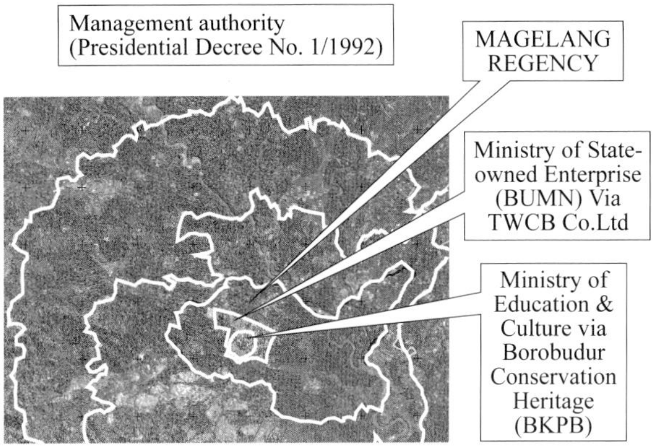

Figure 3.22: Borobudur area as cultural landscape organized by three different management parties (Soeroso 2012)

Misconception about Borobudur and its regional context

The preservation of Borobudur has caused discontinuity to its relationship with the environment. With its designation as a monument, Borobudur becomes susceptible to change. It is not enough that the Government of the Republic of Indonesia only pays attention to the management of Borobudur Temple, without attention to its regional context.

In literature about regional planning, territory is understood as inter-regional relations in environmental or economic fields. The linkage is often emphasized in structural relationships, such as the distinction of central and peripheral areas. The central area plays an important role as the engine of growth and benefits from its status. Furthermore, profits are expected to trickle to the surrounding region or its peripheral areas.

This kind of relationship is shown in Borobudur. The history of Borobudur's preservation shows how the international cultural heritage label marks the gravity of its heritage management. However, in contrast to what happened in the past, the image of Borobudur is also constructed as a center for development and tourism. Suddenly local people flock to take advantage of its presence by selling souvenirs or operating tourism-related businesses. Research by Winarni (2006) discovered that the restoration of Borobudur Temple in 1973 was the generator of rapid spatial growth in the area.

Soeroso (2012) identified and highlighted the division of management zones as the source of problems. The three different management parties in Borobudur – the Government of Magelang Regency, PT. Taman Wisata, and Balai Konservasi – have their own interests in how Borobudur should be treated (Figure 3.22).

According to Soeroso (2012), the implications of the division of roles are that there are differences in:

Plate 3.13: Borobudur view as part of cultural landscape – now the hotel's best view (photo: Adishakti)

- vision and mission management
- management objectives, such as ecological equilibrium versus economic motives
- the target, such as preservation versus local government revenue.

The problem is obvious when Borobudur becomes a prominent tourist destination in Indonesia. Borobudur is at the same time a monument to conserve and a source of economic resources. Development is mostly related to efforts to increase the number of tourists. One proposal for a new market, the Pasar Seni Jagad Jawa (Java Art Market) in 2003, luckily allowed the public to once again redefine the significance of Borobudur to recognize its cultural landscape and living heritage values. Some seminars, supported by a UNESCO mission report, suggested Borobudur Temple should be appreciated according to its various values, which are interpreted not only by experts or governments but by local people also. Those experts also indicated the need for land use control guidance through spatial planning.

As zones IV and V are not yet protected by law, physical construction, especially of large buildings, in the surrounds of the Borobudur area is now uncontrollable. Unfortunately, the intrusion of new buildings such as hotels, high-rise buildings, or cell phone towers and the emergence of billboards block the view to Borobudur. The increasing density of vehicles also causes pollution problems physically, visually, and culturally.

Presently, the problem takes the form of massive tourism facility development or the construction of new hotels. Local culture does not recognize the concept of hotel function. Hotels certainly did not have a role in the development of Borobudur and the surrounding area, but hotels and other new developments have been instrumental in the modification of the land use, which was formerly dominated by agricultural land (Winarni 2006).

In terms of the architectural aspect, hotel design accommodates tourist activities and affects how the image of the Borobudur area is constructed. The luxuriousness of a hotel includes its ability to sell a view or views towards Borobudur (Plate 3.13). This means that hotel construction does not simply follow the usual logic of land use, but takes advantage of the topography. Over the past ten years, and ongoing, many hotels have been built to capture views towards Borobudur (Plate 3.13).

Most striking, however, is the impact on the intangible aspect of the Borobudur area – the slow process of marginalization of local people's daily activities, whose meanings used to be linked to or associated with the Borobudur area. The unique geographical features of the Borobudur area support people's daily activities, such as farming and animal husbandry. But those activities suddenly become meaningless when tourism is associated with the Borobudur area.

Regional spatial plan for Borobudur: could it be a corrective tool?

Through the promulgation of the Spatial Planning Law 26/2007, the Indonesian planning system started to adopt a planning system for land use management. The role of government is strong and especially recognizable in the aspects of spatial plan making and land utilization control, especially in the preparation of National Spatial Plans (RTRW Nasional) and spatial plans for National Strategic Areas (RTR *Kawasan Strategis Nasional* – KSN). The law requires all levels of government to prepare spatial plans to direct development in their regions. In this system, rigid zoning and codes are used for growth management and development control (Figure 3.23). The law also requires governments to prepare zoning regulations (*peraturan zonasi*) as key instruments to control land development. Zoning regulation is supported by environmental and building codes.

According to Law 26/2007, a spatial plan is classified by the main function of areas, administrative areas, activity areas, and the strategic value of the region. Spatial planning based on the strategic value of the region comprises a spatial plan for KSN, provincial/regional strategic areas, and local strategic areas. KSN are areas of national priority because the spatial arrangement has a very important influence. There are several types of KSN related to the following aspects: national sovereignty, national defense and security, the economy, society or culture, and/or the environment, including areas designated as world heritage. Within the framework of implementation of KSN there is a need for a spatial plan for KSN. A spatial plan should be agreed by all stakeholders, both at central and local levels.

The central government, which works closely with the DPR (*Dewan Perwakilan Rakyat* or People's Representative Assembly, i.e. Parliament), is the only level authorized to make laws to be applied throughout the whole country. It seems to apply top-down planning approaches and standards. Unfortunately, it is possible that geographical diversity among regions is poorly considered and accommodated.

As already mentioned, Borobudur, a cultural world heritage site, is designated as one of 75 *Kawasan Stragenis Nasional* or KSN (National Strategic Areas). Borobudur is a Socio-Cultural National Strategic Area. There is no clear guideline yet about the preparation of spatial plans for this kind of KSN. Therefore, comprehensive understanding about Borobudur as world heritage will determine the substance of this spatial plan.

Based on Government Regulation No. 28/2008 on National Spatial Planning (RTRW Nasional), the coverage area of the Borobudur National Strategic Area is 1095 hectares, which comprise three villages: (1) Borobudur village, where Borobudur Temple is located, (2) Wanurejo village, where Pawon Temple is located, and (3) Mendut village, where Mendut Temple is located (Figure 3.24). According to the implementation of national development

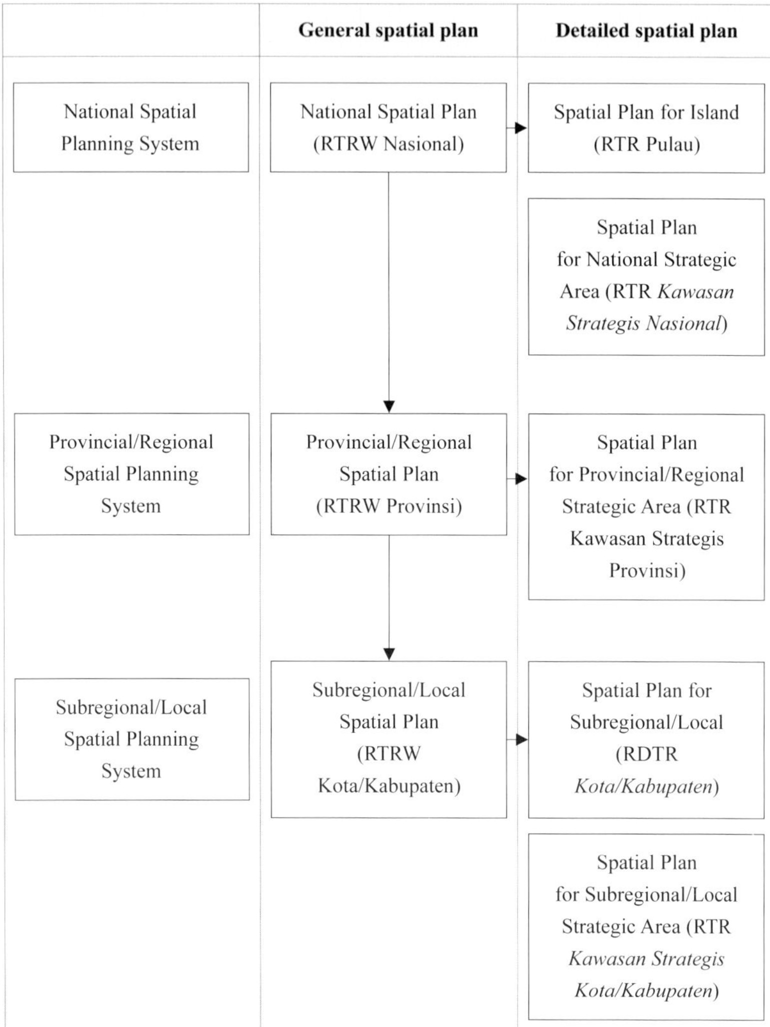

Figure 3.23: Spatial planning system in Indonesia

priorities in 2010, preparation of the Borobudur KSN is a pilot project. The target for completion of the Presidential Decree on Spatial Planning for National Strategic Areas of Borobudur Temple was December 2010.

Understanding of the Borobudur Temple Compound as a comprehensive environment was exposed. It also has a deep meaning for Buddhist teaching, as well as its relationship with

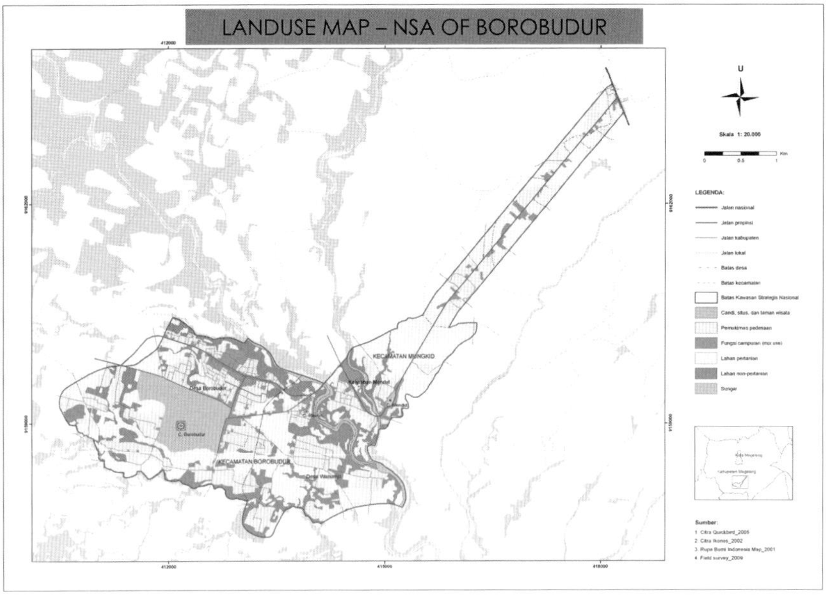

Figure 3.24: Land use map of the Borobudur National Strategic Area (Soeroso 2012)

the surrounding environment (Fatimah, 2012). The understanding was used as a basis for the preparation of the KSN presented in the context of the Borobudur Temple region (Figure 3.24).

However, a spatial plan needs not only to regulate land use, but also all stakeholders affected by the regulation. This understanding means that planning – planning itself and its implementation – requires commitment and power to achieve success.

In fact, a plan is usually difficult to implement because of the possible tension between planning and affected actors (Healey 2003). A regional plan for Borobudur is expected to operate in such a context – as heritage conservation as imagined by the local people. Conservation of Borobudur and the surrounding areas should be the manifestation of the relationship between the world heritage and the surrounding environment. It should be a mutual relationship without causing economic dependency.

Development of participatory process by local people

It can be seen that the challenge for planning for Borobudur is persistently seeking new methods to ensure not only the implementation of the plan, but also the preparation of the plan. The planning process ultimately expects the planner to be a facilitator in the discussions

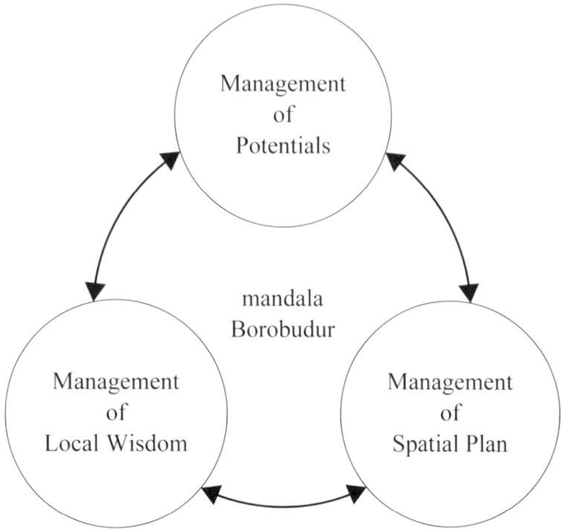

Figure 3.25: A mandala is achieved when there is a balance in the management of potentials, local wisdom, and the spatial plan (Priyana 2013)

of different roles/parties. Its role is not merely to complete a planning work. A planner needs to be observant to see which parties – those that are involved, those that should be involved, and those with no need to be involved – are in the process of building consensus.

One important activity of a planner is to engage the community through empowerment. In the planning process, empowerment provides community members with knowledge on the definition and dimension of use of their power. However, empowerment does not mean stopping the use of public power. It should be in line with and supported by a government that is willing to share the power that it has (Friedmann 1992). Empowerment does not mean dismantling government structures and putting them back together with the community as the main actors. Empowerment aims to improve the structure with the full involvement of the community in social and economic development.

In this situation, the local community is able to be associated with the Borobudur Temple. Development of rural tourism activity sheds light on how to manage the assets of villages through tourism-oriented development. In 2003, for example, a plan for a new market spurred community members to organize themselves to participate in many meetings to discuss the concept and future of Borobudur.

It is recognized that Borobudur, as world heritage, should not only be seen in the frame of monument conservation, but also as an integration of various aspects to achieve balance and harmony. Local people often use the term 'mandala Borobudur' to express Borobudur and its surrounding area. Its conservation can be achieved by management of the following aspects: potentials, local wisdom, and the spatial plan (Figure 3.25).

The potentials of the Borobudur area are the assets owned by the village or hamlet people. Each village or hamlet has a unique way of life, including family life, social interaction,

Plate 3.14: View of the sunrise from Punthuk Setumbu, which gives an impression of Borobudur and its surrounding as a cultural landscape (photo: Adishakti)

culture and traditions, and specific elements. As each village is believed to be unique, the important thing is to identify the assets that exist in the village and can be developed, such as production activities, geographical or environmental conditions, and historical elements.

Borobudur is considered the center of the area and the villages as its periphery. The result is the emergence of souvenir vendors in Borobudur, while the potential that exists in other villages has been forgotten and almost lost. However, Borobudur Sub-district is the poorest area in the Magelang Regency.

To be able to empower the periphery, meaning must be given to the potentials in the periphery. Resources need to be strengthened and encouraged so that they can become icons that are not inferior to Borobudur itself.

One way to develop potential is by using the 'One Village One Product' approach, which was developed in Japan. The approach aims to identify and create local product excellence. The product is developed for not only national, but also regional and even international, acceptance.

So far, the local community in Borobudur has identified and developed icons other than Borobudur Temple alone and other historic sites/artifacts, namely:

- Candirejo, a village known as an eco-tourism village, which was developed with support from an environmental non-governmental organization
- Klipoh, a hamlet known as a pottery craft village
- Punthuk Setumbu Hill at Karangrejo village, a spot best known as the place to enjoy the sunrise over Borobudur (Plate 3.14); introduced by a local photographer, it offers a way to experience Borobudur from a distance
- Tuksongo (Nine Springs) village, which is known for creating glass noodles from palm trees
- the ancient lake of Borobudur, which could be developed as a geo-tourism destination.

In this context, local planning processes should be organized level by level (Priyana

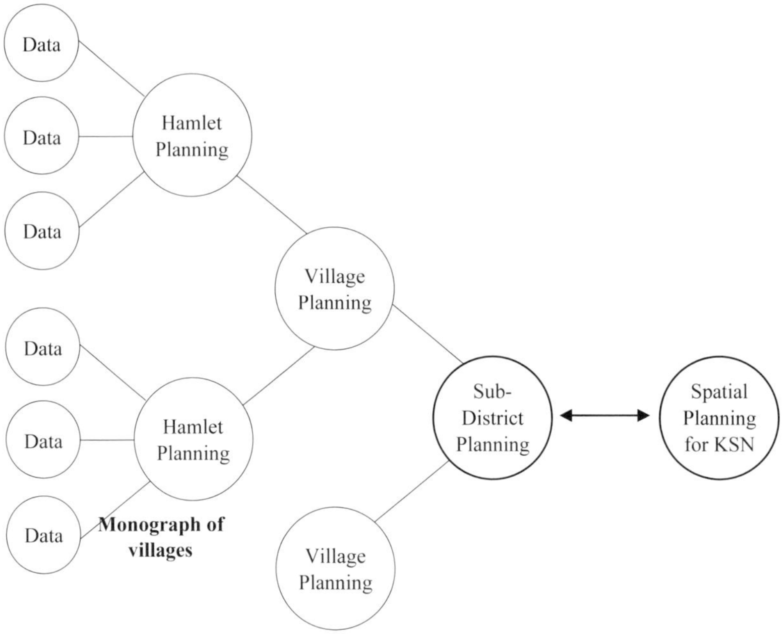

Figure 3.26: Management of spatial plan: sub-district planning is the result of village and hamlet planning (Priyana 2013)

2013), beginning with the hamlet level, then the village level, and finally accumulating in the district level. Data collection should be completed during the process at the hamlet level, where local people certainly recognize their problems. Instead of seeing Borobudur and its region as a single system, it should actually be seen as a total multisystem. With this approach, the issues that are identified could represent everyday life issues.

The formulation of strategic issues, of course, needs to depart from comprehensive data. Villages are usually identified through monograph documents (*monografi desa*), but it is common that the documents contain merely figures that cannot fully represent the potential and local wisdom of the community. Priyana (2013) emphasizes the importance of a good village monograph: it is better if the data are developed and discussed at the hamlet level and by local people (Figure 3.26).

Therefore, the capacity planning of communities involved needs to be improved. The process should be public and involve not only public figures but also local people with expert facilitation. To pass through the public consultation process, planning must be already known and agreed by the community.

Plans that are prepared and agreed upon should be raised and discussed within the scope of the larger territory. It is believed that problems that occur in a village or hamlet cannot be resolved only within the scope of the village or hamlet. District and provincial governments

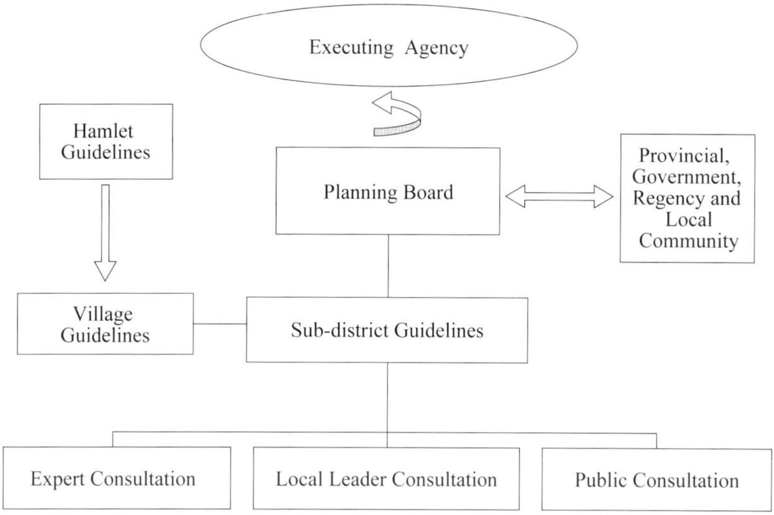

Figure 3.27: Planning process for Borobudur (Priyana 2013)

need to involved and, in addition, should be supported by a network of conservation organizations to allow the involvement of new knowledge about heritage conservation.

Planning can take this role, as well, to take advantage of the planning process rather than relying on existing formal planning mechanisms (Hocs 1996). Once community groups achieve the same awareness of a goal, their power can be more solid. Such a situation is a driver of a real action sequence.

Key planning – as also proposed by Priyana (2013) – involves the emergence of new institutional capacities in the context of the governance of Borobudur and the surrounding area. Institutional capacity is the relationship among various resources, both internal and external, at Borobudur, including local people, local government, and experts in managing Borobudur (Figure 3.27).

Borobudur Field School and the spatial plan for *saujana* heritage

Cultural landscape or *saujana* heritage is a new concept in the Indonesian heritage conservation and management field. There is a need to develop this concept within the Indonesian context with its various geographical settings. Furthermore, the willingness to conserve and manage cultural landscape heritage should be matched by proper tools, including spatial planning, which is also still in the development process. In this context, Borobudur Field School could contribute to the development of cultural landscape conservation and management. Borobudur Field School is open to undergraduate/graduate students, professionals, government officials, and local people who get together to study Borobudur as cultural landscape. The goals of the field school are to introduce participants to cultural landscape heritage field methods and provide them with an understanding of heritage management. The field school does not begin with the confirmed definitions of cultural landscape built into UNESCO frameworks, therefore it is unique and allows all kind of participants to share their expertise by being in the field with the community. This field school can provide a model for interaction among various actors. Timelines, procedures, and formulation of a framework can be proposed to enrich the planning system for Indonesia's social-cultural strategic area.

Borobudur mandala: the temple compound and surrounding villages

Jack Priyana

Introduction

Borobudur is a place of Buddhist worship and is well known as an architectural masterpiece. It functions as a holy place to honor the Buddha, with various symbols of human life and the universe to guide humankind to switch from natural lust to enlightenment and wisdom according to the teachings of Buddha. Established around the eighth century, Borobudur is also known as an archaeological artifact that has played an important role in the development of human culture, especially in Indonesia and the world at large. This important role of Borobudur and its universal outstanding values led to its inscription as a World Heritage Site by UNESCO in 1991.

For the surrounding communities, however, Borobudur is viewed as more than just an archeological site, place of worship, or World Heritage Site. Borobudur is fused with the life of the surrounding communities and has a deeper meaning. Borobudur has become a center for community spiritual activities without restriction (not just for Buddhists). For instance, in past times, the front yard of the temple was often used for traditional *wayang* puppet performances and other ceremonies. The strong character of the temple is not only visualized in Borobudur as a temple but is also blended with nature and the culture around it. Borobudur, and its surroundings, is a perfect combination of nature and culture and forms a unified cultural landscape.

A number of attempts to preserve Borobudur have been carried out by various parties such as the Indonesia government (supported by UNESCO), JICA, and others. However, so far such preservation is insufficient to accommodate the interests of the surrounding communities. Those efforts seem to have focused only on Borobudur Temple as an archeological site, and have not yet touched the local people as the main subjects who live around the temple, although Borobudur, as an architectural masterpiece, should be well connected with the surrounding nature and culture, as well as the people. This section explains the context of the Borobudur Temple compound and its surroundings based on the mandala concept, a scheme and representation of the cosmological significance of Borobudur. The mandala concept hopefully provides another perspective on the current concept of conservation, therefore Borobudur conservation efforts can be more comprehensive and realize the surrounding communities as a new force to protect Borobudur.

Borobudur as a center of spiritual activity

There are a number of hypotheses about the concept and establishment of Borobudur Temple. One says the area was once a lake and the temple was like a lotus flower floating on the lake. This visualization was first mentioned by Nieuwenkamp (1933), a Dutch painter and scholar of Hindu and Buddhist architecture. This idea can be traced from the position of the temple between the hills. Expert examination also indicates that Borobudur was in the middle of an ancient lake (Van Bemmelen 1949; Murwanto et al. 2004).

The lotus flower shape, which is almost symmetrical, also resembles the form and the corner shapes of Borobudur Temple. Thus it is reasonable that the lotus is regarded as the symbol of Borobudur. In Buddhism the lotus flower is the embodiment of purity. The lotus is a flower that floats on the surface of the water and is untouched by mud. It is believed to be the vibrant sanctity moving towards the light of wisdom.

Borobudur itself is like a sacred book that contains messages of scripture translated into beautiful reliefs throughout the walls of the temple that are full of meaning. Borobudur is a center of Buddhist teaching, where humans search for the values of life, and delivers universal messages to guide human life. Borobudur Temple also exists in unity with the surrounding nature, people, and culture. Surrounding communities regard Borobudur as the book to understand nature and the value of life.

Symbolism in Borobudur

Borobudur is a representation of nature (Plate 3.15). Representing a mountain, Borobudur is *Mahameru* that manifests in the form of a pyramid. From its base to the top are different levels (like a staircase), which symbolize the journey of the soul – starting with greedy lust symbolized in the base and climbing to the peak of sanctity in the stupa. This symbolism is also often found in the mountains that are considered as sacred.

Borobudur is also a representation of human life. Each point of human life is depicted in the reliefs. Borobudur looks like scripture that is a role model for life. This important role has positioned Borobudur for human daily life activities, as well as to accommodate the needs of sacred cult activities. Borobudur is like a holy book – it is the center of Buddhist teachings and the search for life wisdom.

Borobudur Temple Compounds

Borobudur Temple is closely related with other nearby temples, hence they are collectively called the Borobudur Temple Compounds, which consist of three temples: Borobudur Temple (the main and biggest monument), Mendut Temple, and Pawon Temple (smaller with similarity in style and craftsmanship). The temples are situated in different locations: Borobudur Temple is in Borobudur village and Pawon Temple is in Wanurejo village, both within Borobudur Sub-district. Mendut Temple, on the other hand, is located in Mendut village within the neighboring Mungkid Sub-district. Figure 3.28 shows a map of the temple

Plate 3.15: The symbolism of Borobudur Temple: (left) Borobudur Temple as a mountain/ *Mahameru*; (right) Borobudur Temple is like a lotus flower floating on the lake

Figure 3.28: Map of Borobudur Temple Compounds, consisting of Borobudur, Pawon and Mendut temples in a straight axis (map modified from Gunawan Kartapranata, 2011)

Plate 3.16: Aerial view of Borobudur Temple (Miksic 1990)

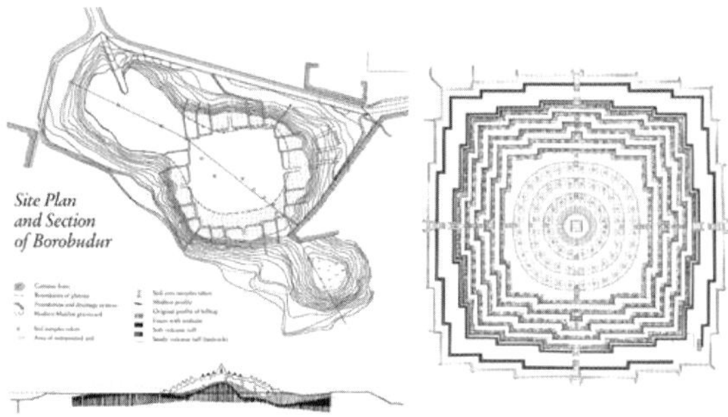

Figure 3.29: The architecture of Borobudur Temple (Miksic 1990)

compounds connected by an imaginary axis. These temples are still used annually for the Vesak ceremony.

Borobudur as a mandala

Borobudur Temple is an architectural masterpiece rich in meaningful symbols. As a center of spiritual activity, Borobudur has a distinctive structure (a combination of square and circular shapes). When viewed from above, the plan of Borobudur Temple reveals a mandala structure (Plate 3.16 and Figure 3.29). The Borobudur mandala is a scheme and representation of the cosmos. The word 'mandala' comes from Sanskrit and literally means 'circle'. The mandala concept originated from Hinduism, but is also used in the context of Buddhism. In tantra the mandala was used as one of the tools for contemplation and meditation. Various types of mandalas are used as meditation tools. Now the term 'mandala' has become a common designation for the plan or graphic or geometric pattern symbolizing the universe (microcosmos) from the human perspective. Local people often use the term 'Borobudur mandala' to express the area surrounding Borobudur.

Based on Javanese philosophy, the mandala concept of Borobudur is also related to the concept of *mancapat*, which means four sides with one center. In the context of Borobudur Temple, one stupa forms the center with four sides: east, west, north, and south. In the microcosmos view, Borobudur Temple represents a small universe, showing the journey of purifying the human soul, while in the macrocosmos view, Borobudur Temple is part of a greater universe represented by its widespread cultural landscape. However, Borobudur Temple and its surrounding cultural landscape is an inseparable unit. It is the Borobudur mandala that should be protected and kept in harmony.

Conservation efforts and challenges

Borobudur Temple currently has a sort of green safety belt in the form of the archeological park (which has been transformed into the Borobudur Tourism Park). To realize the development of the park, the two nearest hamlets were relocated. Although it was risky to move villagers residing around the temple, the effort to preserve Borobudur was implemented. The purposes of this green safety belt development are to:

- support Borobudur Temple as a conservation area
- support local economic growth
- provide an income source for the state and stakeholders
- provide a recreation area.

In line with its intended purpose, the current Borobudur park is attractive and is one of the main tourism destinations in Indonesia. Borobudur Tourism Park has become a commercial tourism site that prioritizes the economic value of the tourist area, which is managed by a state-owned company. The demand of Borobudur as a source of revenue for the state creates a burden for Borobudur. Unfortunately, it has forced Borobudur to be managed in the interests of mass tourism, resulting in such things as ignorance of the temple as a pilgrimage destination, less respect for the spiritual value of the temple, and conservation as exploitation.

Furthermore, until a decade ago Borobudur was managed by the old-fashioned perception of tourism in which tourist visits focused only on Borobudur Temple. Tourism management and stakeholders neglected the rural communities around the temple. Borobudur has been seen only as a building and has gradually lost its sanctity value and has become an economic commodity. Meanwhile, local communities around Borobudur have experienced culture shock in facing tourism. Tourism activities affect the society and the culture of the surrounding communities. If the impacts of tourism are not well managed, they will bring rapid change to the lives of the people around Borobudur – rural communities will turn into urban communities with decreasing traditional values and local wisdom, and so on.

Plate 3.17: Village *andong* tour (photo: Priyana, 2005)

Attractiveness of the surrounding villages

Borobudur Temple is located in Borobudur village, where the administration office and the biggest market of the sub-district are located. It can be said to be a focal point of the sub-district, the most developed area, and the center of administrative and economic activities. There are twenty villages in the sub-district and some are closely located near the temple, where the tourism activities take place. In recent years a new type of tourism has flourished in the Borobudur area. Tourism activities that previously only focused on the temple are now starting to spread out into the surrounding villages. Several tour guides take tourists to explore new experiences of rural tourism, which differs from the temple-centered tourism to date. Usually, tourists ride in *andong* (horse-driven carriages) to visit interesting places in the surrounding villages (Plate 3.17).

The surrounding villages have unique potential to attract tourists. For example, villages and their main potentials include:

- Ringin putih – the myth village
- Tanjungsari – the tofu village
- Klipoh hamlet in Karanganyar – pottery villages
- Tuksongo – the glass noddle village
- Kebonsari – the center of bamboo craft
- Ngargogondo – the language village
- Giritengah – the honey bee center
- Wanurejo – the art and craft village
- Candirejo – the village of scenic views.

At the end of 2002, local communities in Borobudur Sub-district held a forum and decided to establish an organization to mediate of behalf of the community to attempt to solve any problems related to tourism and to support the movement of rural tourism in Borobudur. This non-profit organization is named JAKER (*Jaringan Kerja Kepariwisataan Borobudur/* Borobudur Tourism Network). It was not active at first, but was reestablished in 2005 and

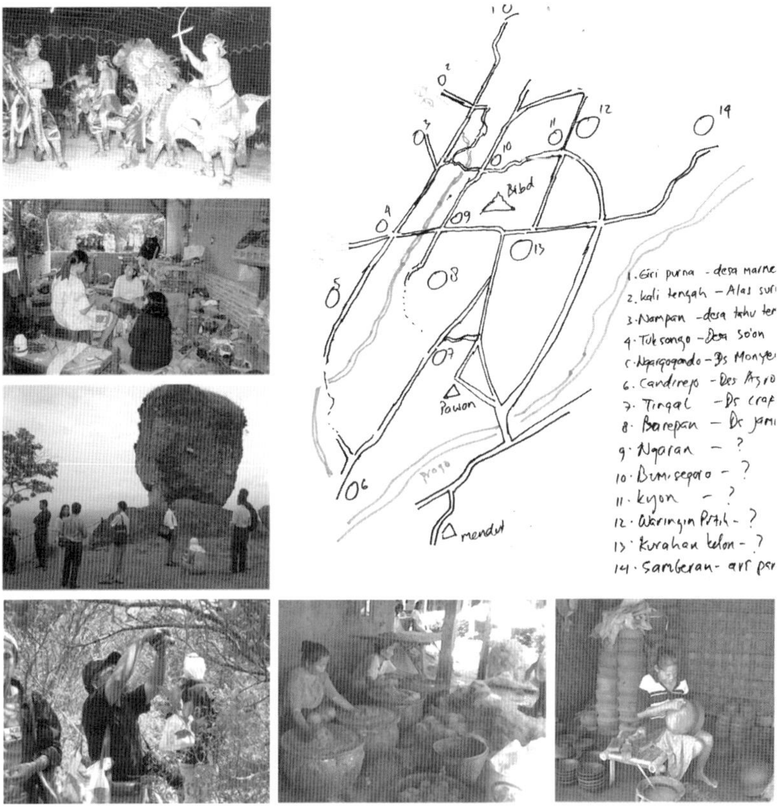

Figure 3.30: Map of villages and their potentials and attractions (photos: Priyana, 2005)

Jack Priyana (the author of this sub-chapter) was appointed as the chairman. With its renewed vision and mission, this organization actively supports local communities to explore the village potentials. One program is OVOP ('One Village One Product'), where each village can utilize its unique potential for tourism attraction.

Rural tourisms and the sustainability of the mandala

As rural tourism activities have flourished in a wider area, many villages are involved. About ten villages are quite active and are visited by tourists. Activities are mostly packaged in the form of village tours that visit the village(s) in a short timeframe, but a number of villages also provide homestays for guests staying overnight.

Attention needs to be paid to rural tourism by various stakeholders in order for development to grow and be well managed. In addition to preserving the culture and environment, rural tourism activities could be another source of income to improve community welfare. Thus the balance of nature and humans could be realized in the scope of the Borobudur mandala. Rural tourism activity needs to be supported by government; for instance, by making community-oriented policies, providing a good master plan, and supporting the implementation of laws so that development of the area can be controlled. However, spatial planning and management is an important tool to oversee the development pace of the area.

The balance of the Borobudur mandala is an important factor for creating a balance for community life in the area. The life of the villages around Borobudur can be regarded as a cultural living buffer zone that can support conservation and development.

Conclusion

Borobudur Temple, a Buddhist worship place, is a worldwide-known architectural masterpiece. It is rich in Buddhist teachings, which are shown in its reliefs and architecture. The temple structure and design represent a universe (microcosmos) symbolizing the journey of the human soul to purification. The Borobudur mandala provides a cosmological philosophy and meaningful symbols of the harmony between nature and humans.

The temples surrounding villages have unique potentials that can be utilized as tourism attractions. Rural tourism activities have spread and flourished widely in the area. Good progress has been made in the balance of the tourist flow, which was temple-centered but is now distributed within the vicinity.

Borobudur Temple Compounds and the surrounding villages, as well as the cultural landscape, represent a universe (macrocosmos). There is an inseparable unity, and one affects the other. Balance and harmony must be maintained in order to support the conservation of the whole area.

Advantages of the field school

I have been involved since the first Borobudur Field School (BFS) was held in 2004. This program allows participants to intermingle with local communities. We feel gratitude that the BFS committee allows local people to attend several parts of the program, such as lectures, discussions, field surveys, and so on. During the program, we can share our ideas and receive opinions and suggestions. We can share problems and discussions to try to find solutions together. It is a good opportunity to recharge our knowledge, as well as to widen our network. It is also a good opportunity to show the local potentials of Borobudur to the BFS participants who come from various countries. I hope the BFS program will succeed and continue to be held regularly. We really appreciate the attention to the Borobudur local communities.

4 Community Initiative in Borobudur

Community-based conservation through rural tourism initiatives in Borobudur

Titin Fatimah

Borobudur Temple has a long history since being built around the seventh to eighth centuries by the Sailendra Dynasty. After being buried for centuries, it was discovered and reconstructed and is now a world-famous tourist destination. Nowadays, not only the temple, but its surrounding villages as well, offer new alternative tourism activities. Several rural tourism movements have flourished in the area.

This sub-chapter aims to explain the rural tourism activities conducted by local communities in the Borobudur area and to analyze how such activities contribute to the cultural landscape conservation. As we know, Borobudur Temple and its surrounding cultural landscape are an inseparable unity. Conservation should be applied to both the temple and its setting.

This sub-chapter consists of six parts. Part one is an introduction to explain the structure of community and entities in Borobudur Sub-district. Part two describes the research methodology of this study. Part three discusses the traditional village community and self-initiated development, with a focus on Candirejo. Part four discusses citizens' organization at the sub-district level. Part five seeks to understand the relationship between cultural landscape conservation efforts and the rural tourism initiatives conducted by the community. It starts with the identification of the progress of rural tourism in Borobudur Sub-district, then searches the impacts of tourism activities on cultural landscape. As a synthesis, the author tries to develop a scheme of cultural landscape conservation through rural tourism activities. The last part of this sub-chapter is a concluding remark showing how rural tourism initiative can contribute to cultural landscape conservation.

The structure of community and entities in Borobudur Sub-district

A community is a group of people living in a certain place or having similar interests. Two types of community are discussed here: 'village community' (at village level) and 'citizens' organizations' (at sub-district level). Village community here refers to the communities that exist in the village, such as traditional community systems called *Rukun Tetangga* (RT; literally 'neighborhood') and *Rukun Warga* (RW; literally 'harmonious citizens'),[1] community groups in hamlets or at village level (youth organizations, women's organizations, farmer organizations, etc.), and regular residents' meetings (for example, *selapanan*, *arisan*, etc.) Citizens' organization here refers to community organizations or associations or community

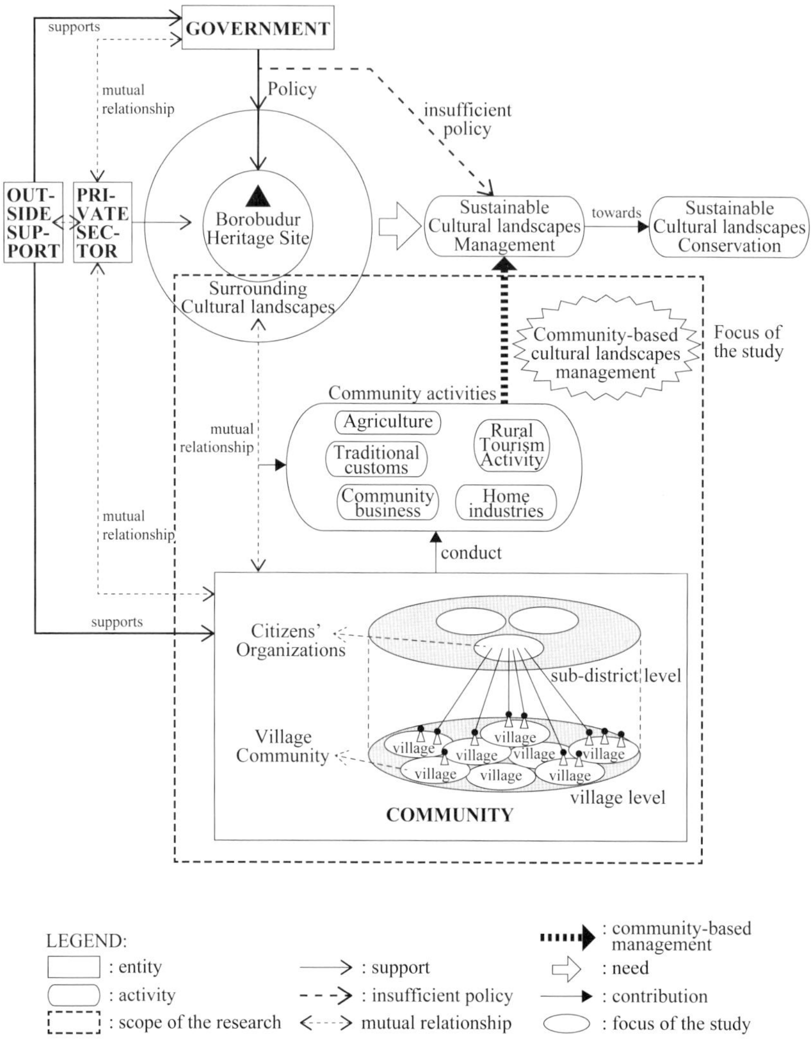

Figure 4.1: Community and related entities in Borobudur (Fatimah, 2012)

forums in which the scope is not village-based but is wider (usually covering the sub-district level), such as tourist guide associations, village chief associations, forums, and so on.

In the case of Borobudur Sub-district, many entities are related to the conservation of Borobudur Temple and the cultural landscape. Figure 4.1 shows that the main entities are:

- government: the central Government of the Republic of Indonesia, the regional

authority of Central Java Province, and the local authorities of the Magelang Regency and Borobudur Sub-district
- the private sector: travel agents, hotels, and various enterprises
- the community: village communities (at the village level) and citizens' organizations (at the sub-district level)
- outside support institutions: international organizations such as UNESCO, ICOMOS, local universities, non-profit organizations (NPOs), donors, etc.

Borobudur Temple is currently managed by the central government through the Ministry of Culture and Tourism, while the park surrounding the temple is under the management of PT. Taman Wisata Candi Borobudur, Prambanan dan Ratu Boko (PT. TWCBPRB/Tourism Park of Borobudur, Prambanan, and Ratu Boko Temple Co. Ltd)[2]. The area outside the park should be managed by the regional government, but this is not necessarily so, and local communities, in collaboration with citizens' organizations, still actively undertake some activities. Sometimes, external parties such as UNESCO, universities, NPOs, and so on provide support (Fatimah 2012).

The discussion in this sub-chapter focuses on community-based initiatives (especially rural tourism), both at the village and sub-district levels, towards sustainable cultural landscape conservation (see the dash-lined box in Figure 4.1).

Research methodology

This topic has been the research subject of author's doctoral dissertation. The field survey in Borobudur was conducted from 2003 as research for my master's thesis. Therefore, this writing is a result of longitudinal field research (Pettigrew 1990; Saldana 2003). This research mainly uses qualitative methodology with a field research approach, which requires the author to go 'into the field' to observe the real phenomenon and conditions, take extensive notes, and gather qualitative data for analysis (Patton 1987). Especially in a rural area of Indonesia, such as Borobudur, it is quite difficult to obtain documents. Therefore, this research uses interviews, field surveys, and a reference study as the main data collection. A participatory survey was also conducted.

Field surveys on rural tourism activities were conducted in Borobudur Sub-district, which has twenty villages, and then focused on selected villages (seven out of the twenty villages) whose local communities are considered to be actively conducting rural tourism activities. The villages are Borobudur, Candirejo, Giritengah, Karanganyar, Karangrejo, Wanurejo, and Wringinputih.

In-depth interviews were conducted with individuals such as village chiefs, prominent community figures, leaders of organizations, actors or performers of events or activities, and so on. Documentary and data archiving was also carried out to obtain important information related to the research from sources such as newspaper articles, project reports, minutes of meetings, published statistics data, strategy- and policy-related documents and publications, maps, and other secondary data.

Traditional village community and self-initiated development, with a focus on Candirejo

As mentioned, village community refers to the communities that exist in the village. Until now, village community traditions are mostly still practiced by village inhabitants.

This part focuses on traditional community activities in villages that have had direct influence with the cultural landscape. Borobudur Temple is surrounded by twenty villages. Candirejo village is located about three kilometers south-east of Borobudur Temple. In the past decade, this village has become known as one of Indonesia's tourism villages.[3] Therefore, I focus on Candirejo village as a case study. This village began its self-initiated development in the 1980s. By searching its development history, we can see how a traditional village community can initiate activity towards a new village industry in a sustainable way. Therefore, this section discusses the development process of Candirejo, especially its community-based rural tourism activities.

Background: the importance self-initiated development

Candirejo village is situated in the area surrounding the Borobudur Temple World Heritage Site, and the area is classified as cultural landscape heritage (Taylor 2003) and should be conserved (Engelhardt et al. 2003).

Borobudur Sub-district has several citizens' organizations (such as JAKER[4]) and NPOs (such as PATRA-PALA[5]) that have tried to collaborate with village communities to carry out agricultural revitalization programs to conserve and utilize village culture and landscape as an alternative solution for recent problems in the Borobudur area such as environmental degradation, decreases in farming benefits, and mass tourism, which is concentrated at the temple. So NPOs are encouraging villages in the surrounding area to maintain the scenery as part of the cultural landscape around Borobudur Temple. For instance, the NRM-LCE (Natural Resources Management for Local Community Empowerment) project conducted by PATRA-PALA covered ten villages scattered on the foot of the Menoreh Hills, and JAKER is in discussion with almost all twenty villages in Borobudur Sub-district. Candirejo became the main focus of the NRM-LCE project from December 2001 to November 2004.

Under such a situation, only Candirejo implemented a concept of 'Community Based Ecotourism', which was named by the villagers themselves and was managed by their own Tourism Village Cooperative. Candirejo has been selected as a pilot project for community-based tourism in Indonesia (May to November 2003) and has also been honored with awards.

Here we should question why only Candirejo could realize such a program while other villages in Borobudur Sub-district could not achieve the same level. Rural tourism is important for village revitalization and it is necessary to understand how it starts, so Candirejo can be regarded as a good case study.

General overview of Candirejo village

Candirejo is situated on the foot of the Menoreh Hills on the south side, while the north side is bordered by the Progo River, a big river which is the main river in the Kedu Plain; a small river, the Sileng River, flows through the village (Figure 4.2). Topographically, this village has two types of land: hilly areas on the south side and a plain area on the north side. The village is

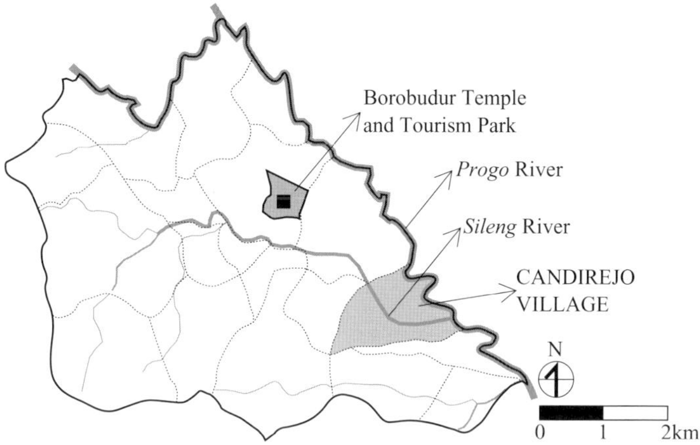

Figure 4.2: Candirejo village site context (Fatimah 2012)

situated at 100–600 meters above sea level. Candirejo village has an area of 366.25 hectares, which include rice fields, dry fields, *pekarangan* (yards), settlements, and so on.

Physically, the settlement area has a unique character, with wide yards planted with rambutan tress and bordered by green fences. Traditional houses are still in use. A number of historical sites in the village offer potential as tourist attractions.

Tourism activity in Candirejo is under the management of the Tourism Village Cooperative. There are a number of tour packages such as village tours by bicycle, foot, or *andong*, sunrise treks to the Watu Kendil site on the top of the Menoreh Hills, cooking lessons, lunches in traditional houses, homestays, and so on. Visitors can enjoy the atmosphere of daily life in the village, the beautiful scenery, and traditional music (*gamelan*), and so on, and a homestay program has been offered since 2002, with traditional houses mostly serving as accommodation facilities (Plate 4.1).

Social systems and community organizations

The residents of Candirejo village still live in a traditional way. They have their own social system and social customs that are still practiced in their daily lives; for instance, they practice *gotong-royong*[6] spirit to keep their surrounding environment clean (Gumisawa 2007) and still highly appreciate the principle of *tepo-seliro*[7] as one of their common wisdoms (Atmosumarto 2005).

The village residents have a regular community forum called *selapanan* in which they discuss any problems that have occurred in their village. This meeting is also called *rembug desa*, which means 'village meeting'. The forum is held every thirty-five days, either at the village level or at the hamlet level. There are other meetings such as *arisan* and *pengajian*, which also function as a gathering place for smaller groups such as at the RT or RW level. Several main organizations (LSD/LPMD, BPD, PKK, POKJA)[8] form the institutional

Plate 4.1: Candirejo village: (clockwise from top left) village greenery; a house used for homestays; view from a hill top; yards in the settlement area (photos: author's field survey, 2005)

framework of Candirejo's community system (Figure 4.3).

The realization process of community-based ecotourism in Candirejo

This part uses interviews and supporting documents to analyze the realization process of Community Based Ecotourism in Candirejo village, which is summarized in Figure 4.4. In this figure of interviewed events related to the realization of green tourism, we can read 'the developing process' by vertical order (↓) and 'the mechanism of each process' by horizontal order (→). From left to right, the village community is considered from the resident level to the administration level.

The first phase: agricultural development (1980–90)

The rural development program began around 1980 through a yard cleaning program (★1 in Figure 4.4). The residents cut unnecessary and overcrowded trees (bamboo, coconut, jackfruit, etc.) inside their settlement area and replaced them with more productive trees (e.g. rambutan, papaya). Figure 4.5 compares Candirejo's bamboo trees distribution in 1980 and 2008, and shows the distribution of rambutan trees in 2008. This program was supported

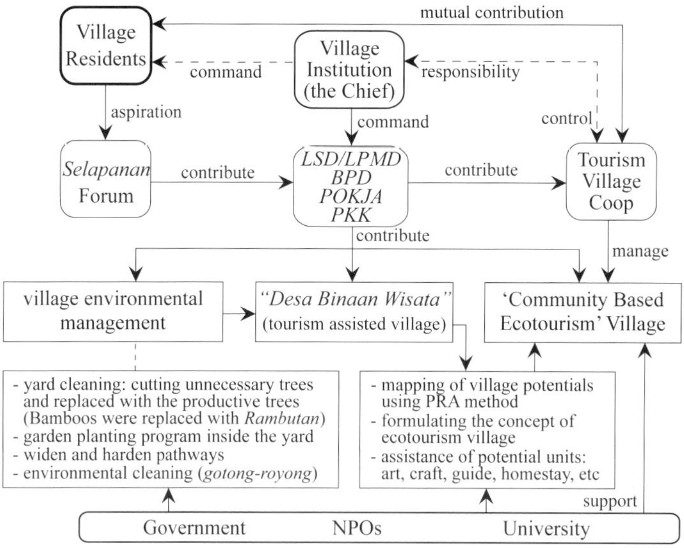

Figure 4.3: Community system in Candirejo village
(source: compiled by author, based on field survey)

by government through P2WKSS[9] and Pucungan hamlet became the pilot project. Once it seemed to be successful, the program was applied to other hamlets in the village (★2 in Figure 4.4). In addition to planting rambutan trees, yard space was also optimized by cultivating smaller vegetables and fruits between the rambutan trees (★3). The interviewees said that village residents implemented the program together hand in hand. Therefore, it raised a spirit of togetherness among them. The implementation of this program also brought other good effects to the village. The environment inside the settlement area became clean and well organized, and showed a better appearance.

The second phase: cultural improvement and community empowerment (1991–98)

After the vegetation replacement program, improvement programs for nonphysical aspects (such as managerial skills and art, craft, and home industries) were also carried out. Candirejo received support from government, academic institutions, and NPOs. Training and assistance on farming were held to increase the benefit of farming activity. Training in crafts such as bamboo carving, wood carving, batik, and so on was carried out to increase skills. Assistance was also provided to train art performance groups in each hamlet, such as in traditional dances (e.g. *jatilan*, *kobrasiswa*), traditional theatre (e.g. *gatholoco*, *ketoprak*), and so on (★4).

The implementation of the yard cleaning program in the first phase resulted in a better environment in Candirejo village. As a result, the village received awards in several village competitions (★5). The interviewees said these achievements renewed the motivation of

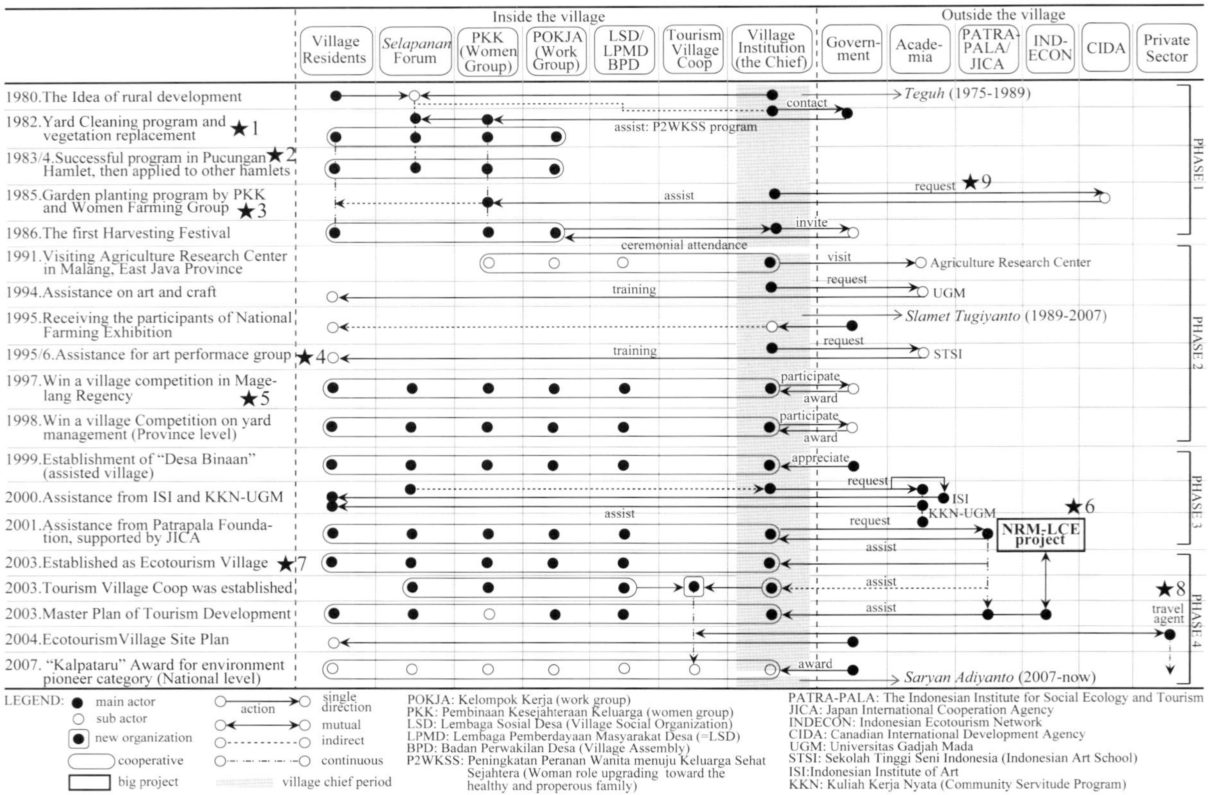

Figure 4.4: The realization process of Community Based Ecotourism in Candirejo village (author's analysis, 2008)

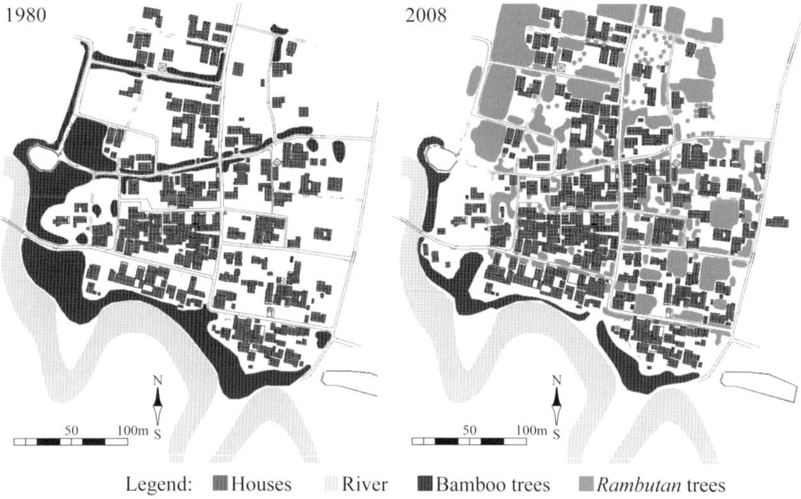

Figure 4.5: Vegetation changes in Kedung Ombo and Mangundadi hamlets, Candirejo village (author's analysis, 2008)

Plate 4.2: Cultural events in Candirejo village (Candirejo Village Cooperative and author's field survey, 2009)

village residents to participate in the program and maintain their surrounding environment. It has raised pride and a sense of belonging among residents.

The third phase: tourism activity and concept formation (1999–2003)

Candirejo village has good potential, both in natural and cultural aspects, to develop tourism activity. The village is easily accessible because it is only three kilometers from Borobudur Temple and one-and-a-half hours from Yogyakarta by car. Hence, this village has good potential to attract the tourists who visit those places (Silalahi et al. 2003). After twice receiving awards in village competitions, Candirejo became a good example of village environment management for other villages. In 1999 Candirejo was established as a *Desa Binaan Wisata* (Tourism Assisted Village) by the Government of Magelang Regency.

In order to develop further, Candirejo contacted PATRA-PALA and, supported by JICA in 2001–04, received assistance through the NRM-LCE project (★6), which develops the concept of Community Based Ecotourism. Village potentials were mapped using Participatory Rural Appraisal (PRA).

In 2000 the village adopted the principle of *catur daya* (four powers) as the basic philosophy of tourism activity. It consists of *daya tarik* (the power of fascination), *daya tumbuh* (the power to grow), *daya manfaat* (the power of benefit), and *daya tangkal* (the power to parry). This principle obliges the village residents to be members of a conducive-dynamic-active community. Conducive means they obey the leader, respect each other, and highly appreciate the common convention and spirit of *gotong-royong*. Dynamic means they are innovative and highly motivated to participate in programs. Active means they always pursue the program actively and proactively (Suhandi et al. 2003). This village also has a slogan, *Candirejo Bersatu*, which means 'Candirejo Unite'.

The fourth phase: independent management and wider promotion (2003–now)

Tourism activity in Candirejo formally started in 2003 when this village was designated as an ecotourism village by the Ministry of Culture and Tourism. Since then, the number of visitors, especially foreign visitors, has been increasing (Adiyanto et al. 2008).

The Tourism Village Cooperative was established in 2003 (★7), just after the designation of Candirejo as a Community Based Ecotourism village. This organization was created to manage the operation of tourism activities in the village. Membership is open but limited and, until now, the members are representatives of village organizations such as art performance groups, the *andong* association, the homestay association, youth groups, and chiefs of each hamlet. In interviews, they explained that the reason for the establishment of a cooperative instead of a company is that the cooperative is more suited to the character of village residents. Traditional customs and a sense of togetherness are still dominant in the social system of Candirejo village.

An annual meeting is held to report on activities throughout the year (Plate 4.3). This meeting is attended by all members. During the meeting, each representative can freely show opinions or suggestions. Recently, the Tourism Village Cooperative has collaborated with the private sector (such as travel agents and several hotels around Borobudur Temple) to promote its tourism packages (★8 in Figure 4.4) and the number of foreign visitors has significantly increased.

Village residents' roles and participation

The development through four phases, including the first two phases before 2001 when PATRA-PALA came to assist, shows that developments were initiated by the local community. During the process, the community took an important and significant role as the main actor throughout the process, while government, NPOs, academic institutions, and the private sector played a role as supporters or facilitators.

The local community initiated a 'request' to the organizations (represented in Figure 4.4

Table 4.1: Candirejo village residents' roles and participation

Program		Participation type					
		Time/ attendance	Idea	Labor	Skills	Money	Goods/ possessions
1982	Yard cleaning and vegetation replacement	■		■		■	■
1985	Garden planting program (vegetable plots)	■	■	■			■
1991	Visiting other places for comparative study	■	■				
1994	Assistance for art performance groups, crafts, and home industries	■			■		
1999	Pathways renovation (asphalt and paving)			■		■	■
2001	Collaboration with NPOs			■	■		■
2002	Homestay program		■				■
2003	Establishment of Tourism Village Cooperative	■	■	■	■		
2003	Idea of tourism village development	■	■		■		
2003	Master Plan of Tourism Development		■				

Plate 4.3: Village cooperative's annual meeting, 29 March 2008 (Fatimah, 2008)

Table 4.2: Borobudur visitors (source: Borobudur Conservation Office, 2014)

Year	Domestic tourists	Foreign tourists	Total	Year	Domestic tourists	Foreign tourists	TOTAL
1984	NA	NA	1,082,363	1999	1,764,934	86,258	1,851,192
1985	NA	NA	1,080,568	2000	2,559,527	11,444	2,570,971
1986	NA	NA	1,178,668	2001	2,470,647	111,136	2,581,783
1987	NA	NA	1,060,303	2002	1,998,355	107,972	2,106,327
1988	NA	NA	1,017,052	2003	2,008,949	61,744	2,070,693
1989	NA	NA	1,149,298	2004	1,935,918	90,517	2,026,435
1990	1,582,942	217,402	1,800,344	2005	1,903,582	89,144	1,992,726
1991	1,592,884	241,536	1,834,420	2006	1,182,212	60,850	1,243,062
1992	1,677,481	312,535	1,990,016	2007	1,681,122	299,443	1,980,565
1993	1,742,242	310,886	2,053,128	2008	1,824,873	120,816	1,945,689
1994	1,814,097	347,805	2,161,902	2009	2,370,293	146,965	2,517,258
1995	2,053,488	325,149	2,378,637	2010	2,218,971	150,017	2,368,988
1996	1,980,949	311,315	2,292,264	2011	1,952,163	160,163	2,112,326
1997	1,991,404	283,818	2,275,222	2012	2,830,892	186,841	3,017,733
1998	1,279,460	115,309	1,394,769	2013	3,148,156	217,963	3,366,119

by arrows from the village community) (★9). These initiatives were followed by 'assist' from the organizations. In other words, Figure 4.4 indicates that some programs would not have been carried out without local community initiatives (contact and requests to organizations outside the village).

In addition, residents play an important role in the process through their contributions (Table 4.1). They contribute time/attendance, ideas, labor, skills, and money, as well as goods. Both Figure 4.4 and Table 4.1 show evidence of the importance and significance of local community initiatives. The community system in this village is still strong, as are social and traditional customs. Some organizations accommodate the residents' ideas and hope to be used as communication media among the residents.

Citizens' organizations in the sub-district

Background: excessive tourist development

Since its public opening in 1983, Borobudur Temple has become a famous tourist destination and attracts many visitors to the temple and the surrounding park. The tourism park is located in Zone II, where facilities for tourists are available, such as an information center, museum, toilets, restaurant, hotel, parking area, and so on.

The economic crisis and political instability that started in late 1997 has had detrimental effects on tourist visits to the temple. The number of visitors decreased during 1997–98,

Plate 4.4: Mass tourism and crowded street vendors; (top) during peak season there are many visitors to the temple and buses park on the road when the parking area is full; (bottom) street vendors aggressively sell souvenirs, causing some discomfort to visitors (photos courtesy of JAKER, 2005)

although domestic tourist numbers increased again gradually after 1998 and peaked in 2001, with double the number of visits (Table 4.2).

Unsurprisingly, the crisis has also had serious impacts on the life of the villagers around Borobudur Temple. Economic difficulty had forced villagers to come to the Borobudur Tourism Park and become street vendors. Many people become street vendors because they can earn money more quickly and easily by selling souvenirs than by farming. Vendor activities include selling souvenirs, clothes, and postcards, renting out umbrellas, operating food stalls and souvenir kiosks, and so on. Some offer services as photographers, tourist guides, masseurs, toilet attendants, cleaners of cars, and so on (Ahimsa-Putra 2003).

The number of vendors is still increasing,[10] causing difficulties to PT. TWCBPRB in managing vendors who are becoming crowded and more competitive. The more street vendors, the more pressure there is to compete against each other to sell souvenirs or food to visitors.

The problem of vendors in Borobudur has become so serious that it has forced PT. TWCBPRB and local governments to take action. The Government of Central Java Province,

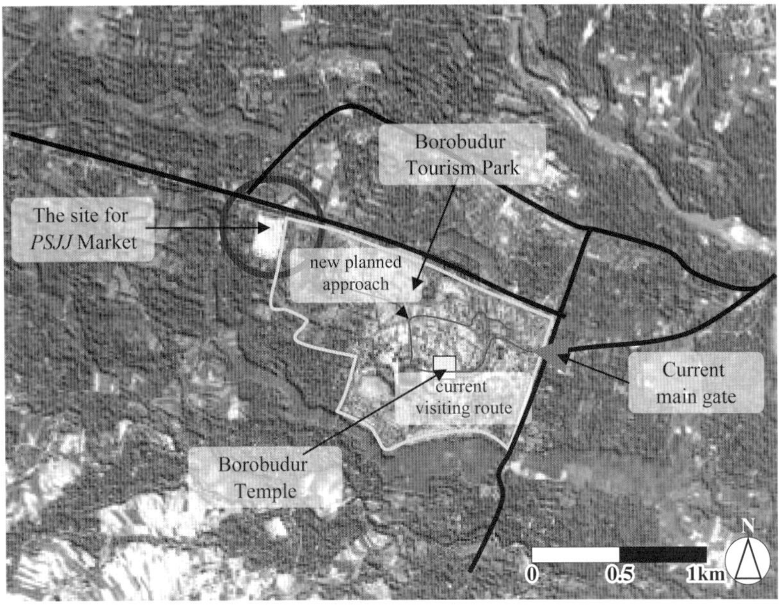

Figure 4.6: Borobudur Tourism Park and the PSJJ site (plan made by author based on Ikonos satellite image and field investigation, 2004)

for example, asked a consultant to design a vendor management system in Borobudur Tourism Park. This plan, the *Pasar Seni Jagad Jawa* (PSJJ),[11] aimed to gather the vendors in an art/souvenir market integrated within the parking area (Engelhardt et al. 2003). The market is similar to a huge shopping mall and is located very near to the temple.

There is an intention to change the entrance and approach to the temple from the current east gate to the rear of the temple. The model and location of the PSJJ thus may cause problems in terms of landscape conservation. The PSJJ plan raised polemics and invited reactions from both local communities and several organizations about heritage concerns. Protests and demonstrations against the proposal were held. Following this opposition, a new proposal[12] was drawn up but in the end both proposals were rejected after an evaluation by the UNESCO-ICOMOS Reactive Monitoring Mission Team (Engelhardt et al. 2003). Figure 4.6 shows the site plan.

At the same time, a declaration pointing out the uselessness of the PT. TWCBPRB was announced by Borobudur communities to mark the twentieth anniversary of the Borobudur Temple restoration. They also asked the government to revise Presidential Decree No. 1/1992 about the management of PT. TWCBPRB. This meeting was held by FLMB[13] and facilitated by PATRA-PALA. The event was attended by village chiefs within Borobudur Sub-district and by youths, representatives of the tourism industry, and heritage activists. During the meeting, they decided to establish the JAKER organization to represent the community.

Table 4.3: Profile of citizen's organizations in Borobudur Sub-district (field survey, 2008)

No.	Name of organization	*Est. Year	Form of organization	The reason/purpose of establishment	Main activities	Scope	Key person /leader	Funding sources	Current condition
1	HPI (Himpunan Pramuwisata Indonesia/Indonesian Tourist Guide Association)	1988	Professional association	A nationwide organization for supporting guides in every tourism spot at the smallest level.	Coordinating the guides, workshop, training, etc. (members: >50 persons)	Guide in Magelang Regency	★Nurrochmad (guide), ★Hatta (guide)	Self-help, incentive from government	●
2	PKDKB (Paguyuban Kepala Desa se Kecamatan Borobudur/Village Chiefs Association in Borobudur Sub-district)	1990	Professional association	To provide a media to communicate among village chiefs in Borobudur Sub-district. ■	Meeting, sharing information, and solving ongoing problems. (members: 20 persons)	Borobudur Sub-district	★Slamet Tugiyanto (village chief)	Contribution from each village	●
3	KOPARI (Koperasi Pariwisata/Tourism Cooperation)	1996	Tourism services cooperative	First, to support the special needs of photographers, then open to guides, vendors, etc. ▲	Support the member needs, training, micro credit, etc. (members: >500 persons)	Borobudur Sub-district	Suherman (ex-policeman, businessman) ☆1	Member dues, incentive from government	●
4	PTJ (Paguyuban Turonggo Joyo/Horse Carriage/Andong Driver Association)	1998	Professional association	To avoid conflict among the andong drivers in Borobudur Sub-district. ▲	Managing and coordinating the andong drivers. (members: <80 persons)	Andong driver in Borobudur	Aan (andong driver) ☆2	Member dues, incentive from government	●
5	MAPAN (Masyarakat Peduli Lingkungan/Community for Environmental Awareness)	1999	NPO	To keep and conserve the environment in Borobudur, especially against pollution from tourism activities. ▲	Advocacy, training, workshop, assisting small business groups, etc. (members: ±10 persons)	Borobudur Sub-district	★Aji Luhur (entrepreneur)	Self-help, incentive from government	□

6	PSWB (Paguyuban Sambya Waharing Boro/Association of Retailers & Vendors in Borobudur)	1999	Professional association	To avoid conflict among retailers and vendors. ▲	Coordinating and managing the vendors, making consensus, etc. (members: >700 persons)	Vendor in Borobudur Park	Maladi (entrepreneur, now village chief) ☆3	Incentive from PT. TWCB-PRB	□
7	PJWB (Paguyuban Jasa Wisata Borobudur/Borobudur Tourism Services Association.)	2003	Professional association	To accommodate people working in tourism (not only vendors) in Borobudur. ▲	Coordinating the members, negotiating with PT. TWCBPRB and government. (members: >1000 persons)	Vendor in Borobudur Tourism Park	Tri Basuki (vendor) ★Sarnun (vendor)	Self-help/ member dues	◎
8	TANKER (Tim Anti Kekerasan/Anti-Violation Team)	2001	NPO	To minimize the bad attitudes of some local people towards visitors, to create a comfortable sociocultural condition in Borobudur. ▲	Sweeping, controlling, patrolling, and making sure the situation in Borobudur is safe for visitors.(members: ±20 persons)	Borobudur Sub-district	★Jack (guesthouse owner, guide), ★Kirno (entrepreneur)	Self-help, incentive from government, event/ project	●
9	JAKER 1 (Jaringan Kerja Kepariwisataan Borobudur/ Borobudur Tourism Network)	2002	NPO	To mediate on behalf of the community and to problem solve any issues related to tourism.	After the establishment, there was no activity. (participants: <40 persons)	Borobudur Sub-district	★Slamet Tugiyanto (village chief)	Self-help,	□
10	JAKER 2 (Reborn after JAKER 1 was idle)	2005	NPO	To reactivate JAKER 1, with renewed vision and mission. ■	Advocacy, assisting local community, etc. (main members: ±7)	Borobudur Sub-district	★Jack (guesthouse owner, guide)	Self-help, partnership	●
11	GG (Gagas Gapura/Discussion forum)	2003	Discussion group	To contribute thoughts on Borobudur issues in more intellectual ways, especially against PSJJ plan.	Discussion, publishing newsletter to share thoughts. (members: ±5 persons)	Magelang Regency	★Lasmito (consultant), ★Ruwido (consultant),	Self-help	□

12	WI (Komunitas 'Warung Info Jagad Cleguk'/Community Information Center)	2003	Discussion group	To collect and spread information and issues related to Borobudur, as well as local art and culture. ▲ ■	Documentation, discussion, art performance, demonstration, etc. (main members: ±4 persons)	Magelang Regency	★Sucoro (artist)	Self-help, partnership	●
13	LEPEK (Lembaga Perekonomian Rakyat/Micro Economic Foundation)	2003	NPO	Local people always treated as objects; therefore it is important to make them participate in every process. ▲ ■	Advocacy, training, assisting some small-scale businesses such as crafters.(members: ±5 persons)	Magelang Regency	★Wito (management consultant)	Self-help, partnership	◎
14	BCA (Borobudur Care Association)	2004	NPO	To support local people against PSJJ plan. ▲	Participating in discussion and demonstration. (main members: ±4 persons)	Borobudur Sub-district	Priyoto (hotel owner), ★Nurrochmad (guide), ★Sarnun (vendor)	Self-help	□
15	FMSW (Forum Masyarakat Sadar Wisata/Tourism Awareness Community Forum)	2005	Forum	To raise local awareness about tourism, especially to support PSJJ plan. ▲	Discussion, mobilization, demonstration.(participants: >70 persons)	Borobudur Sub-district	Agus Rochmad (driver), ★Wito (management consultant)	Self-help	□
16	FPD (Forum Putra Daerah/ Local Genuine Generation Forum)	2005	Forum	To gather local community strength to support PSJJ plan▲	Discussion, mass mobilization, demonstration (participants: >200 persons)	Vendors in Borobudur Park	Suripto (vendor), ★Wito (management consultant)	Self-help	□
17	FRKPB (Forum Rembug Klaster Pariwisata Borobudur/Borobudur Tourism Cluster Discussion Forum)	2005	Forum	To be a mediator between government and local community and avoid conflict among organizations. ▲	Meeting, making funding proposal to government, monitoring, evaluation, etc.(participants: >15 organizations)	Borobudur Sub-district	★Kirno (entrepreneur)	Fully supported by government	●

18	PRL (Pertemuan Rebo Legi/ Crafters Association)	2006	Professional association	To accommodate crafters (focusing on environmental-friendly craft). ■	Regular meeting every 35 days on Rebo Legi day, workshop, assistance, etc.(members: +25 persons)	Crafters in Borobudur-Menoreh	★Purnomo (craftsman)	Self-help	●
19	FLMB (Forum Lintas Masyarakat Borobudur/ Borobudur Cross Society Forum)	2002 2005	Forum	To accommodate various organizations into one forum, to unite the voice and build the strength of local community in Borobudur.	An incidental forum held when needed, i.e. gathering local people against PT. TWCBPRB.(participants: >30 persons)	Borobudur Sub-district	Priyoto (guesthouse owner), ★Sucoro (artist)	Self-help	△

Legend: ●existing and active □not existing/already dispersed ▲tourist conflict *Est. Year: year of establishment ☆ 1: interview with KOPARI staff ☆ 2: interview to Aji Luhur ◎ existing but not so active △ unclear ■ promoting village culture ★ : interviewed key person ☆ 3: interview with Wito and Sarnun

Table 4.4: Socioeconomic condition for timeline analysis (author's analysis, 2011)

Year	Socioeconomic condition in Borobudur	Highlight
1983	Opening of Borobudur Tourism Park to the public	Tourism activities start
1983	Beginning of tourism-related jobs	
1997	Economic crisis hits Indonesia	Due to economic crisis, some problems start to emerge
1997~	Impacts of economic crisis started to emerge (economic difficulty → increasing number of street vendors → overcrowded and aggressive street vendors)	
2003	PSJJ plan issued	Peak of many problems
2003-2005	Peak of many problems in Borobudur: community against PSJJ plan	
2006~	PSJJ problem calming down	Recovery situation

Unfortunately, the government ignored this local initiative. This situation forced some citizens to take action by establishing other organizations to accommodate their aspirations.

Such tourist development activity, especially the peak of the PSJJ problems in 2003, shows a certain impact on community-based activities at the sub-district level.

Profile of citizens' organizations in the sub-district

According to interviews during the field survey, supported by secondary materials, Table 4.3 lists citizens' organizations in Borobudur Sub-district since the 1980s. This data consists of basic information such as organization name, year of establishment, form of the organization, the reason or purpose for establishment, main activities, scope of the organization, key people or leader, funding sources, and the current condition of each organization.

The progress of citizens' organizations

Based on the explanation of each citizens' organization shown in Table 4.3, a timeline method was used to compile and analyze the growth process of each organization. This timeline analysis uses a time range from 1988 (the year of establishment of the first citizens' organization) until 2009 (reflecting the recent condition). In this time range, the socioeconomic condition in the Borobudur area was analyzed and then referred to the establishment of citizens' organizations. According to the field survey result, the socioeconomic condition in Borobudur Sub-district could be explained chronologically as shown in Table 4.4.

The socioeconomic conditions in Borobudur Sub-district, as shown in Table 4.4, highlight three important events or conditions: the economic crisis (1997), the PSJJ plan (2003), and a calmer situation after the PSJJ problems. Based on this, four periods can be recognized. Each period is considered to have a different state. The establishment of citizens' organizations was then analyzed along the different phases. Therefore it is possible to analyze the conditions and activities of citizens' organizations during certain periods. Accordingly, the dynamic progress in Borobudur Sub-district can be divided into four phases:

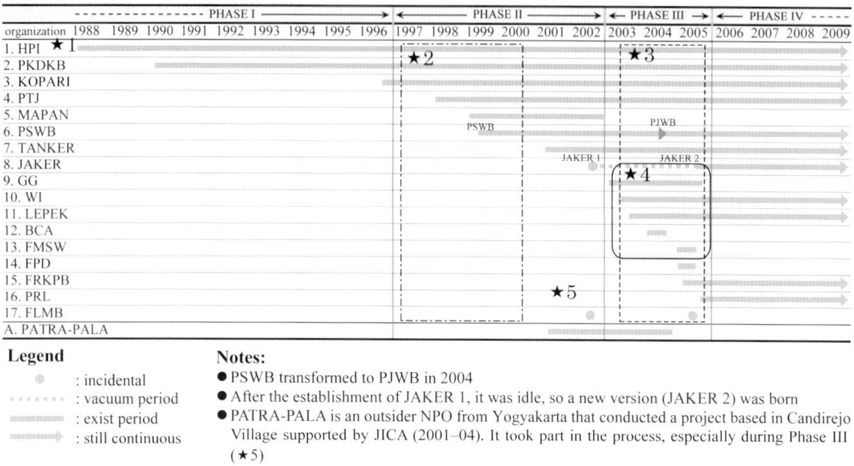

Figure 4.7: Timeline analysis of citizens' organizations in Borobudur Sub-district (author's analysis, 2008)

- Phase I: the start of the tourism period (…–96)[14]
- Phase II: the economic crisis period (1997–2002)
- Phase III: the peak of PSJJ problems period (2003–05)
- Phase IV: the recovery period (2006–…).

Figure 4.7 shows that in Phase I many people started to work in tourism as tourist guides, photographers, vendors, and so on, therefore organizations were needed to accommodate their needs. HPI was established for tourist guide coordination and training (★1). KOPARI initially focused on supporting photographers' needs, but then opened to guides and vendors. One of its programs to provide micro credit is open to the public.

Phase II saw the start of problems in Borobudur, caused first by the national economic and political crisis during 1997–2000 (★2). Many problems in Borobudur raised awareness among the locals, and a number of organizations were established to assist in problem solving. PSWB was established to avoid conflict among *andong* drivers and vendors by coordinating and managing them. MAPAN, TANKER, and JAKER were the first NPOs concerned with advocacy and assisting local communities.

Phase III saw the peak of many problems in Borobudur (★3), especially with local communities against the PSJJ plan. During this period, grassroots movements arose, as well as many discussion forums, associations, and organizations such as GG, WI, LEPEK, BCA, FMSW, and FPD (★4). Most of their activities were discussions, advocacy, and demonstrations to push the government and PT. TWCBPRB for better management of Borobudur and the surrounding area.

Table 4.5: Classification of citizens' organizations (author's analysis, 2008)

Category	Activities	Name of organization
Tourism service actor	□ Professional association	HPI, PTJ, PSWB, PRL
	■ Tourism service cooperative	KOPARI
Thinker	Study/discussion group	GG, WI
	△ Action mobilization	BCA, FMSW, FPD
	Self-managed program executor	MAPAN, TANKER, JAKER, LEPEK
Forum	General forum	FRKPB, FLMB
	○ Village chief forum	PKDKB

In Phase IV, after the PSJJ problems in 2005, the situation became more settled. In this period, a new awareness of promoting local village potentials has been arising. A review of the master plan and related laws has taken place, and now the government is formulating a new master plan. About eleven citizens' organizations still exist and continue their programs.

Besides local Borobudur organizations, an NPO from outside Borobudur, namely PATRA-PALA, took part in the process, especially during Phase III. As an experienced NPO, it has enough capability and competence to assist and supervise local communities (★5). PATRA-PALA facilitated several meetings, seminars, and workshops to help the process of problem-solving.

Transformation of citizens' organizations

According to the activities shown in Table 4.3, the citizens' organizations within Borobudur Sub-district can be classified into the three categories shown in Table 4.5:

- tourism services actor (e.g. association of vendors, tourist guides, etc.)
- thinker (e.g. local NPO, discussion forums, etc.)
- forum (e.g. PKDKB, FRKPB (a forum initiated by JAKER and local government to accommodate organizations in Borobudur Sub-district)).

Each organization has relationships to others depending on how it conducts activities. Based on Phases I to IV, activities of organizations, as well as relationships, change. So an attempt was made to map their connections. This mapping placed each organization based on its existence during Phases I to IV (Figure 4.7) and the classification group (Table 4.5). Afterwards, lines were drawn to indicate the connections between organizations according to interview results and the documents studied (see Figure 4.8).

Figure 4.8 shows that the relationship in each period is different. During Phase I there was no relation between villages and the tourism sector. They started to be connected in Phase II when thinkers and outsider NPOs entered the network. Phase III was the peak of problems, therefore many citizens' organizations were established as the manifestation of local initiatives, which is why the connections between all sectors were quite complex during Phase III. Entering Phase IV, the PSJJ plan was stopped, and the problems calmed down.

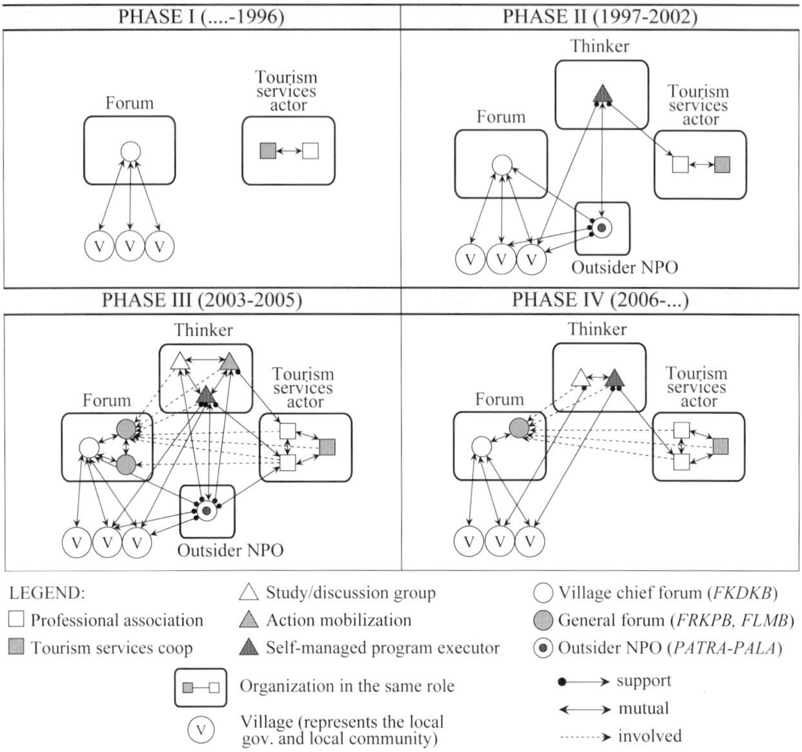

Figure 4.8: The relationship of organizations in Borobudur (author's analysis, 2008)

Several initiatives that appeared during the peak of problems in Phase III also dispersed, such as GG, BCA, FMSW, and FPD, while other organizations still exist. The reason they dispersed is that their establishment was a reaction to the PSJJ plan. Other organizations with long-term programs still continue their activities today (Fatimah and Kanki 2009).

Conservation and rural tourism initiatives

Nowadays, rural cultural landscape conservation efforts take numerous forms, such as through the introduction of rural tourism. The concept of sustainability in rural tourism must be a multipurpose one if it is to succeed. It should aim to sustain the culture and characteristics of host communities, as well as the landscape and habitats (Lane 1994). Tourism is seen as an agent of rural economic regeneration and as a way of valorizing conservation (Bramwell

Figure 4.9: Signage showing attractions that can be visited during village tours (Fatimah, 2008)

1990; Brown and Leblanc 1992; Jamieson 1990).

A number of researchers have addressed the concerns on community-based tourism development (Morishige 2009) and community-based cultural landscape conservation (Buggey and Nora 2008). Hampton (2005) pointed out the chance of local communities benefiting from a new approach of planning and managing local assets. He also emphasized that heritage sites may be able to generate real economic and social benefits for their local hosts.

In the case of Borobudur, several rural tourism movements have flourished. Borobudur Temple is a major tourist destination in Indonesia and attracts around three million domestic and foreign visitors annually. The average number of visitors is 8000 tourists per day. During peak seasons, the temple can attract an average of 40,000 tourists per day, and both foreign and domestic tourists often stay in the nearby city of Yogyakarta, Indonesia's second-most popular destination after Bali, and take day trips to Borobudur, usually on coaches and with a guide (Dahles 2001).

Typically, tourists visiting Borobudur spend three to four hours exploring the temple and the enclosing Borobudur Tourism Park without visiting other places adjacent to the site. This type of tourism is not ideal for Borobudur's conservation efforts, especially as Borobudur Temple is also surrounded by vast cultural landscape heritage (Taylor 2003). Hence, integrating these landscapes into a Borobudur tourism scheme is important in conserving the temple. Today, there are initiatives by some local people to spread awareness among Borobudur residents of the importance of conserving the surrounding villages.

This study shows that a number of citizens' organizations were established and some community initiatives were undertaken in Borobudur during 2003–05. Some parties such as local guides and local NPOs, for example, took tourists to the villages surrounding the temple in order to reduce the overcrowding problems that started to emerge during this time. Figure 4.9 shows welcoming signage containing information of several villages' attractions that are worth visiting during village tours. The signage is situated at an intersection in Tuksongo village, which is often passed by tourists in *andong*.

One important step was the establishment of Candirejo village as a Community Based Ecotourism village in 2003. In recent years, noticeable development includes the spread of various village tours carried out by local guides around the temple. There are also rural tourism activities held by other villages in Borobudur Sub-district. The successful story of Candirejo village has inspired other villages to initiate similar activity. This type of rural tourism can be categorized as 'new tourism' or 'alternative tourism' rather than conventional tourism.

The progress of rural tourism in Borobudur Sub-district

The history of Borobudur rural tourism is summarized in Table 4.6.

Before rural tourism activities started, Candirejo village had already implemented environment improvement programs and developed the community since the 1980s. It was acknowledged as a *Desa Binaan Wisata* (Tourism Assisted Village) by the Government of Magelang Regency in 1999 and was established as an ecotourism village in 2003.

After the opening of the Borobudur Tourism Park in 1983, tourist visits gradually increased. In the 1990s several local guides and lodge owners started to bring tourists to the village area independent of any coordination with the tourist guide association (for example, a guide from Candirejo took tourists to his house and on sightseeing visits around the village).[16] Another place that is frequently visited is Klipoh, in Karanganyar village, a traditional hamlet known for its pottery industry. It is also popular because there is a nearby place with a good view to Borobudur Temple and a spot to enjoy the sunrise.

In 2000 local guides and *andong* drivers agreed to better organize these tours. They agreed on a standard package tour, route, price, and so on. They also included visits to other villages such as Wanurejo, Tuksongo, and Tanjungsari. Village tours became a popular alternative around 2004–05 after the PSJJ plan issue appeared in 2003 (Table 4.6). When the problem concerning the Borobudur Temple management was exposed by the press and frequently featured in mass media, it also brought increased attention to the temple.

Current conditions of village tours

In recent years guided tours started to visit the villages surrounding Borobudur Temple. Typically, the tours are organized in the form of *andong* rides in which tourist are guided to explore the villages along several predetermined routes (Figure 4.10). During the tours, tourists can enjoy the rural atmosphere, watch traditional art performance, and so on (Plate 4.5).

The routes illustrated in Figure 4.10 are the standard routes but are flexible depending on the situation, time availability, and the tourists' interests. The existing routes can be classified into three types:

- single village route (Route B~H: visiting and exploring only one village)
- multiple village route (Route A: visiting and exploring several villages)
- temple visit route (Route I: special route visiting Borobudur, Mendut, and Pawon temples).

Usually, before conducting a tour, the guide consults with the local people, especially when the tour itinerary needs preparation, such as to schedule an art performance, a pottery-making experience, a lunch, and so forth (Fatimah and Kanki 2012).

Table 4.6: Timeline of rural tourism progress in Borobudur Sub-district (field survey, 2009)

Year	Events at sub-district level
1983	Borobudur Temple was opened to the public
1988	HPI was established
1990	Village tour was first started by local guides and lodge owners
1991	Borobudur Temple was inscribed in the World Heritage List
2000	*Andong* reformation, divided into two groups: *andong* for local market and tourism market❷ Village tours organized/standardized among the guides❶❷❸
2003	PSJJ plan appears → Borobudur publicized by press → village tour activities become widely known UNESCO-ICOMOS Reactive Monitoring Mission Candirejo Ecotourism Village established ①
2004	Indonesian government established a steering committee for the second stage of Borobudur restoration focusing on community empowerment Spirit to explore village potentials → 'One Village One Product' (OVOP) ❺① First Borobudur Field School ②
2005	Second Borobudur Field School ② JAKER actively supports villages through various programs First stage of Borobudur village mapping by Green Map ③❺
2006	Third Borobudur Field School ②
2007	Fourth Borobudur Field School ②
2008	Second stage of Borobudur village mapping by Green Map ③❺
2009	Borobudur Field School organized by local people❹

Citizens' organizations in Borobudur Sub-district that are involved:
❶ HPI: *Himpunan Pramuwisata Indonesia* (Indonesian Tourist Guide Association)
❷ PTJ: *Paguyuban Turonggo Joyo* (*Andong* Driver Association)
❸ MAPAN: *Masyarakat Peduli Lingkungan* (Community for Environmental Awareness)
❹ WI: *Warung Info Jagad Cleguk* (Community Information Center)
❺ JAKER: *Jaringan Kerja Kepariwisataan Borobudur* (Borobudur Tourism Network)

Other institutions from outside Borobudur that are involved:
① PATRA-PALA
② CHC-UGM: Center for Heritage Conservation-Gadjah Mada University, Yogyakarta)
③ Green Map Yogyakarta (a branch of worldwide Green Map System network that engages in helping communities in mapping green living, nature, and cultural resources, based in Yogyakarta)

After the success of Community Based Ecotourism in Candirejo village, other villages are trying to initiate rural tourism activities in their villages. According to field investigations in seven villages (Borobudur, Candirejo, Giritengah, Karanganyar, Karangrejo, Wanurejo, and Wringinputih), each village has its own unique potential to explore. Some activities and improvements have also been done by village communities. They usually try to utilize the village attractiveness and potential to attract tourists.

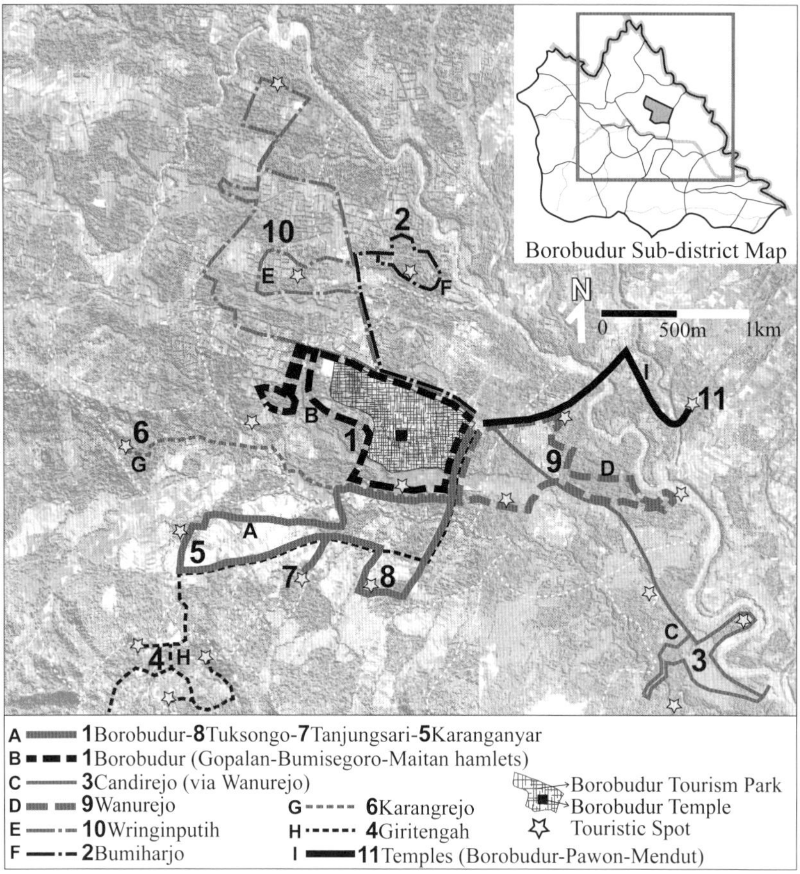

Figure 4.10: Routes of village tours (field survey, 2009)

Impacts of tourism activities on cultural landscape

With rural tourism activity, villagers make some improvements to their village environment to increase the potential and level of attractiveness. These improvements, whether physical or non-physical, have impacts on the village environment and landscape elements. For instance, facilities are built in places visited by tourists or existing facilities are customized to suit the new needs, tourist functions, and so on. These changes impact the cultural landscape – intentionally or otherwise. According to field investigation and interviews, impacts on physical aspects caused by rural tourism activities are evident. Figure 4.11 summarizes and

Plate 4.5: Rural tourism activities: village tour by *andong* (left); traditional festival (right) (photo: Fatimah, 2009)

compares these impacts by looking at the conditions of the elements before and after tourism activities.

As Figure 4.11 shows, there are five categories of change in physical aspects of landscape elements:

- additional: the process of adding something new to the current object in order to fulfill a requirement or to make something functionally better, for example:
  - building a wooden/bamboo hut on a hilltop to view the landscape
  - adding a handrail along a footpath up a hill to help visitors climb up
  - providing night lamps
- continue: this keeps things as they are without changes, for example:
  - maintaining an old traditional house in its original condition
  - continuing activities such as local home industries, art performances, and agricultural methods/traditions
- customize: a process of changing something to fit new requirements, with minor changes, for example:
  - adding facilities for guests in houses that are used for homestays
  - practicing the *tumpangsari* system for agriculture (planting various plants in one place to optimize cultivation in limited farmland)
- transform: a process of changing an object with major alterations, for example:
  - reusing vacant old houses as models of traditional houses and as lunch venues
  - replacing concrete fences with green fences
- repair: a process of fixing or renovating an existing object that is broken or out of date to ensure that it is able to carry out its function properly, for example:
  - repairing access to the village/places to be visited
  - repairing an old bamboo bridge with new bamboo materials.

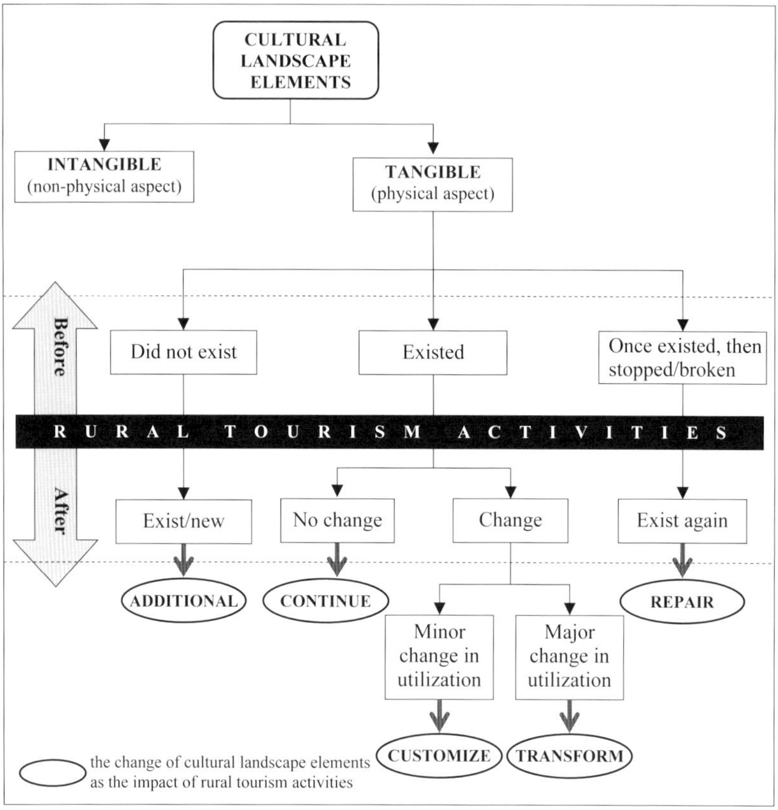

Figure 4.11: Impacts of changes (author's analysis, 2011)

A scheme of cultural landscape conservation

Cultural landscape continuously changes (Palang et al. 2005), therefore it is necessary to manage those changes in sustainable ways. This is called 'evolutive conservation' (Architectural Institute of Japan 2011).

Landscape conservation is best when it is adaptive and continual – a long-term process rather than a short project (Naveh 1995). Community-based rural tourism participates in the effort of cultural landscape conservation as it is embedded in the villagers' ordinary activities. Village potential can be nourished and maintained through daily activities such as farming, keeping the environment clean, growing and keeping greeneries, practicing traditional customs, and so on. Those village potentials are elements of cultural landscape and therefore maintaining village resources and potentials contributes to cultural landscape conservation.

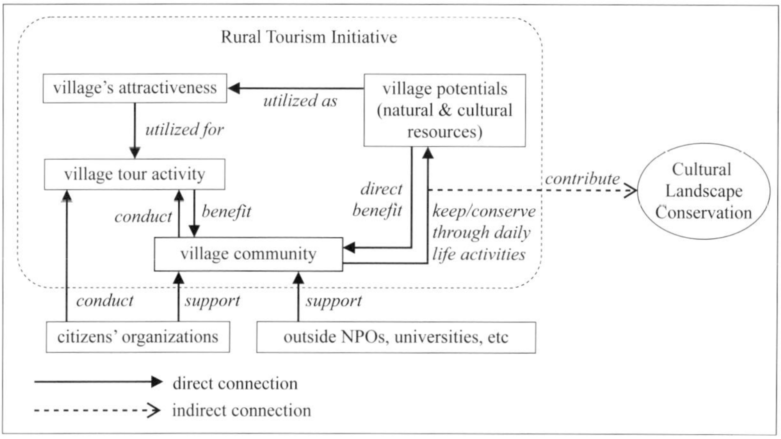

Figure 4.12: Scheme of community-based conservation for cultural landscape through rural tourism (author's analysis, 2011)

Figure 4.12 shows the scheme of rural tourism initiatives and its relation with cultural landscape conservation. Although there are several problems in its implementation, if the rural tourism initiative scheme proposed in this figure can be managed successfully, it can play an important role in cultural landscape conservation in the long term.

Taylor (2003) points out that places, traditions, and activities of ordinary people create a rich cultural tapestry of life, particularly through our recognition of the values people attach to everyday places and the concurrent sense of place and identity.

Since 2003 a number of discussions regarding the new perspective on Borobudur cultural landscape have taken place. These discussions give some insights and awareness (especially for the local people) that Borobudur Temple and its surrounding area is a part of cultural landscape. It is an inseparable unity which is both important to be conserved and sustained (Fatimah et al. 2005). Points that have emerged concern the importance of exploring and promoting the surrounding village potentials for alternative tourism attractions, as well as accommodating community initiatives and participation in such initiatives. All the activities for cultural landscape conservation planning have to be knitted together and cohere in a framework conceived to sustain the whole character and significance of the landscape, not just its individual parts (Mason 2008).

Concluding remark: rural tourism and landscape

In summary, rural tourism initiatives in Borobudur Sub-district have been shown to be the result of collaborations between villagers, local NPOs, and tourist guides. It is also confirmed that rural tourism activities in Borobudur take the form of exploring village potentials and locality. The rural tourism initiatives in each village differ in term of progress and conditions, but each village has its own community initiative, which is an important part of tourism development in Borobudur. The villages' attractiveness and potentials that are used for rural tourism are part of the landscape elements used in the villagers' daily lives.

According to field investigation and evaluation, improvements have been carried out by village communities due to rural tourism activity in their villages. These improvements have brought some changes to the village environment, which inevitably also affects the whole cultural landscape. As cultural landscape continuously changes, we can consider any changes as a natural phenomenon, but we should also be aware of the possibility of destructive impacts.

Landscape changes can bring positive and negative impacts. Those changes should maintain the authentic value of landscape elements. As long as the changes are intended to upgrade the landscape value and are not against the norms and principals of cultural landscape conservation, they are tolerable. Community knowledge, awareness, and consciousness of cultural landscape conservation are very important. With sufficient knowledge and awareness, people will consciously make good changes in their daily life activities, as well as in rural tourism activities.

Rural ecotourism and landscape in Candirejo village

Wahyu Utami and Tatak Sariawan

Rural ecotourism in Candirejo village is supported by local government and local community. To become a rural ecotourism village, government and local communities created a tourism cooperative. Through providing the best service, the local economy can be improved and the ecology maintained.

'Rural ecotourism' has become a boom in Indonesia, especially in Borobudur with its World Heritage listing and many tourists. It is believed to be generating rapid movement in villages that are preparing for rural ecotourism, especially based on central government directives. This phenomenon is about tourists, potential areas, nature, culture, economic movement, and environment issues.

This sub-chapter aims to describe the participation of the local communities in Candirejo village in rural ecotourism. Rural-ecotourism is one way to equip the rural economy, particularly in terms of contributions from communities. The specific objective is to explore the participation of local communities.

This sub-chapter is based on presentations, papers, and interviews on local organizations that support the local communities and on interviews conducted with local people, especially the main actor in the rural-ecotourism program.

Rural ecotourism and landscape

Fennell (2008) describes ecotourism as responsible travel to natural areas which conserves the environment and improves the welfare of local people. In line with this definition, MacCannell (in Fennell 2008) connected ecotourism with empirical relationships between a tourist, a site, and a maker. Ecotourism is related to the conservation of natural areas and sustainable resource management as the link between economic development and conservation of natural areas (Wearing and Neil 2009). The tourist represents the human component, the site includes the actual destination or physical entity, and the maker represents some form of information that the tourist uses to identity and give meaning to a particular attraction (MacCannell in Fennell 2008).

It cannot be achieved if there is no committed environmental performance, especially by the communities working together (Clarke in Fennell 2008). An activity that supports the local economy and occurs in nature automatically qualifies as ecotourism (Fennell 2008) with some component of the activity associated with the sociocultural context (Fennell and

Dowling 2003; Theobald 2005). To support the rural ecotourism program, participation of the local community is very important. Theobald (2005) stressed that, for rural areas, local community is the dominant player.

Ecotourism development is based on four aspects – economic, ecological, social, and cultural – that minimize negative effects on the environment and local values (Theobald 2005; Stefanica and Gurmeza 2010): 'Integrated in sustainable development, ecotourism involves activities that directly contribute to the nature protection and to keeping the old human creations unaltered' (Stefanica and Gurmeza 2010). Theobald (2005) emphasized the control of ecotourism:

> Tourism which is developed and maintained in an area in such a manner and at such a scale that it remains viable over an indefinite period and does not degrade or alter the environment (human and physical) in which it exists to such a degree that it prohibits the successful development and wellbeing of other activities and progresses.

Candirejo as an ecotourism village

Candirejo is located in Borobudur Sub-district close to Borobudur Temple. Some researchers have explored Candirejo as a tourism village. PATRA-PALA, an outsider NPO from Yogyakarta, conducted a project based in Candirejo, supported by JICA, in 2001–04. Candirejo village became the main focus of the NRM-LCE (Natural Resources Management for Local Community Empowerment) project by PATRA-PALA from December 2001 to November 2004 (Fatimah 2012; Rahmi 2012).

Borobudur Temple is a World Heritage Site that has spectacular villages surrounding the temple, which is part of its uniqueness. Candirejo was proposed in 1999 as a tourism village and established by the Minister of Tourism in 2000 (Rahmi 2012). Based on a decree by the Magelang Regency on 13 May 1999 (No. 0556/1258/19/1999), Candirejo was chosen as an ecotourism village because of its proximity to Borobudur Temple and the potential of its natural and cultural resources (Tatak 2012b). Socialization, environmental management, and the establishment of potential managers were important first steps at the hamlet and village levels.

In 2000 the village adopted the principle of *catur daya* (four powers) as the basic philosophy of tourism activity in the village. It consists of *daya tarik* (the power of fascination), *daya tumbuh* (the power to grow), *daya manfaat* (the power of benefit), and *daya tangkal* (the power of parry) (Tatak 2012b). The slogan *Candirejo Bersatu* – 'Candirejo Unite' – was created to support *catur daya*.

Local people contribute to building tourism as guides, caterers, and in other roles in rural tourism (agriculture). Fatimah (2012) mentioned that Candirejo village has been successful with its community-based ecotourism program and has been selected as a pilot project for community-based tourism in Indonesia (May–November 2003).

At first, local people did not believe that Candirejo village could be a tourism village

Plate 4.6: Traditional houses are used for homestay accommodation in Candirejo (photos: Utami and Tatak)

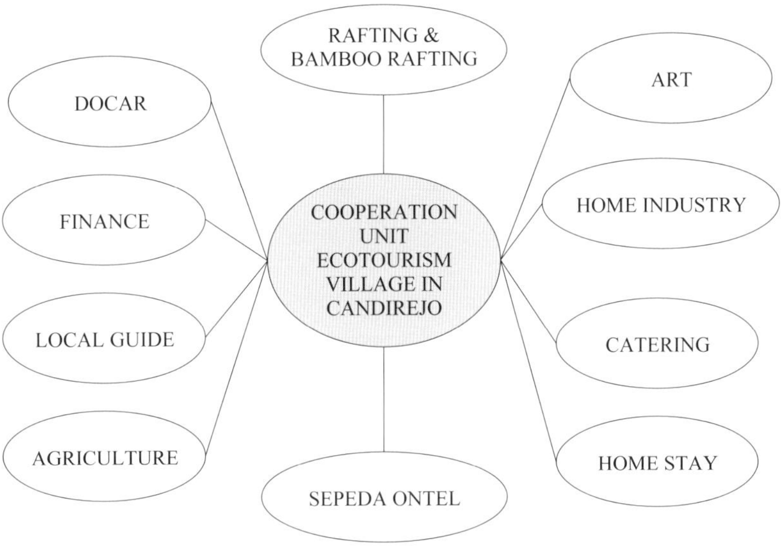

Figure 4.13: Facilities of an ecotourism village (Tatak 2012a)

because it has no specific building like Borobudur Temple. However, training and exploration of other communities and organizations suggested that many interesting and potential areas could be developed and reordered to support the village as a tourism village, especially an ecotourism village. As a result, the people were ready to prepare and support the entire program. To achieve the goal, local people used *gotong royong* to make the village interesting for tourists without changing its original nature (interview with Tatak, 2013).

An action plan for rural ecotourism in Candirejo

Ecotourism has been growing based on cooperation with a friendly local people:

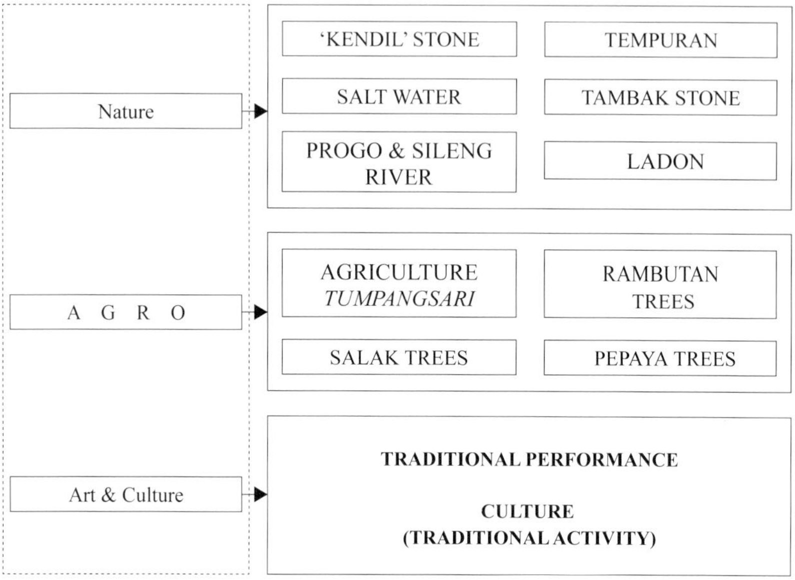

Fig 4.14: Potential village as ecotourism village (Tatak 2012b)

Plate 4.7: Natural resources in Candirejo (photos: Utami)

Plate 4.8: Local people in Candirejo act as guides (photos: Utami)

> not only specific people can be an actor, but all of the people in Candirejo can be an actor of the local tourism…young people were prepared as guide[s] with English exercises, some families were prepared as the best host[s] with their houses as homestay [accommodation] and as original people in the village. (interview with Tatak, 2013)

To support Candirejo as an ecotourism village, facilities such as homestay accommodation (Plate 4.6) were created and support facilities were reinvigorated, such as *andong* (traditional horse carriage) and bicycles for local transportation, art groups for performances, home industries for tourist activities, and catering services to provide local food; Figure 4.13). Agriculture and its supporting elements were also renewed by the local people (Plate 4.7) (interview with Tatak, 2013; Tatak 2012a).

To support Candirejo as an ecotourism village, a popular local saying – *gupuh* (friendly), *lungguh* (let them sit), and *suguh* (good service) (Tatak 2012b) – is very well known. It means to provide kindness and the best service for guests. The people always host their guests with *gupuh*, *lungguh*, and *suguh.*

Local and non-local people

The goal of ecotourism is to generate a tourist economy and to strengthen the village and the local community. All the local people help each other and review the best methods or strategies – not only for guides, but also other local actors for tourism in farming, home industries, transportation, traditional food, and so on, who can all support rural ecotourism in Candirejo village:

> …with ecotourism village…so many people get a new challenge as the actor[s] of the local tourism… (interview with Tatak, 2013)

Some local people act as guides (Plate 4.8) and narrate the story of Candirejo village and

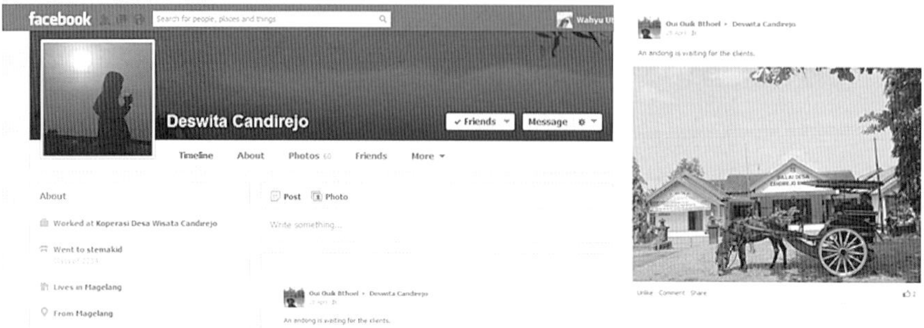

Figure 4.15: Local social media for Candirejo (source: facebook)

Figure 4.16: Examples of Tatak's presentations (sources: Tatak 2012a, Tatak 2012b, Tatak 2012c)

provide a description of its potential value, not only the physical values but also the intangible values in the village. They have to be knowledgeable about Borobudur Temple and the surrounding villages. Some are trained by the Tourism Village Cooperative and others work in cooperation with the organization. For example, local transportation – by *andong* (cart) and *kusir* (the *andong* driver) – brought local people to the traditional market before Candirejo became an ecotourism village. Since the development of ecotourism, *kusir* offer their services to many tourists, which allows the tourists to enjoy Candirejo and the surrounding villages (interview with Tatak, 2013). So we can say that ecotourism in Candirejo provides a positive value and generates local income (private and public).

Today there are six local people who are always concerned to support Candirejo as an ecotourism village. The main function is to strengthen the local potential of the village and, importantly, to provide interesting information for tourists. Usually, a guide builds a narrative with detailed information about Candirejo village and the surrounding villages. Based on this, the tourist receives the best information and enjoys the ecotourism package (interview with Tatak, 2013).

Plate 4.9: Tourists in Candirejo (photos: Utami)

Virtual hosts – for example, social media sites such as facebook (Figure 4.15) – can also provide much information about village activity. Local people interact with virtual hosts to attract tourists to Candirejo, besides visiting Borobudur Temple.

Because Candirejo is an ecotourism village and has been voted as one of the best ecotourism villages, some local people present the strategy of village potential to other interested parties in Indonesia. One such person is the chairman of the Candirejo Tourism Village Cooperative, Mr Tatak Sariawan, who has made many presentations about Candirejo (Figure 4.16).

Many tourists come to Candirejo village to enjoy all the interesting activities and attractions – houses, the environment, art performances, and so on (Plate 4.9). In recent years, many tourists have been attracted to the village by information from Borobudur Temple guides, from the experiences of other tourists, and by online information on websites, facebook, and so on:

> …tourists that have [visited] before, come again [for a second or third time] with the other [people] or…some tourist[s] come to Candirejo because of the information from the tourist that [has come] before… (interview with Tatak, 2013)

Tourist come to Candirejo as part of a group or individually. Some have a fixed schedule, and some come and leave in a day, but they enjoy the ecotourism provided by members of the Tourism Village Cooperative. Generally, the cooperative schedules a suitable village tour. Sometimes, tourists or guests stay in Candirejo for several days, in which case the cooperative provides a varied schedule that includes traditional food each day. In these cases, the main facilities, beside the guide, involve homestay accommodation and catering.

Plate 4.10: BFS participants enjoying Candirejo ecotourism (photos: Utami)

Tourists who come to Candirejo can bring many positive effects to the local people. They generate other tourists (from the same country or other countries) and one day may come again and bring their friends. In this case, all the people of Candirejo, as the actors in the ecotourism village, can participate as guides and as service providers (of traditional food, transportation, agriculture, home industry, and so on) (interview with Tatak, 2013).

The Borobudur Field School and tourism in Candirejo

Borobudur Field School participants are among the people who can enjoy Candirejo's ecotourism (Plate 4.10). For Candirejo village, programs like BFS can promote the village as an ecotourism destination in Borobudur Sub-district. As a regular program, BFS is well known by local people.

BFS inspires the local people and motivates them to continually update information and facilities. For them, BFS is an interesting program because BFS participants are not only Indonesian people but also foreigners (interview with Tatak, 2013).

Every year, BFS is held in Candirejo and participants stay in homestay accommodation for seven days. The local people contribute to this program and, because of the regular schedule, there is good collaboration and a good relationship.

Conclusion

Candirejo, as a rural ecotourism village in Borobudur Sub-district, is well managed and has good links between local community, local organizations, and local government. The people all support the program and have specific tasks in each function or position. The various elements of the rural ecotourism village build the best service and best program based on balancing nature, culture, and economic considerations. So we can say that Candirejo is concerned not only about the economic aspect, but also about the sustainable aspect of tourism. This suggests that the best conditions will result in a positive value that can generate local finances. Balancing ecology – nature – economic – sociocultural aspects is important for the local people.

Landscape photography for sustainability

Suparno (photographer) and Kusumaningdyah Nurul Handayani

Community initiative in Borobudur has a great impact in ensuring that the environment of the Borobudur landscape is sustained. This community initiative has been instigated by individuals and many sectors within society, including photographers. Borobudur Temple and its landscape and surroundings have long been famous for their sophisticated and photogenic objects. One community leader of Borobudur village who has successfully and consistently documented Borobudur and its surrounding areas over the past ten years is Suparno.

Suparno Harjoutomo (often called Parno as his nickname) was born fifty-six years ago as the first son in a family of eight siblings. He grew up and lived and worked until retirement in Borobudur village, and has done much to document the process of community initiative through his landscape photography in Borobudur.

Working at Borobudur Conservation Office from 1973 until 2008, Suparno began his career in the Restoration Department, where the focus was on taking care of Borobudur Temple, such as cleaning and caring for the stones in the temple. His expertise is derived from his father, who worked as a clerk at Borobudur Temple. Since his teenage years, Suparno has been interested in photography as a hobby and, due to his skills, he was assigned a specific task in his department to document the various deterioration of rocks at Borobudur Temple using a special camera lens. His photography, initially a hobby, eventually became part of his daily work at Borobudur Conservation Office.

'Borobudur as a role model of life…'

Over time, Suparno's love for the masterpiece that is Borobudur Temple is no longer as an object of his work. After twenty-five years he feels that the glory of Borobudur Temple is like a teacher of life.

When entering retirement, the question of what he could return to the Borobudur community crossed Suparno's mind. Since his retirement in 2008, the pleasure and the knowledge of the world of landscape photography has become increasingly active, and has led Suparno to highlight four places of Borobudur landscape photography. Presenting the cultural landscape of Borobudur and its surroundings from various angles, his works inspire the local people of Borobudur.

The process of discovery is not instant. It takes time to discover, explore, and promote Borobudur landscape photography to a public audience. Suparno started by inviting friends, professional photography colleagues, and a journalist to participate in landscape photography in Borobudur. Slowly, awareness of the landscape photography highlighting the beauty of Borobudur started to spread to the general public through the stories of friends who had experienced the landscape and through media reviews of Borobudur.

Since 2006, when the open sources of digital media arose, many people have uploaded their photographs to the virtual world. This has led to the landscape photography of the surroundings of Borobudur Temple becoming well known and desirable as an alternative tourism destination, besides Borobudur Temple. Gradually, this process has created an influx of visitors who pay for services (such as parking, food, and beverages) and can help local people to manage the existing revenue wisely. Although not all twenty villages in Borobudur Sub-district offer opportunities for Borobudur landscape photography, Suparno highlights four places: Punthuk Setumbu in Karangrejo village; Kedok in Ngadiharjo village; and Kapling Janan and Maitan in Borobudur village.

Punthuk Setumbu, Karangrejo village

The discovery of the Punthuk Setumbu location was via a meaningful process. It began, in 2004, when Suparno wanted to visit the family home of his old friend Yu Jumput who had died. Yu Jumput was older than Suparno and was respected by him. To express his condolences, Suparno decided to visit her family home.

Finding the family's house in the village of Karangrejo was not an easy trip because of its location in the hills and, by accident, Suparno found the Punthuk Setumbu area was a good spot to see Borobudur Temple from above the hills (Plate 4.11). The view amazed him. Suparno visited this area once more, even though the road is winding and slippery, to photograph the panoramic landscape. Gradually, Punthuk Setumbu became well known and was opened to the general public to view the Borobudur landscape.

The most appropriate time to enjoy this scenic area is at dawn around 4.30 am. The opening view is of the sun rising behind Mount Merbabu, followed by hedges and trees silhouetted against Borobudur Temple, which is banded by morning dew and golden yellow light. Sometimes an extra ray of light appears to pierce the clouds. This moment does not last for long, no more than an hour after sunrise.

The changing seasons greatly affect the image. May and June are the best months to photograph Borobudur Temple and the panoramic landscape from Punthuk Setumbu – the position of the sun is right between Mount Merapi and Mount Merbabu, while Borobudur Temple is positioned in the southern sun.

Punthuk Setumbu is approximately three kilometers west of Borobudur Temple. As a village treasury, the land is managed by the local community organization and can earn approximately 2.5 million rupiah per day. The community organization has built new tourism facilities on the kindly advice of Suparno. The new tourism location is a vast area of approximately 600 square meters and has been improved and developed with facilities such as benches, a cafeteria, and a parking area so that tourists can easily enjoy the views of Borobudur Temple from the top of the hill.

Plate 4.11: Views of the sunrise and Borobudur Temple from Punthuk Setumbu (photos: Suparno)

Kedok, Ngadiharjo village

The Mount Merapi eruption in 2010 brought Suparno to Ngadiharjo village. At that time all the plants in the area were covered by volcanic ash, which made all the plants *mingkup* (close down). At the time, the view to Borobudur Temple was clearly visible.

Located approximately five kilometers from Borobudur Temple, Kedok hamlet is now well known among professional photographers of landscape photography. Unlike the situation in Punthuk Setumbu, where the area of land is owned by the village, Kedok's places are owned by local individuals. Limitations on visitors can be enforced in this location, said Suparno. It is much easier to deliver the concept of sustainability and to maintain landscape photography through the individual owner compared to the public ownership in Punthuk Setumbu.

The most appropriate time to enjoy this scene is at dawn around 4.30 am (as in the Punthuk Setumbu area). July is the best month for landscape photography. The advantage of this spot is that Mount Merapi and Mount Merbabu can be seen much more clearly without the mist seen from Punthuk Setumbu. Mount Menoreh dominates the background hills. The power of raw lighting illuminates the landscape.

Plate 4.12: Views from Kedok (photos: Suparno)

Plate 4.13: Views from Kapling Janan (photos: Suparno)

Kapling Janan, Borobudur village

Kapling Janan is located close to the Borobudur Temple complex. It is approximately 500 meters from the complex. Unlike other areas, Kapling Janan village is not in the hills.

The most appropriate time to enjoy this scene is at midday. Photographs can be taken from the rooftops of people's houses, which makes this spot private. This spot is available only with special permission.

Maitan, Borobudur village

The latest location that Suparno has surveyed is in Maitan. Located in Maitan hamlet of Borobudur village, this location has the advantage of offering a sophisticated angle of the main stupa of Borobudur Temple and the sun beside the scenic Mount Merapi and Mount Merbabu. Unlike in the other locations in the hills, both mountains are clearly visible through the coconut trees. For the particular height and shooting angle, Suparno, with the assistance of local residents, made a semi-permanent stage. The width of the stage is only approximately three meters, which limits the number of visitors who can enjoy this location.

The most appropriate time to enjoy this scene is as the sun rises. In March and September, the best months for landscape photography, the sun's position can be right in the middle of the main stupa of Borobudur Temple (Plate 4.14).

Plate 4.14: Views from Maitan hamlet (photos: Suparno)

Sustainability and cultural landscape photography

To maintain the sustainability of Borobudur's cultural landscape photography in the future, Suparno makes efforts to educate the local people to maintain their places for landscape photography. He delivers the concept of cultural landscape sustainability through the local community by advising on such things as the hospitality that the local community can provide to visitors – how to treat visitors as if they are relatives who have come from far away, so that these visitors will feel like coming to their hometown (to feel the warmth and friendliness of the people) and have a sense of duty to keep the surrounding environment clean. He also campaigns on the importance of locales being maintained by the local people – investors from outside Borobudur village should not be allowed to occupy potential tourist places. Borobudur and its surroundings are strategic areas that should not be explored only in the interests of a particular class of people. A doctrine that values life is the one that Suparno was taught to maintain landscape photography and sustain the local community into the future.

Currently, Suparno resides in Kapling Janan village with his wife and family. Since 1989 he has operated a culinary business – a traditional noodle shop – as a side job. His noodle stall is very well known and is a major culinary destination when visiting Borobudur Temple. In retirement, Suparno remains committed to always finding new spots to appreciate Borobudur and the surrounding landscape. He has a certain satisfaction in finding places where landscape photography can be an inspiration for many people. People can enjoy the satisfaction and amazement he feels when appreciating Borobudur through landscape photography.

Dusun Maitan: a lesson learned from villagers

Muhammad Hatta

Over the past few years in Indonesia many tourist villages have emerged, promoted by the notion that tourism activities can be used as a driver of economic activity. Touristic activities can also be seen as the locomotive that realizes poverty reduction in rural areas. The government has taken part in promoting tourist villages through village community empowerment programs. Unfortunately, an understanding of the tourist villages is often only on the surface. Tourism can have negative and unavoidable impacts and villages are often not fully aware that tourism activities can become a boomerang for the preservation of the village.

Maitan hamlet is a good example to consult as a lesson for a tourist village. The hamlet is located not far from Borobudur Temple and has experienced ups and downs as a tourist village. It once almost lost the spirit to manage tourism but it bounced back from adversity thanks to assistance from active local community networks.

Maitan hamlet is one of ten hamlets located in Borobudur village and is located at the western side of Borobudur Tourism Park on the opposite side of the main park entrance, so it is far less accessible to the tourists who come to Borobudur Temple. The hamlet has a lot of people, mostly within the religious community, and is friendly and open. Economic activities in this village mostly involve farmers, artisans, cassava chip makers, and building construction laborers.

At the beginning of the development of Borobudur Tourism Park, Maitan had almost been forgotten. Although less than five kilometers from Borobudur Temple, for decades the village name had not been heard. The identification of Maitan hamlet as an attractive location in Borobudur village originated from the development of the special interest in tourism in Borobudur Temple. Around the 1990s some tour guides at Borobudur Temple, seeing a gap in developing tourism activities, and travelers who saw that Borobudur Temple was not the only attraction, began to understand the further context of Borobudur. In particular, they understood that Borobudur Temple is part of the landscape heritage of the Menoreh Hills. The tour guides began to help the tourists enjoy the landscape heritage by conducting illegal[17] activities in Borobudur Temple to allow them to view the sunrise and sunset at Borobudur Park. Sunrise can be enjoyed at the top of Borobudur Temple at around 6.00 am and sunset can be enjoyed at around 5.00 pm. The extraordinary uniqueness of these experiences became a new attraction of Borobudur Temple and attracted more tourists to Borobudur.

In a further development, the tour guides found new attractions that are no less interesting. The sunrise can be seen from Bakal Hill in Maitan hamlet, a simple ten-minute walk from Borobudur Temple. When spending the morning at Bakal Hill, tourists can enjoy Borobudur Temple as a focus in the expanse of misty landscape beauty.

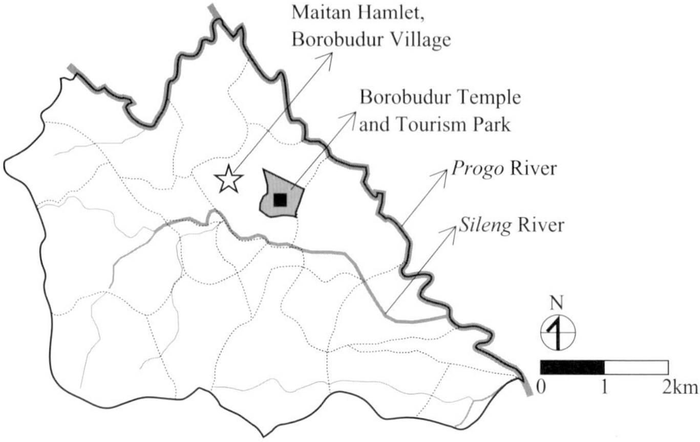

Figure 4.17: Location of Maitan hamlet, Borobudur village (source: Fatimah, 2012)

Rural tourism activities in Maitan hamlet

Around the year 2007, Bakal Hill became the forerunner to the development of the hamlet as a tourist village. Together with the community, tour guides assisted people to manage places and attractions for visitors and to form networks to help in management. A tourism awareness group (*Kelompok Sadar Wisata - POKDARWIS*) was formed, spearheaded by village youths. They nominated their own guides and arts, crafts, and homestay managers, and others. The Borobudur Temple guides helped in tutoring local guides in foreign languages, especially English.

Tourism activities were slowly bankrolling the economy and people were starting to understand the importance of opening up tourism activities. The next important and necessary step in the development of the village was community capacity building. The community had come to understand, little by little, that tourism is certainly not easy. Through the networks owned by the community groups, they learned how to get help. Independently, they began to learn about tourism awareness, including, among other things:

- financial management and accounting
- techniques for identification of interesting assets (activity map derived from the Green Map,[18] a kind of database development in the village for the early formulation of the Village Development Plan)
- management of local and tourist attractions; among the activities in Maitan are:
  - watching the sunrise from Bakal Hill
  - watching the process of making palm sugar
  - watching craft processes (making woven pandanus mats and baskets)
  - visiting traditional houses
  - enjoying art attractions by local children

Plate 4.15: Tourism activities in Maitan hamlet; (clockwise from top left) riding *andong* for village sightseeing, visiting a traditional house, making bamboo craft boxes, homemade bamboo craft boxes (photos: Fatimah, 2012)

- establishment of a ranger (local integrator) for tourist activity
- management of division teams, such as catering groups, transportation, and others.

Figure 4.18 shows the land use of Borobudur village and its village tour itinerary, which is focused in Maitan hamlet. There are ten hamlets in Borobudur village, but the rural tourism activities are mostly located in Maitan hamlet. One reason is that the local community is very active and able to collaborate easily with outside partners, such as the Indonesian Tourist Guide Association (*Himpunan Pramuwisata Indonesia* – HPI), Green Map, and so on.

Turning point

Technology and social media are becoming important marketing tools for Maitan hamlet. Photographers who capture the interesting spots in Maitan hamlet have introduced the hamlet to the world via photo uploads and travel reviews on the internet. From a forgotten hamlet, Maitan has become famous as one of the special spots to photograph and view the sunrise above Borobudur Temple.

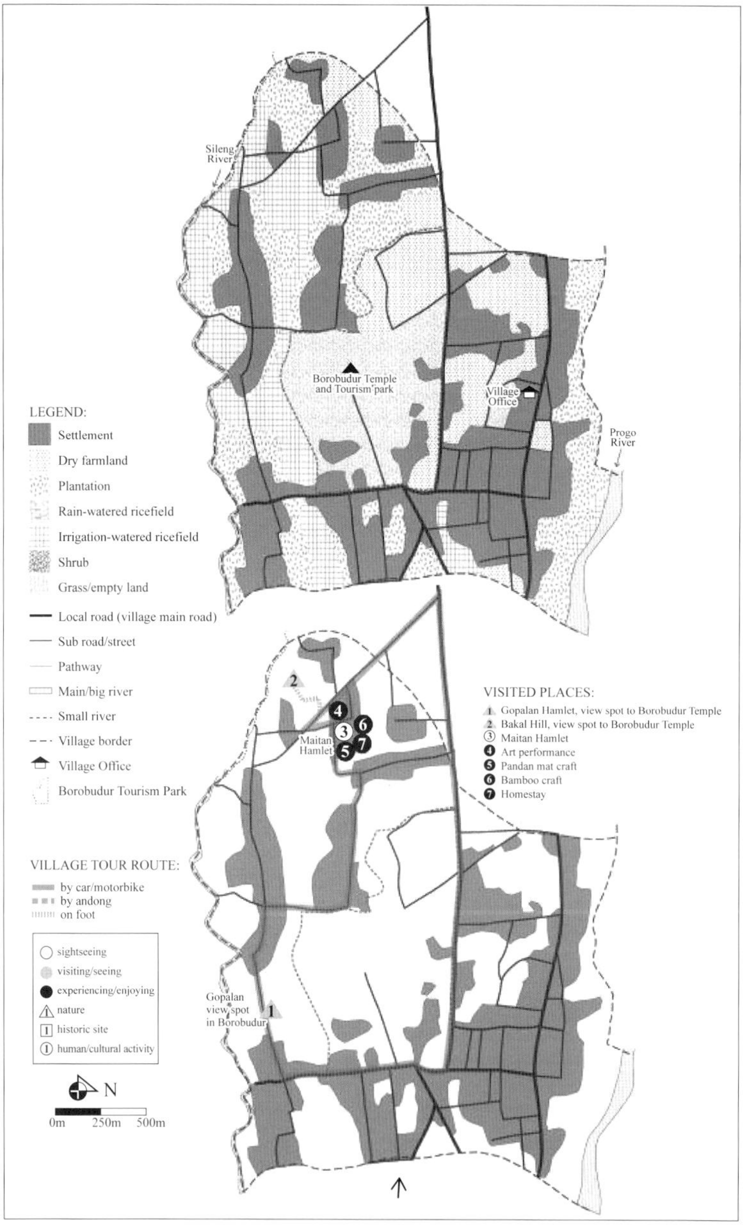

Figure 4.18: Map of land use and detailed tour itinerary in Borobudur village, focused in Maitan hamlet (source: Fatimah, 2012)

Plate 4.16: View to Borobudur Temple from the top of Bakal Hill (Gunung Bakal) before and after the development of a new hilltop resort
(photos: Fatimah, 2012, and Adishakti, 2012)

Plate 4.17: The Plataran Resort Hotel is built on the top of Bakal Hill
(photos: Adishakti, 2012)

As the name of Maitan hamlet began to grow, the private sector became interested in business opportunities. Bakal Hill, as the main tourist destination of the village, became very valuable. Around 2009, the prime sunrise location on Bakal Hill was sold by the village and a luxury private resort hotel was finally permitted (Figure 4.16). Based on the regulation, the site is located in a zone for water absorption and no building construction should be developed there.

Statistically, the physical development of Maitan hamlet looks good due to the existence of the beautiful luxury resort. But the statistical values also affect the arrival of other investors. Bakal Hill, the main place of tourism activities in Maitan hamlet, is now closed to the general public and can only be enjoyed by hotel guests (Plate 4.17). In addition, the village people had to accept a reduction in water catchment areas in Bakal Hill and the resultant decrease of springs in the village.

Revival

The appearance of a luxury hotel in the middle of Maitan was a turning point and a lesson for the society. The village lost its main tourist destination. Other tourist activities also gradually became minimal because some tourists replaced coming to Maitan hamlet with efforts to find another spot like Bakal Hill. With Punthuk Setumbu and Pos Mati in other villages as new favorite locations to watch the sunrise, the economy slowly changed.

In such a difficult situation, activists in the tourist village still encouraged Maitan hamlet to keep up the activities and find a solution by maintaining and widening their network. The greatest support came from the tour guides who are always actively and creatively searching for new locations of interest for tourist activities. Other support came from Universitas Gadjah Mada with its Borobudur Field School activities and Green Map, among others, as well as from the Japan Foundation. Although these networks and support systems had a wide recognition of the problems in Maitan, the hamlet began to unravel.

In July 2010 one of the instigators in the Maitan community, Muhammad Hatta, received a chance to implement a youth exchange student program in Japan for two weeks through Jenesys (Japan–East Asia Network of Exchange for Students and Youth), supported by the Japan Foundation. The program offers insights and learning through experiences in visiting Japan. Lessons include the application of the concept of planning by involving the community (the concept of *machi-zukuri* – community/neighborhood planning). In this concept, people in the community are the main users of the environment and space, for it is very important to involve the community in all phases of planning, monitoring, and evaluation of development. Public awareness about the surrounding environment, the vision, and the mission is very important to the future and is embodied in a collective agreement that is then implemented and maintained together. This sense of community inspired Hatta to put the concept into practice, together with the Maitan hamlet community.

Associated with what was learned in Japan, Hatta then tried to embrace all Maitan hamlet stakeholders to again be involved in planning the tourist village Hamlet Maitan Plan. All components of the community were involved, including mothers and children, and various key figures such as *Kyai* (local Muslim leader) were involved in the discussion stages. The aim was always to maintain a shared commitment.

Collaborating groups began to gather around with the help of governmental support through PNPM *Mandiri Pariwisata* (PNPM is the *Program Nasional Pemberdayaan Masyarakat*/National Program for Community Empowerment). PNPM *Mandiri Pariwisata* is support focused on tourism development. Tourism and several new tourist destinations began to be identified. Creative ideas associated with the management of tourist destinations began to form, including:

- assembling the stories as the background of the places
- *Jathilan* (traditional dance) activities for children
- activities for processed cassava (cassava flour) initiated by a group of mothers; this activity is expected to be the forerunner of a growing snack food business
- the establishment of a community library, with shelves of books donated by *Persatuan Pelajar Indonesia*–PPI Jepang (Indonesian Students Association in Japan) to the victims of the 2010 Mount Merapi eruption, as well as the books of domestic and foreign tourists who visit the village
- a package of activities to enjoy the sunrise around Maitan hamlet, including having breakfast
- public awareness of the conservation of traditional buildings as tourist attractions
- public awareness on environmental management so that the environment is clean and beautiful
- public awareness of the importance of maintaining bamboo as part of the ecosystem that ensures the availability of spring water
- the involvement of local workers at the hotels, which started to ameliorate problems with hotels on Bakal Hill; furthermore, the CSR tried to operate with the target community for various village activities.

With awareness and shared commitment, public confidence increased and Maitan hamlet again began to rise. Although the sunrise spot on the hill is still not freely accessible, tourist activity is resuming. Society must be creative and optimistically face all challenges.

Lessons learned

The case of rural tourism activities in Maitan hamlet provides a number of lessons to be learned.

- Tourism can bring benefits, but it also can be dangerous and very fragile. Therefore, the community is an important actor in the whole process. A strong community can face obstacles and convert them to opportunities. Based on the experience in Maitan hamlet, a spirit of togetherness among the community members resulted in good impacts on the sustainability of activities.
- Capacity development and training is important for the community, as it can raise awareness and skills to maintain village potentials. It can also help in building self-confidence and enhancing traditional skills.
- Women play an important part in rural tourism activities. They are aware of the benefits of tourism and realize that their skills can be used to earn an income by producing

attractive souvenir items.

- Training in enterprise development, tourism promotion, and business management has significantly helped even illiterate women to lead community organizations, enabling them to develop leadership qualities and to enhance their knowledge and ability to seek external resources for development plans.
- Business development training courses have taught business skills and encouraged entrepreneurs to establish new small enterprises such as lodges, teashops, stores, and souvenir and agricultural production. Creating income generation is very important to support the economy of the local community and to maintain the rural tourism activities.
- Networking and collaboration with stakeholders and many parties from outside the village is important to accelerate the progress of rural tourism development in the village.

Notes

1 RT is the smallest community group in a neighborhood environment and usually consists of twenty to twenty-five households. RW is the bigger group formed from some RTs. RT and RW group systems usually have their own informal rules for community daily life.

2 PT. TWCBPRB is a state-owned company chosen by the government to manage the stated tourism park.

3 In Indonesia, three villages are listed as tourism villages by the Indonesian Ecotourism Center: Candirejo (Borobudur, Central Java), Cinangneng (Bogor, West Java), and Sibetan and Nusa Ceningan (Bali) (Indecon n.d.).

4 JAKER (*Jaringan Kerja Kepariwisataan Borobudur*/Borobudur Tourism Network), led by Jack Priyana, pursues the idea of 'One Village One Product' to encourage the local product of each village in Borobudur. It also started to manage an alternative tourist heritage trail package, visiting many villages in Borobudur Sub-district by *andong* (traditional horse carriage).

5 PATRA-PALA Foundation is an outsider NPO based in Yogyakarta that focuses on social ecology and ecotourism. It was established in 1993 with N. R. Wibowo as the Executive Director.

6 The formal definition of *gotong royong* originated in a Javanese dictionary published in 1938. The essential meaning is that several people work together to carry a large and heavy object – it means traditional mutual cooperation among villagers and between the villagers and the village administration (Gumisawa 2007).

7 Javanese advice that a person should not do things he expects others would not do for him (Atmosumarto 2005).

8 See the legend in Figure 4.3 for an explanation of these organizations.

9 P2WKSS (*Peningkatan Peranan Wanita menuju Keluarga Sehat Sejahtera*/Women's Role towards a Healthy and Prosperous Family) is a governmental program to optimize the yard space to increase family income by planting productive trees. The government gave rambutan seeds to the village residents.

10 Based on statistical data, there were about 793 vendors in 1997, + 2500 vendors in 2003 (2800 during the peak season), and + 3500 vendors in 2008.

11 The Java Art Market. *Jagad Jawa* means 'Javanese universe'.

12 'The Grand Strategy' is a new proposal that offers to undertake PRA analysis of the wants of the community of informal vendors around Borobudur and then to rezone the area to meet those wants (Engelhardt et al. 2003).

13 FLMB (*Forum Lintas Masyarakat Borobudur*/Borobudur Cross Society Forum) is a community forum

to accommodate various organizations in Borobudur.

14 HPI was established in 1988 but far before this year tourism activities existed (although in a simple version), as indicated by the ellipsis.

15 This data is based on the latest information from the management, PT. Taman Wisata Candi Borobudur, in a seminar to commemorate 200 years of the Borobudur Temple discovery (4 September 2014).

16 Based on a personal interview with Taryudi, a local guide who is a native of Candirejo; he said that he took tourists to the village to offer a different atmosphere from the temple. The first tourist he took to his house and around the village was impressed, so he continued the scheme.

17 Activities to enjoy the sunrise and sunset cannot be done during operational hours of Borobudur Tourism Park, which is why it is 'illegal'.

18 Village potential mapping was first held by JAKER in collaboration with the Green Map community from Yogyakarta in 2005. The initial step was to map village potentials in Borobudur Village. This effort continued in 2008 for more comprehensive mapping.

5 International Borobudur Field School 2004–13

Sinta Carolina and Yeny Paulina Leibo

The Borobudur Field School program has been running for a decade now, during which time seven field schools have been held. The field school is organized by the Center for Heritage Conservation, Department of Architecture and Planning, Faculty of Engineering, Universitas Gadjah Mada, in collaboration with Kanki Laboratory, Kyoto University, Japan.

In organizing the field school, an organizing committee is usually responsible for managing all aspects related to preparation (pre-field school), the duration of the field school, and post-field school. The organizing committee usually consists of a small group of people – a chairperson, a secretary, a treasurer, and people in charge of program/guidebook/materials, equipment and transportation, and accommodation.

This chapter provides detailed information on how the field school is organized and on the effort, hard work, and consistency required. From the first field school until the latest, all the data come from the field school archives.

Field school programs

Borobudur Field School programs generally consist of lectures, field trips and visits, a working group studio, meetings with local communities, and group presentations at the end of the program.

Lectures are delivered by facilitators who come from different backgrounds, including academic backgrounds (lecturers from Universitas Gadjah Mada (UGM), Kyoto University, Wakayama University, Universitas Pembangunan Nasional Yogyakarta, and Universitas Tarumanagara Jakarta) and practical background (local people, local organizations, and non-governmental organizations related to Borobudur Temple).

The three types of field trips are enthusiastically awaited by participants – a field trip around Borobudur villages guided by an experienced local guide, a sunrise trip, and a field trip to surveyed areas. During the week there is a visit to Borobudur Temple and the Borobudur Conservation Office, where participants can find information on the temple from trusted sources. There is also a very interesting visit to discover the trails of the ancient lake around Borobudur Temple.

In the working group studio, participants gather in their respective groups to discuss and work together to prepare for the final presentation.

At the end of the program, the participants make a presentation according to the topic given to the groups. The presentations are usually held in the Borobudur Conservation Office

Table 5.1: Borobudur Field School (BFS) time schedules

1st BFS, 2004

Time	Morning	Afternoon	Evening
Friday, Sept. 10	Depart to Borobudur, opening, field trip, lecture		
Saturday, Sept. 11	Lecture(s) in Candirejo village	Visit to Borobudur	Discussion, group division
Sunday, Sept. 12	Field trip		Meeting with community
Monday, Sept. 13	Sunrise & field trip		Guest lecture
Tuesday, Sept. 14	Visit to Conservation Office, field trip		Working group studio
Wednesday, Sept 15	Group presentation		Cultural activities with local community
Thursday, Sept. 16	Back to Yogyakarta and visit Losari Coffee Plantation Departure of the participants		
Thursday, Sept. 17	Optional trip		

2nd BFS, 2005

Time	Morning	Afternoon	Evening
Monday, Sept. 12	Depart to Borobudur, opening, lecture, village tour		Lecture
Tuesday, Sept. 13	Sunrise trip, lecture(s) in Candirejo village	Field trip	Lectures
Wednesday, Sept. 14	Field trip		Working group studio
Thursday, Sept. 15	Field trip		Working group studio
Friday, Sept. 16	Visit to Borobudur Conservation Office, field trip		Working group studio
Saturday, Sept 17	Group presentation		Closing & cultural activities with local community
Sunday, Sept. 18	Back to Yogyakarta and visit Sendangsono Pilgrimage Departure of the participants		
Monday, Sept. 19	Optional trip		

3rd BFS, 2006

Time	Morning	Afternoon	Evening
Monday, March 27	Depart to Borobudur, opening, lecture, village tour		Lecture
Tuesday, March 28	Field survey, lectures in Candirejo village	Field trip to Borobudur	Lectures

Wednesday, March 29	Sunrise in Klipoh, visit to Borobudur Conservation Office, Borobudur Heritage Trail		Working group studio
Thursday, March 30	Field trip	Meeting with community	Working group studio
Friday, March 31	Working group studio		*Kubrosiswo* performance
Saturday, April 1	Group presentation		Closing & cultural activities with local community
Sunday, April 2	Back to Yogyakarta and visit Selogriyo Temple Departure of the participants		
Monday, April 3	Optional trip		

4th BFS 2007

Time	Morning	Afternoon	Evening
Monday, April. 19	Arriving of participants	Opening, lectures	Free time, sightseeing
Tuesday, April 20	Depart to Borobudur, village tour	Field lecture in Borobudur Conservation Office	Opening Borobudur Exhibition at Jogja Gallery
Wednesday, April 21	Sunrise in Klipoh, visit to Borobudur Conservation Office, Field trip		Cultural night: *Kubrosiswo*
Thursday, April 22	Borobudur cultural landscape trip (Kedu Plain trip)	Kedu Plain trip	Bakmi night at Pak Parno's
Friday, April 23	Sunrise trip, visit Ngawen Temple, Ancient lake tour	Working group studio, bicycle ride to Tempuran	Working group studio
Saturday, April 24	Group presentation		Closing & farewell dinner
Sunday, April 25	Back to Yogyakarta and visit Sendangsono Pilgrimage Departure of the participants		
Monday, April 26	Optional trip		

6th BFS, 2012

Time	Morning	Afternoon	Evening
Sunday, July 1	Arrival of participants		
Monday, July 2	Lecture(s) in UGM Yogyakarta	Depart to Borobudur Check in	Trail in Candirejo village
Tuesday, July 3	Lectures in Candirejo village		Lectures
Wednesday, July 4	Sunrise trip	Borobudur Heritage Trail	
Thursday, July 5	Field survey and discussion with local community		Working group studio

Friday, July 6	Field survey and discussion with local community	Working group studio	
Saturday, July 7	Group presentation		Cultural activities with local community
Sunday, July 8	Kedu Plain trip and back to Yogyakarta		
Monday, July 69	Optional post-summer school excursion to Merapi Mountain post-eruption (budget excluded)		

7th BFS, 2013

Time	Morning	Afternoon	Evening
Tuesday, Sept. 3	Arrival of participants in Yogyakarta		
Wednesday, Sept. 4	Lecture(s) in UGM Yogyakarta	Depart to Borobudur Check in	Trail in Candirejo village
Thursday, Sept. 5	Lectures in Candirejo village		
Friday, Sept. 6	Sunrise trip	Borobudur Heritage Trail	
Saturday, Sept. 7	Field survey and discussion with local community		Working group studio
Sunday, Sept. 8	Field survey and discussion with local community	Working group studio	
Monday, Sept. 9	Group presentation		Cultural activities with local community
Tuesday, Sept. 10	Back to Yogyakarta and visit Merapi Mount area Departure of the participants		

or in the headquarters of the Kembang Setaman Homestay and people from the village are invited.

Table 5.1 shows sample time schedules for the Borobudur Field School.

Field trips

Several places are always included as destinations in the Borobudur Field School. These places are chosen for their special features and form part of a giant mosaic of rural *saujana* heritage in Borobudur. They are mostly located in areas surrounding Borobudur Temple – villages, mountain ranges, hills, rivers, and temples – as well as places related to Borobudur Temple that are located outside the Borobudur area, such as Mount Merapi, Ketep Pass, and so on.

Menoreh–Borobudur region

The Kedu Plain, popular as a sacred region in olden times, is surrounded by mountains and the Menoreh Hills – in the east by Mount Merapi, Mount Merbabu, Mount Telomoyo, and Mount Ungaran, which each has a specific value; in the southwest by Mount Sumbing, Mount

Sindoro, and Mount Prahu, which each has a specific value also; and in the west and south by the Menoreh Hills. The Menoreh Hills and mountains are like jewels in the island. The Kedu Plain has many rivers, but two have important values; the Progo and Elo rivers converge into one and continue south to the sea as the Progo River.

Menoreh–Borobudur and Borobudur Sub-district, as part of the Kedu Plain, have specific values. Built in an exceptional area, Borobudur Temple is a miracle of the Old Mataram Kingdom, whose property included the surrounding landscape. From this district, especially from Borobudur Temple, we can enjoy the magical and beautiful scenery. Borobudur Temple and the villages are the main attraction of this area.

Candirejo village

Administratively, Candirejo village is located in Borobudur Sub-district, Magelang Regency, Central Java, and geographically is located on the foot of the Menoreh Hills, approximately three kilometers from Borobudur Temple. For the past ten years, with its great potential, the village has become an important destination for people to enjoy the beautiful landscape and the culture, traditions, arts and crafts, and village daily life.

The natural environment, farming, and plantations comprise the main potential of the village. Candirejo is an agricultural society that depends mainly on farming and plantations.

Candirejo homestays

For the past ten years Candirejo village has been the place where all participants of Borobudur Field School stay during the field school. The village community prepared the homestays – houses owned by the locals with rooms rented to tourists or visitors who stay in the short term (one to seven days). The tourists/guests live in the same house with the owner, so feel like they are living in a relative's house in the village. The house owner usually serves breakfast for the guests, and the guests can enjoy delicious homemade cooking.

Kembang Setaman Homestay is the site where all participants have gathered since the first Borobudur Field School. It is owned by Mr Tatak, who is also in charge of the Candirejo Tourism Village Cooperative. In the homestay, there is a main hall, where all the lectures are held and where participants can gather together. In the corner of the hall is a set of gamelan, which is usually played by participants, together with the owner of the house. Dinner and lunch are served at a long table on the terrace. Participants can choose to sit on the verandah or inside the house/ hall for meals.

Wanurejo village

Wanurejo village is located next to Candirejo village. This village has great potential and is often visited by tourists. At Wanurejo village we can visit Pawon Temple and view the beautiful panorama, a local handicraft shop, and the house of Mr Soni, an artist whose house is usually visited by participants for lunch and to enjoy the meeting place of three rivers (Progo, Elo, and Sileng rivers).

Karanganyar village (pottery village)

Karanganyar village was the focus of the third field school. Administratively, it is located in Borobudur Sub-district, Magelang Regency, and geographically is located at the foot of the

Menoreh Hills, about five kilometers from Borobudur Temple. The village shares borders to the north with Karangrejo village, east with Tanjungsari village, south with Giritengah village, and west with Ngadiharjo village. Covering 156.525 square kilometers, this village has a quite dense population of about 1872 people, consisting of 426 families. The religious majority is Islamic. Karanganyar village is divided into four hamlets: Dusun Banjaran I, Dusun Banjaran II, Dusun Ngadiwinatan I, and Dusun Ngadiwinatan II.

The people of Karanganyar village are mainly farmers who depend on the farming and plantation of tobacco. But the people also have skills in the field of pottery, in the *tahu* (tofu) industry, and in bamboo carving, and are vendors at the Borobudur Tourism Park. The pottery craftsmen are mostly located in Dusun Banjaran I.

Karanganyar village has an amazing natural environment, and offers sunrise views from the tobacco fields with the scenery of Borobudur in the foreground.

Other potential elements are the fields of ripe yellow paddy, which are like a carpet in the rainy season, and the green carpet of the tobacco plantations in the dry season.

Dusun Banjaran I: the history of the pottery village

Dusun Banjaran I is the center of the pottery craft activities and the place of residence of pottery makers. Traditional houses still dominate in this area and the characteristic feel of this village as a craft center emanates from the *tobong* or the pottery burning area located not far from the workshops.

In 2002 the pathways in Dusun Banjaran I were upgraded to cement blocks, a project the residents considered appropriate to create a much cleaner and nicer village, given the impression that this area was still economically undeveloped. Above all, Dusun Banjaran I has the potential of its local architecture and natural environment.

Karanganyar village has been renowned for its pottery for a long time. Usually these products are used as daily household equipment such as *kendil* (for holding food), *tempayan minum* (for drinking), and *kuali gerabah* (for cooking).

The pottery village has been around for centuries according to folklore and has a connection with the building of Borobudur Temple. According to the stories, in the times of the Borobudur Temple construction, pottery from Karanganyar was used by the builders.

The process of pottery making is a daily activity for each family. The raw material of clay is obtained from village-owned land and the pottery-making process starts with the smudging of the clay by rolling it or by stomping it so that it can be used easily in the next step. The clay is then placed on the pottery wheel, ready to be shaped, after which, to obtain the best result, it is dried first under the sun before being fired at the *tobong* (Plate 5.1). Wood, dry leaves, and coconut skin (*sabut kelapa*) are used to obtain the ideal heat to fire the pottery. The final product is sometimes polished or painted.

The craftsmanship of making pottery has been inherited for generations, from parent to child, from elders to youths. This cultural activity is characteristic of Karanganyar village, even though some of the people consider that their skills are out of date and cannot provide sufficient financial income.

Dusun Banjaran II

Dusun Banjaran II is the exit point of Karanganyar village. Several higher-class houses are

Plate 5.1: Pottery-making process in Karanganyar village (photos: Carolina, 2007)

located here, as are public facilities such as a football field and a mosque. The tourist potential comes from the fresh water spring from the Suroloyo Mountains, which the locals believe can cure many diseases.

Dusun Ngadiwinatan I

Dusun Ngadiwinatan I has natural beauty, including a wonderful sunrise viewing spot with the Merapi and Merbabu mountains.

Dusun Ngadiwinatan II

Dusun Ngadiwinatan II consists of ninety-three families whose members are mostly occupied in the home industry sector of *tahu* (tofu) making with traditional methods.

Tanjungsari village (tofu village)

Tanjungsari village is one of the three villages that are the objects of our field trips. Administratively, Tanjungsari village is located in Borobudur Sub-District, Magelang Regency, and geographically is located at the foot of the Menoreh Hills.

The village is bordered by the Sileng River, a natural resource with tourism potential. Another potential offered by the natural environment can be seen in Gopalan hamlet. The road that crosses the hamlet has spectacular views of the top of Borobudur Temple sprouting out of the trees with the yellow fields of paddy and coconut trees in the foreground.

A potential home industry in Nampan hamlet is *tahu* (tofu) production, which is still done traditionally.

Tuksongo village (glass noodle village)

Tuksongo village is another of our three village destinations for field trips. Administratively, Tuksongo village is located in Borobudur Sub-District, Magelang Regency, and geographically is located at the foot of the Menoreh Hills.

This village covers an area of 228.44 square kilometers. The majority of the people are Muslim. The village is divided into seven *dusuns* (hamlets), six RW (the neighborhood head), and eighteen RT (the head of hamlets).

The people in Tuksongo village are mainly farmers; others are glass noodle merchants. The production of glass noodles, which can be then processed into dishes such as *cendol* (a traditional drink), is part of the village's main source of income and has potential as a tourist attraction.

The pathways in Tuksongo preserve the natural village scenery. The Menoreh Hills are part of the natural scenery with the paddy fields and tobacco plantations.

The process of making glass noodles takes a long time and is done on a large scale. It is usually done in the morning as a home industry. The raw material comes from the Aren tree (*Arenga pinnata*) and can be obtained in Purworejo, Central Java.

The process of glass noodle production is as follows:

- the fibers of the Aren tree are obtained from the stump of the tree and dried in the sun
- the flour from the fiber is separated and mixed with water and then dried again, and the water is used to produce juice
- the dried sediment is once again dried under the sun and then cooked in a large bowl
- the cooked result is pressed with a special machine that creates the strings of glass noodles ready to be dried
- the dried noodles are then packed and are ready to be distributed.

Punthuk Setumbu Hill

Punthuk Setumbu offers fantastic views and is one of the best spots to enjoy the Borobudur sunrise from 400 meters above sea level. Many people climb the hill to wait for the sunrise and relax and enjoy hot coffee or tea and meals while watching this magical view.

From the top of the hill, Borobudur looks like a lotus floating on an ancient lake, surrounded by white clouds and fog. We can also see Mount Merapi and Mount Merbabu in the background.

Punthuk Setumbu Hill is very popular among photographers. This spot was found by a local photographer, Suparno, who used to work in the Borobudur Conservation Office.

The temples in *saujana* Magelang

Asu Temple

Asu Temple (Plate 5.2) is located at Sengi village, Dukun District, Magelang Regency. The temple lies 650 meters above sea level at the eastern edge of Mount Merapi. It has been renovated several times because of eruptions from Mount Merapi. During the last eruption in

2010, Asu Temple was endangered due to its location along the main river flow from Mount Merapi.

Asu Temple faces west and its form is fairly square, with a size of 7.49 meters by 7.49 meters. The temple is constructed from andesite stone. The roof has been broken and most of the stones lost, so it is impossible to reconstruct perfectly.

Asu Temple has few decorations and it seems that it may not have been finished. Asu Temple was abandoned by the workers before they had finished work due to an eruption from Mount Merapi. The original name of this temple in Javanese is Aso, derived from *Ngaso*, which means to take a rest. The people around the temple mispronounced it as Asu, which means dog.

Plate 5.2: Asu Temple (photos: Carolina, 2011)

Lumbung Temple

Lumbung Temple is located 200 meters west of Asu Temple in the region of Tlatar village, Krogowanan, Sawangan District, Magelang Regency. This temple has a width of 8.7 meters x 8.7 meters, a ladder height of 2.5 meters x 2 meters and a temple height of 8 meters and is encircled by the Pabelan River. After the 2010 Mount Merapi eruption, Lumbung Temple was renovated. To avoid further damage, part of the temple was removed and rebuilt as closely as possible (Plate 5.3).

Lumbung Temple is constructed from andesite stone and its structure is in relatively good condition. The temple faces west and its form is fairly square. The temple is not intact because the roof has been broken and most of the stones lost.

The decoration at Lumbung Temple is richer than at Asu Temple. Reliefs were carved on the body of the temple at the south, east, north, and west sides. Damage to the temple was caused by natural disasters because it is near Mount Merapi. Moreover, many people have stolen the stones to build their houses. *Lumbung* in Javanese means a place for saving the harvest of the farmers.

Plate 5.3: Lumbung Temple renovations after the Mount Merapi eruption in 2010 (photos: Carolina, 2011)

Pendem Temple

Pendem Temple is located at Candipos hamlet, Sengi village, Dukun District, Magelang Regency. The temple was buried two meters below ground, with only the foot of the temple above the ground (Plate 5.4). Its form is fairly square, with a size of 11.9 meters by 11.9 meters, and this temple was also made from andesite stones. Like Asu and Lumbung temples, Pendem Temple was affected by Mount Merapi eruptions.

The roof is broken. In the temple there is a well, which still holds water and has a depth of 3.2 meters. The decorations carved on the wall have a floral pattern, but it seems that this temple was not finished because a Makara (a mythical sea creature) near the stairs is half finished. *Pendem* in Javanese means buried.

Plate 5.4: Pendem Temple (photo: Carolina, 2011)

Umbul Temple

Umbul Temple is a bathing place located on the Elo River at Kartoharjo village, Grabak District, Magelang Regency. A pool made from andesite stone is 21 meters by 7 meters in size and 2 meters depth, and is full of warm water (Plate 5.5).

This ancient bathing place is now used by the people around the temple as a swimming pool. Their ancestors built it in the ninth century and dedicated it for the king's family. It faces north-east and is decorated with a beautiful *kala* (symbol of time) relief at the entry point. At the pool there are statues depicting the Hindu stories of Durga Mahisasuramardhini and Agastya. It seems that in the past this pool was also used for religious rites.

Plate 5.5: Umbul Temple (photo: Carolina, 2007)

Selogriyo Temple

Selogriyo Temple is located at Campurejo Hamlet, Kembang Kuning village, Windu Sari District, Magelang Regency. It was built on a hill named Bukit Condong at the eastern edge of Mount Sumbing in the ninth century during the Hindu period. This temple is a single building and its form is unique in Central Java. Its size is 4.2 meters by 4.2 meters, with a height of 4.96 meters. This temple does not have stairs.

To get to Selogriyo Temple, we have to traverse the slope of the hill. The views are breathtaking – the beauty of the scenery is not only due to the contours of the land but also the small surrounding hills. Like other temples around Borobudur, Selogriyo Temple unites with nature (Plate 5.6).

Plate 5.6: Selogriyo Temple and the landscape to the temple (photo: Utami)

Places outside the Borobudur area

Ketep Pass

Ketep Pass is located at Sawangan (between Mount Merapi and Mount Merbabu) and is 1200 meters above sea level. This location is known as Panca Arga (*Panca* means five and Arga means mountain in Javanese) because five mountains (Merapi, Merbabu, Sindoro, Sumbing, and Prahu) can be seen clearly from the pass, as well as Tidar hill, the Menoreh Hills, Mount Telomoyo, and Mount Andong (Plate 5.7).

Plate 5.7: Ketep Pass (photo: Carolina)

Merapi mountain area

Mount Merapi is one of the most active volcanoes in the world. Based on the history of Merapi eruptions, the Borobudur area is also impacted. The recent 2010 eruption covered the Borobudur Temple with volcanic ash, and it took many months and hundreds of people working together to clean the ash from the temple. It is also said that according to history, the Merapi eruption in the year 1000 BC caused the people of Central Java to abandon the area and move to East Java. An eruption also caused Borobudur Temple to be buried for hundreds of years before it was rediscovered by Thomas Stamford Raffles in 1814.

Participants and management

Participants of the Borobudur Field School come from many countries, such as Japan, Malaysia, Vietnam, Egypt, China, Thailand, Korea, Indonesia, and France. Almost every field school has had Japanese participants, who mostly come from connections with Kanki Laboratory. Indonesian participants have come from several regions, including Buton Island, Makassar (South Sulawesi), Yogyakarta, Jakarta, Bandung, Ternate (Moluccas Islands), and Papua. The participants are mostly students (undergraduate and master's students); others are lecturers, government staff, heritage activists, architects, and so on. Table 5.2 lists participants.

The field school is organized by the Center for Heritage Conservation, Department of Architecture and Planning, Faculty of Engineering, Universitas Gadjah Mada. In 2004–06 it

Table 5.2: Borobudur Field School participants

Participants of 1st BFS, 2004
Andhika Priyatama
Agus
Ade Maulani Sabri
Dyah Arnawati
Endah Ciptaning
Fristho Setyawan
Hadhiratul Kudus
Mayu Kitagawa
Mine Kaneko
Miyuki Takami
Koji Matsuo
Nedyomukti Imam Syafi'i
Niswatul Azizah
Kyoto Hayashi
Kusumaningdyah Nurul Handayani
Rahadea Baswara
Sinta Carolina
Soesiloyono
Titin Fatimah
Valentina
Wijanarko
Yuichi Takaragawa
Yusuf Cecep Fajarudin

Participants of 2nd BFS, 2005
Dimas Wihardyanto
Granita Zulaycha
Isamu Takama
Indah Sulistiana
Maria Carmelia
Nicolas Zaegel
Niswatul Azizah
Natsuji Hashimoto
Raditya Jati
Satrio Utomo Dradjat
Seika Oishi
Sinta Carolina
Tomoko Miyagawa
Tomoki Motozuka
Titin Fatimah
Winarni
Yosuke Sato
Yumi Kanki (Terakawa)
Yuta Kimura

Participants of 3rd BFS, 2006
Arif Budi Sholihah
Abrilianty Octaria
Granita Zulaycha
Iwan Imam Sujai
Kusumaningdyah NH
Maria Carmelia
Mayu Kanatani
Ngurah
Nicolas Zaegel
Retno Ayu
Sinta Carolina
Satrio Utomo Drajat
Siswanto
Seika Oishi
Tomoki Motozuka
Takayuki Kawane
Titi Handayani
Tomoko Miyagawa
Winarni
Yvonne Tarore

Participants of 4th BFS, 2007
Arief Budi Sholihah
Ayang Cempaka
Han Seoung Wook
Kusumaningdyah Nurul Handayani
Kana Shiraki
Le Quynh Chi
Maulana Ibrahim
Morinda Frida Anjarsari
Maeda Masahiro
Ning Purnomohadi
Ratna Yunnarsih
Seika Oishi
Sinta Carolina
Satrio Utomo Dradjat
Titin Fatimah

Yeny Paulina Leibo

Participants of 6th BFS, 2012
Ain Noun Kornita Deny
Anne Yuen Kam Peng
Annika Eska Larasati
May Sherif El Sabbahy
Erik Agus Saputra
Selia Jinhua Tan
Kamsiah Mohammad Bostock
Mathew TK Cheng
Maya Raina
Priyo A. Sancoyo
Sigit Pramana Putra
Sinta Carolina
Su Mei Tan
Vincentia Lucinda
Wahyu Nur Isnain Novianto
Wahyu Utami
Yeny Paulina Leibo
Yonanda Rayi Ayuningtyas

Participants of 7th BFS, 2013
Alfons M. Wakum
Ama Billy Yusrianto
Bencharat Sirichirachai
Chantanee Chiranthanut
Dussadee Summart
Grace Damaris
Hamzah Saefuddin
Hiroto Ota
Krittapard Kitkoson
Nafi'ah Solikhah
Naruemon Teefuey
Peerasuk Poolthong
Priyo A. Sancoyo
Punto Wijayanto
Septi Indrawati Kusumaningsih
Witch Chuay-Uea
Raisya Nur Nasich
Inas Nur Atika

was held in collaboration with the Miyagawa Seminar, Department of Environmental Systems, Wakayama University, Japan, and in 2007–13 with Kanki Laboratory, Graduate School of Architecture and Architectural Engineering, Faculty of Engineering, Kyoto University, Japan, with the Chairperson of the Sub-committee for Rural Cultural Landscape, Committee for Rural Planning, Architectural Institute of Japan, and with the Jogja Heritage Society.

For the duration of the program (seven days) participants stay in Candirejo village. Apart from receiving activity materials from facilitators, participants can also obtain data and information directly from other resources, especially the local community. To broaden their understanding and experience, several field trips are arranged in the Menoreh–Borobudur region, in the countryside, and in several heritage areas of Yogyakarta. Activities consist of lectures, field studies/observations, field trips, discussions with local community members, and presentations.

Each field school is limited to twenty-five participants, who are recruited through invitations sent by post and email to cultural and tourism agencies, and to universities that offer subjects in architecture, culture, or tourism in Indonesia and abroad. Leaflets are also distributed with information on the activities, facilitators, facilities included/not included, program options, and registration information (costs, application deadline, the contact person, and so on). Posters are also put up at various universities in Indonesia and the program is advertised through social media.

Anyone who is interested in the conservation of landscape heritage can participate, including people from government organizations and associations, tourism experts, culture and heritage experts, environment experts, researchers from Indonesia and abroad (with backgrounds that relate to the program's theme), and students from universities in Indonesia and abroad who are interested in the field of cultural landscape heritage conservation.

The Center for Heritage Conservation usually recruits students to the organizing committee, which requires much assistance. Ten volunteer students are members of the committee and also attend the field school as participants. The Center has minimal criteria for inviting students, but they have usually entered their last year of study, are able to grasp the content quickly, and have good English language skills.

In calling for participants, the following information is included.

- Facilitators:
  - Prof. Dr. Kiyoko Kanki, Kanki Laboratory, Architecture and Human Environmental Planning, Dept. of Architecture and Architectural Engineering, Graduate School of Engineering, Kyoto University, Japan
  - Dr. Ir. Laretna T. Adishakti, M.Arch., Center for Heritage Conservation, Dept. of Architecture and Planning, Faculty of Engineering, UGM
  - Dr. Ir. Dwita Hadi Rahmi, M.A., Center for Heritage Conservation, Dept. of Architecture and Planning, Faculty of Engineering, UGM
  - Ir. Titi Handayani, M.Arch., Jogja Heritage Society
  - Dr. Amiluhur Soeroso, SE., MM., M.Si, Center for Heritage Conservation, Dept. of Architecture and Planning, Faculty of Engineering, UGM
  - Dr. Titin Fatimah, S.T., M.Eng., Dept. of Architecture, Faculty of Engineering, Universitas Tarumanagara
  - Jack Priyana, JAKER (Borobudur Tourism Network).
  - Dr. Ir. Helmy Murwanto, M.S., Dept. of Geology, University of National Development "Veteran", Yogyakarta.
- Facilities included in the program:
  - modest accommodation (homestay), meals and drinks during the program in Borobudur (six days)
  - modest accommodation in Yogyakarta (one day)
  - meals during the program
  - transportation, Yogyakarta to Borobudur, Borobudur to Yogyakarta, and during the program in Borobudur
  - program materials.
- Facilities not included:
  - transportation to Yogyakarta from original country/city
  - passport and visa arrangements
  - health insurance
  - additional field trip/heritage trail (post-summer school) in Yogyakarta
  - accommodation in Yogyakarta outside the BFS program
  - personal expenses and equipment during the program.

Rules and guidelines for participants

The following rules are set for participants:

- each participant is required to participate in every activity scheduled by the Borobudur Field School
- each participant is responsible for every assignment and work division in the field trips
- all participants are responsible for their own and their groups' luggage and personal accessories and belongings
- all participants are to bring the necessary stationery and other tools for observation according to their own assignments
- participants and officials leaving the location for urgent needs require a permit from the head of officials
- if photographs, slides, or videos for observation are needed, confirmation is required from the documentation official
- each participant must be able to coordinate and work together with any other participant
- each participant must act politely and respect daily customs of the local community
- each participant must keep the environment clean
- each participant is to attend the activities on time.

The following guidelines are provided to participants on the customs of village communities:

- if you meet with locals, it is polite to greet them; greetings can be done by smiling, saying *monggo* (please pass), *nderek langkung* (ask permission to get through), or *kulo nuwun* (ask permission to be a guest), or just nod your head
- dress appropriately; according to local customs, women usually wear long clothes/dress and clothing that covers the shoulders
- men usually wear clothes/shirts and trousers or shorts; the village people still have taboo values
- control your emotion; protests are better expressed in a gentle manner, or better expressed while joking
- if you wish to become a guest of a house, always say *kulonnuwun* (ask permission to be a guest), *asalamualaikum* (greetings in Arabian language *or* Islamic people in general), or *permisi* (ask permission to enter a person's house) while knocking on the door; if the person is home, he or she will answer with *monggo* (please come in) or *walaikumsalam* (the answer for greeting guests)
- the village people are not accustomed to punctuality, since they usually tell time by observing the natural weather or the environment.

Objectives

Places to be studied during the Borobudur Field School vary depending on the theme. Each year there are different places to study:

- Candirejo village (1st BFS)
- Karanganyar village (Klipoh), macro scale (2nd BFS)
- Klipoh hamlet, micro scale (3rd BFS)
- Kedu Plain, Central Java (4th BFS)
- Borobudur as National Strategic Area (6th BFS)

- Candirejo village, Klipoh, Maitan, and special spots to enjoy the beautiful scenery (Punthuk Setumbu Hill and Karanganyar village) (7th BFS).

Field school activities: a photo record by participants

Plates 5.8 to 5.13 show field school activities.

Plate 5.8: BFS 2004; (left) discussion (photo: Rahadea), (right) field survey (photo: Fatimah)

Plate 5.9: BFS 2005; (left) heritage trail, (right) field survey (photos: Fatimah)

Plate 5.10: BFS 2006; (left) night school, (right) field survey (photos: CHC)

Plate 5.11: BFS 2007; (left) discussion (photo: Adishakti), (right) field survey (photo: Maulana Ibrahim)

Plate 5.12: BFS 2012; (left) Candirejo village, (right) visiting Borobudur (photos: Inas)

Plate 5.13: BFS 2013; (left) visiting Punthuk Setumbu Hill, (right) visiting Borobudur (photos: Ama Billy)

Outcomes of the field schools

BFS 2004

BFS 2004 focused on implementing techniques of cultural landscape conservation, including enhancing participants' skills in inventory, documentation, and presentation of the unique villages surrounding Borobudur Temple that have been ignored in the Borobudur Temple conservation and development. Participants were divided into three groups, which each choosing a village to study. The villages were:

- Wringinputih village
- Candirejo village
- Giritengah village.

Wringinputih village

Wringinputih village is located in the northern part of Borobudur Sub-district, about two kilometers from Borobudur Temple to the north-west. The village consists of nine hamlets, fifteen RW (the head of hamlets), and forty-two RT (the neighborhood head). The majority of villagers are subsistence farmers.

The village has an area of about 377.46 square kilometers and a fairly dense population of 4033 people, made up of 1027 households. Wringinputih is an agrarian society.

There is potential for crafts, the food industry, art, agriculture, accommodation, and so on. Generally, the sugar industry has dominated the area, which is filled with coconut trees.

Candirejo village

Borobudur is located in Magelang Regency, with the mountains as a buffer. Borobudur Temple is supported by a beautiful natural landscape. Borobudur has twenty villages and Candirejo is one of the prettiest. With its natural potential and typical rural atmosphere, the customs and traditions are interwoven to provide an incredible visual experience. Agriculture and plantations form the mainstay of the local community, which is an agrarian society.

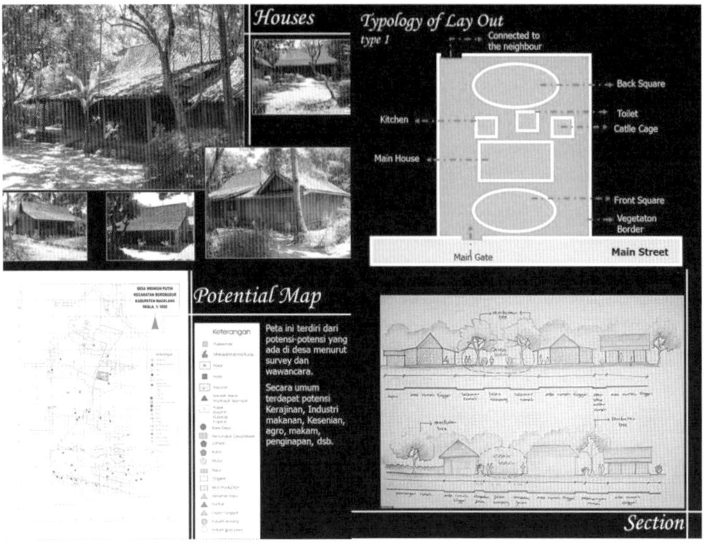

Figure 5.1: Final presentation slides of Wringinputih village by BFS 2004 group

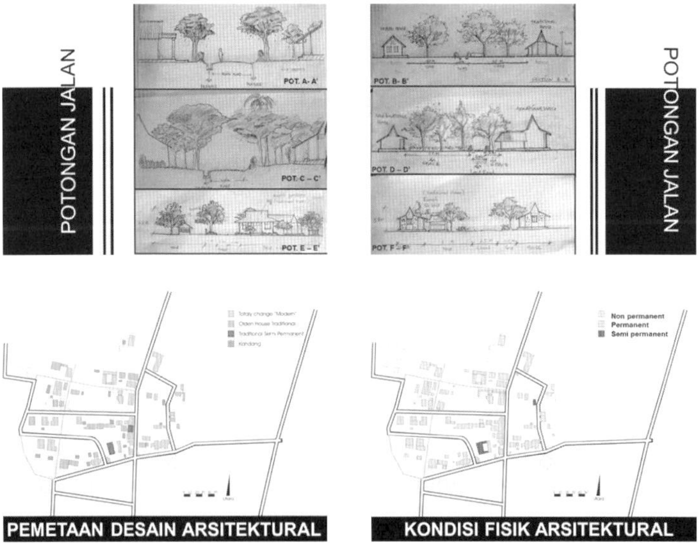

Figure 5.2: Final presentation slides and architectural mapping of Candirejo village by BFS 2004 group

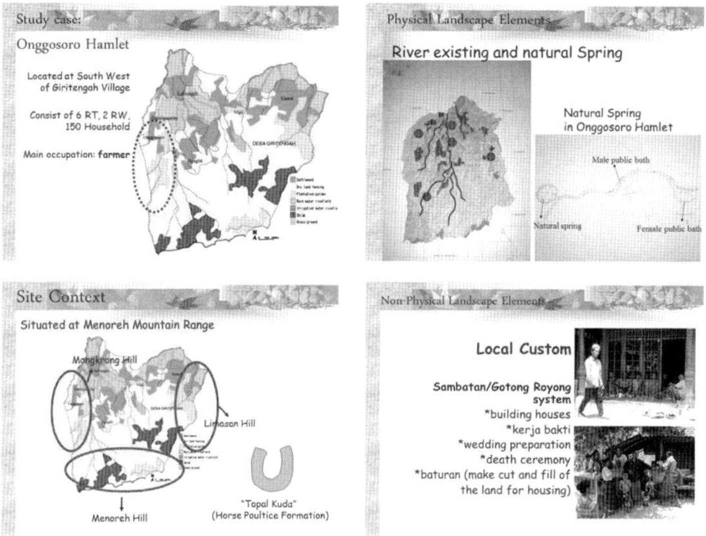

Figure 5.3: Final presentation slides, landscape elements of Giritengah village, by BFS 2004 group

Candirejo is located approximately three kilometers east of Borobudur in the foothills of the Menoreh Hills and has an area of 366.250 square kilometers. The fifteen hamlets have a population of 4056 consisting of 1055 households (the majority are Muslim).

Giritengah village

Giritengah village is located in the south-west of Borobudur Sub-district, with an area of 4.3 square kilometers and a population of 3222 people. There are 886 households in six hamlets, twelve RW, and thirty-seven RT. The landform consists of 60% hilly areas and 40% plains area.

The six hamlets are Mijil, Kalitengah, Gedangsambu, Onggosoro, Ngaglik, and Kamal.

BFS 2005

BFS 2005 focused on Klipoh and the assignment was to develop village design guidelines. Participants were divided into three groups, each with a different theme:

- water analysis
- Klipoh hamlet
- region, scale, and facade.

Water analysis

Mr Hashimoto proposed the need to purify the Klipoh River. When he analyzed the river he

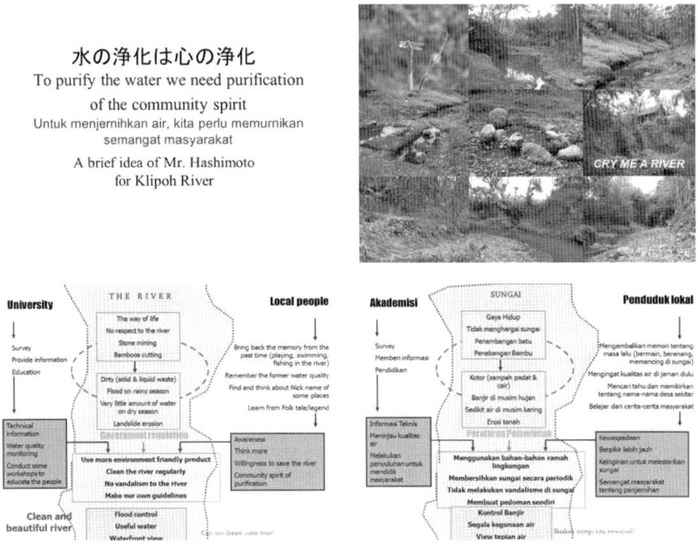

Figure 5.4: Final presentation slides of river analysis by Mr Hashimoto, a participant from Japan

found problems such as stone mining and bamboo cutting and a lack of respect for the river, problems that led to dirty water (with solid and liquid waste), flooding in the rainy season, very little water in the dry season, and landslide erosion.

To achieve the objectives of flood control, useful water, and improved waterfront views, three sectors need to be involved in the purification activity:

- universities – to provide information, surveys, and education in the form of technical information, water quality monitoring, and workshops to educate the people
- local people – to renew the memory of past times (playing, swimming, and fishing in the river), remember the former water quality, find and consider nicknames of places, and learn from folk tales/legends
- government – to regulate a more environmentally friendly use, clean the river regularly, prevent vandalism to the river, and set guidelines.

Klipoh hamlet

Klipoh hamlet in Karanganyar village has long been renowned for its pottery. Usually these crafts products are used as daily household equipment like *kendil* (for holding food), *tempayan minum* (for drinking), *kuali gerabah* (for cooking), and other uses.

According to folklore the pottery village has been around for centuries and has a connection with the construction of Borobudur Temple (according to the stories, the builders used Karanganyar pottery). It is located at the foot of the Menoreh Hills approximately five kilometers from Borobudur Temple. Karanganyar village shares borders to the north with

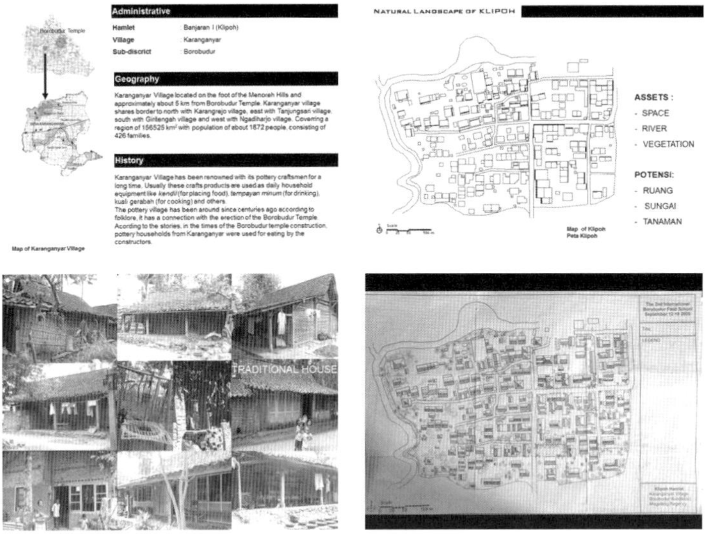

Figure 5.5: Final presentation slides of Karanganyar village analysis by BFS 2005 group

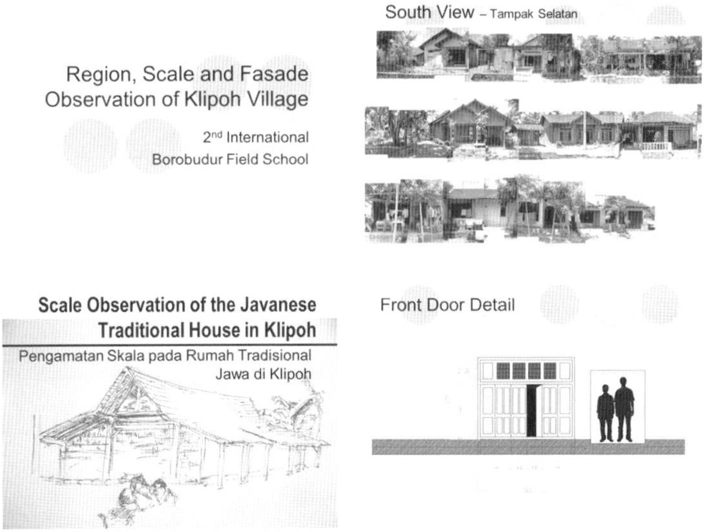

Figure 5.6: Final presentations slides of region, scale and facade observation by BFS 2005 group

Karangrejo village, east with Tanjungsari village, south with Giritengah village, and west with Ngadiharjo village. It covers an area of 156.52 square kilometers and has a population of about 1872 people, consisting of 426 families.

Region, scale and facade

Klipoh is a unique hamlet in the mosaic of the Borobudur area and plays an important role in Borobudur cultural landscape heritage. Klipoh needs to be conserved and sustained.

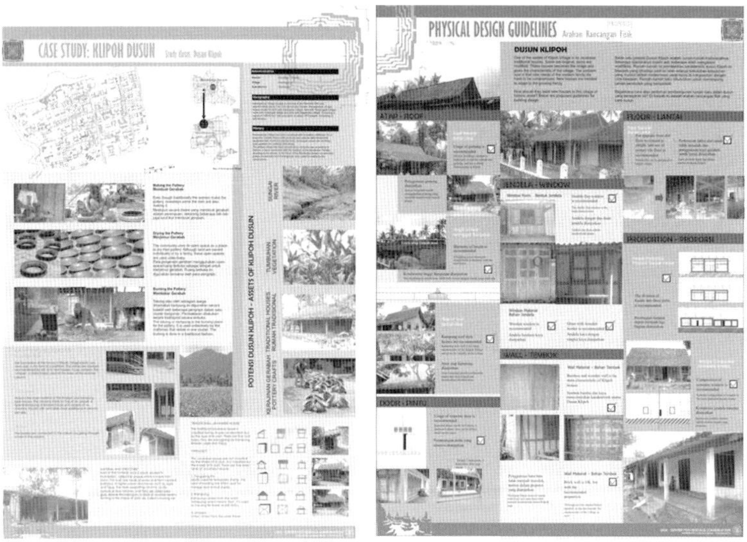

Figure 5.7: Posters of case study and physical design guidelines – Klipoh

BFS 2006

The BFS 2006 assignment was to formulate village design guidelines (Figure 5.8).

The first step was to undertake an analysis and evaluation at Klipoh:

- physical problems:
  - ground exploitation for raw materials for pottery
  - flood plain: erosion, polluted water, and silting up of river/sedimentation
  - 'new design' of buildings
  - pottery and construction material stock arrangement
  - building arrangement related to limited land resources
- economic problems:
  - limited skilled human resources
  - limited design/creativity
  - limited financial capital

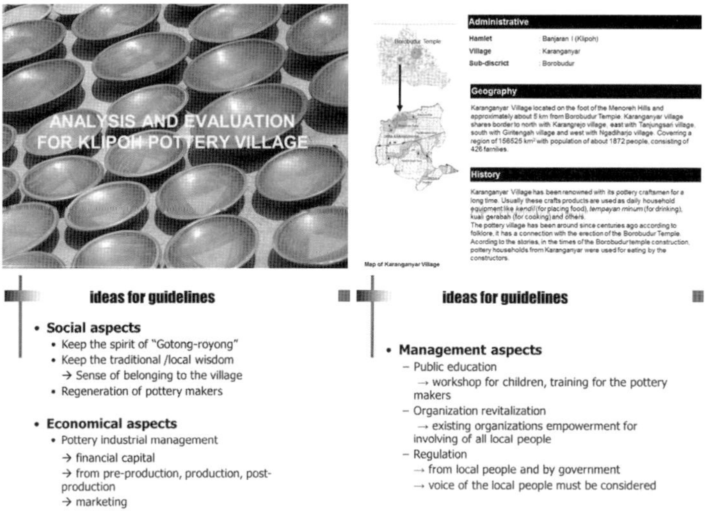

Figure 5.8: Final presentation slides, analysis and evaluation for Klipoh pottery village, BFS 2006

- cheap sale price
- distribution network
- social problems:
  - lack of knowledge and skills
  - industrial pottery management
  - limited human resources
  - no regeneration
  - gaps between young and old generations (especially on product design capacity).

Recommendations were then made for various aspects (Figure 5.8):

- marketing – find buyers who have the capacity to provide training in new designs and technology and to buy and market the product
- environmental – think about the environmental sustainability of pottery
- tourism – tourism is a side effect of being a pottery village, so conserve the uniqueness of the village
- physical – local guidelines from and for the community; new houses must be well designed (give more attention to human scale and traditional form)
- management – revitalize local organizations
- linkage – create links to other villages in the Borobudur area (glass noodle village, tofu village, etc.) for cultural landscape unity
- design – conserve old designs and reinvent new designs.

The field school produced a 'Process and techniques of cultural landscape conservation

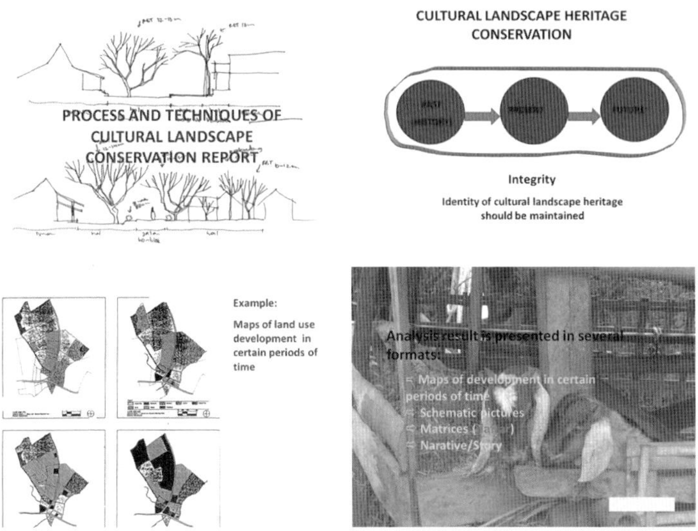

Figure 5.9: Final presentation slides, process, and techniques of cultural landscape conservation report, BFS 2006

report' (Figure 5.9). A description of the landscape through every historic period up to the present was compiled, and included:

- documentation of physical development (character, attributes, features)
- description of the social history and cultural history related to the physical development.

Documentation sources included:

- written sources:
  - newspapers, diaries
  - published secondary sources: guidebooks, books
  - unpublished secondary sources: research and seminar papers, theses, dissertations, reports
  - journals, periodicals, catalogs
  - manuscript collections
- visual sources:
  - maps, site plans
  - design plans
  - photographs
  - paintings, prints, drawings, and illustrations
- oral histories
  - tapes and transcripts of interviews with residents
  - interviews by people who have done earlier research on the village.

Components for documentation included:

- site research prior to field work and a review of various source materials:
  - databases
  - files
  - reports and special studies
  - other site materials (maps, photographs)
- site survey: on-the-ground field work to document the existing landscape characteristics through techniques such as:
  - existing conditions plan
  - narrative text
  - photographs
  - condition assessments.

BFS 2007

BFS 2007 focused on the various principles and issues of the regional context of Borobudur conservation planning. The participants were divided into two groups, the Macro Scale and the Micro Scale groups.

Kedu Plain and surrounding mountains – Macro Scale Group

The cultural landscape is fashioned from a natural landscape by a cultural group. Culture is the agent, nature is the medium, and the cultural landscape is the result.

Elements of cultural landscape in the Kedu Plain setting include:

- paddy fields

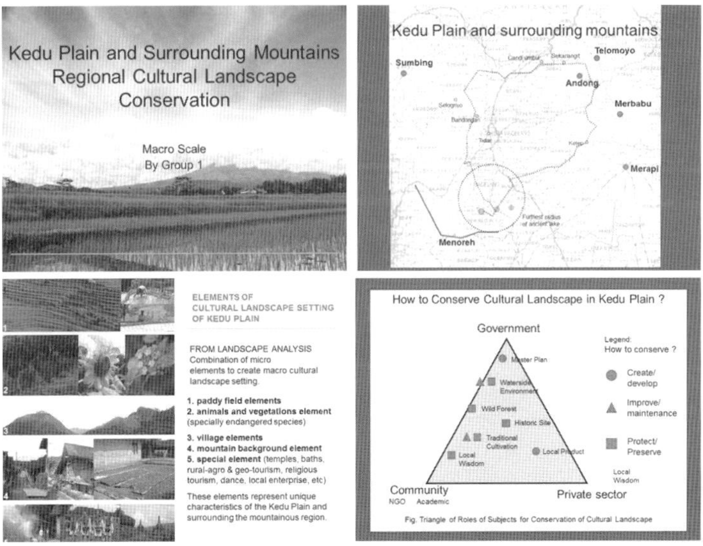

Figure 5.10: Final presentation slides by Macro Scale Group, BFS 2007

- animals (especially endangered species) and vegetation
- villages
- mountain backgrounds
- special elements (temples, baths, rural-agro and geo-tourism, religious tourism, dance, local enterprise, etc.).

These elements represent unique characteristics of the Kedu Plain and the surrounding mountainous region. Landscape analysis reveals that a combination of micro elements creates the macro cultural landscape setting.

Integrated management of the cultural landscape requires:

- large-scale environmental management, which should be done by government (e.g. a master plan and regulation/law)
- small-scale environmental management, which should be done by the local community (e.g. daily cultural activities).

Heritage Trail Program – Micro Scale Group

The Micro Scale Group considered the response of local people to visitors with different backgrounds; for example, by:

- organizing a Heritage Trail (BFS in collaboration with local community)
- enhancing homestay programs in different villages.

Impressions of villages surrounding Borobudur Temple involve aspects in the:

- non-physical category:
  - skill or ability (communication, interaction, friendliness, hospitality)

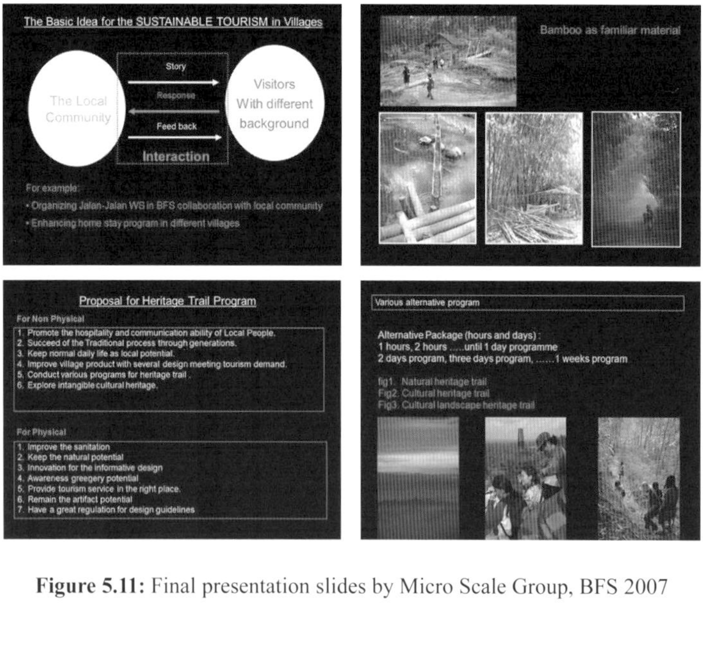

Figure 5.11: Final presentation slides by Micro Scale Group, BFS 2007

- traditional processes
- normal daily life
- promotion of village products
- intangible cultural heritage
- physical category:
  - sanitation
  - natural potential
  - tourist information (maps, signboards, brochures, leaflets)
  - greenery
  - tourisms service (accommodation, toilets, public phones, information centers, access)
  - artifact potential
  - regulations for design guidelines.

BFS 2012

BFS 2012 participants were assigned a study on the Borobudur National Strategic Area and were divided into four groups to discuss specific themes:

- environment
- spatial planning
- tourism
- architecture.

Environment

In considering how to conserve the National Strategic Area, the Environment Group discussed:

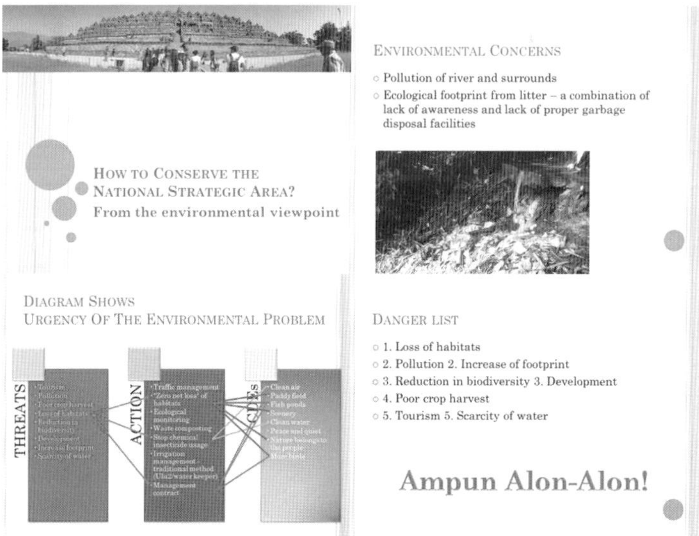

Figure 5.12: Final presentation slides by Environment Group, BFS 2012

- environmental concerns:
  - pollution of river and surrounds
  - ecological footprint from litter – a combination of lack of awareness and lack of proper garbage disposal facilities
- initial ideas to address the problems:
  - fish ponds benefit land
  - the grass verges and roadside trees are both picturesque and beneficial
  - wise use of water resources
  - rice farming along the highway corridor is picturesque, but use of pesticides is degrading the environment
  - we must not presume to teach the farmer about paddy planting or fish farming; the locals used to have innate knowledge of environment.

Spatial planning

The Spatial Planning Group considered cultural landscape heritage planning for the National Strategic Area based on nature. Borobudur was built on the Kedu Plain, and the mountains, hills, and rivers are part of the *saujana* heritage of the Borobudur area. The ancient lake is also part of the history of the cultural landscape.

A draft spatial plan proposed mixed land use and farming in Palbapang:

- along Borobudur/Ngrajek roads
- small farms and fishing in Palbapang

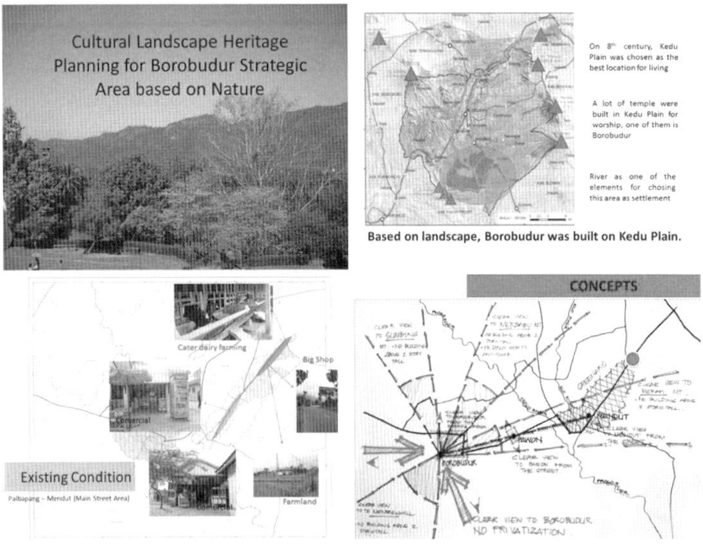

Figure 5.13: Final presentation slides by Spatial Planning Group, BFS 2012

- two kinds of government facilities to promote high-value tourist-orientated policies (policies should not benefit local communities only as vendors).

Tourism

The Tourism Group listed the types of tourism around Pawon and Mendut temples:

- pilgrim tourism
- history tourism
- education tourism
- recreation tourism
- adventure tourism
- natural tourism
- cultural tourism
- ecological tourism
- culinary tourism.

The group also considered commitments in the tourism business:

- empowering local people
- benefits are mostly for local people
- open management
- maintaining environment and heritage
- promoting local cultures and products.

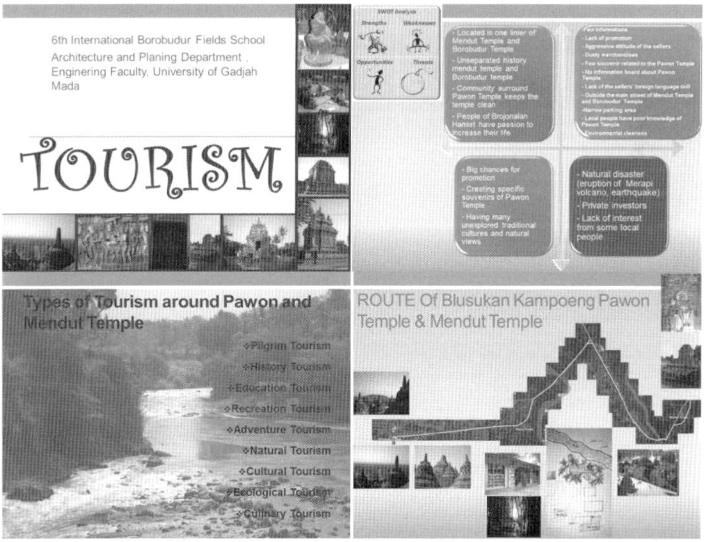

Figure 5.14: Final presentation slides by Tourism Group, BFS 2012

Architecture

The Architecture Group considered three zones/conservation areas and their guidelines:

- Zone 1: paddy fields and fish ponds:
  - strictly conserved area
  - no businesses/construction allowed to disturb paddy fields and fish ponds
  - pedestrian zone introduced so people can enjoy the paddy fields and fish ponds
- Zone 2: commercial
  - current potential commercial development allowed
  - no new applications/buying land for business use
  - all business need a pedestrian zone
  - limited to two stories high and to a local building style
  - parking for owners around the back
  - expansion needs to take the form of traditional houses (*Jokulu* style) instead of large modern buildings
  - business needs to maintain the vernacular method of building
- Zone 3:
  - existing local business only allowed, no new construction
  - introduce conversion of small local shops and residences to the local character
  - only rentals allowed, priority given to local home industry or other kinds of adaptive reuse
  - pedestrian zone introduced.

The group also made suggestions for building new structures:

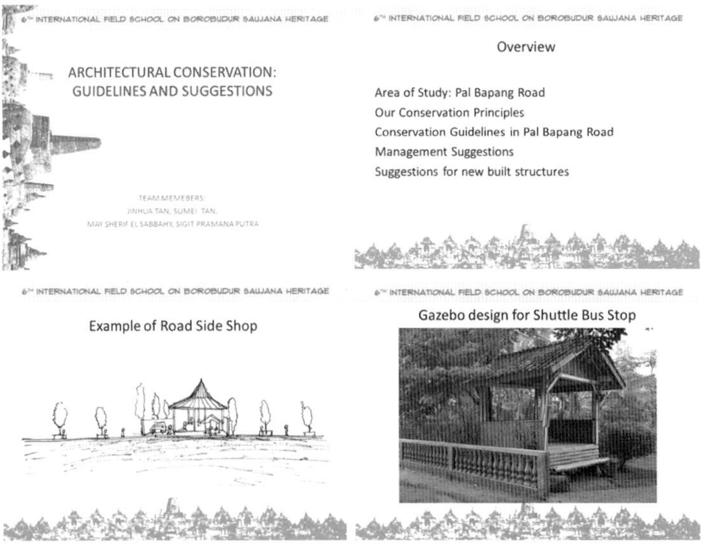

Figure 5.15: Final presentation slides by Architecture Group, BFS 2012

- to follow traditional dwelling architectural characteristics such as floor plans, roof style, and bamboo features
- to ensure longer-lasting residences, allow the use of local-made bricks for walls (roofs, doors, and windows to remain traditional bamboo style)
- to use traditional styles and materials for business buildings; however, in some instances, allow brick walls in-between the bamboo mats.
- to use local style, scale, and materials for extensions (avoiding large buildings).

BFS 2013

For BFS 2013 participants were divided into four groups:

- Regional Group
- Architecture Group
- Temple Group
- Village Group.

Regional Group

The Regional Group investigated the changing landscape due to land conversion and the following elements of heritage planning:

- building design
- historical landscape
- agricultural activity
- scenery and vista

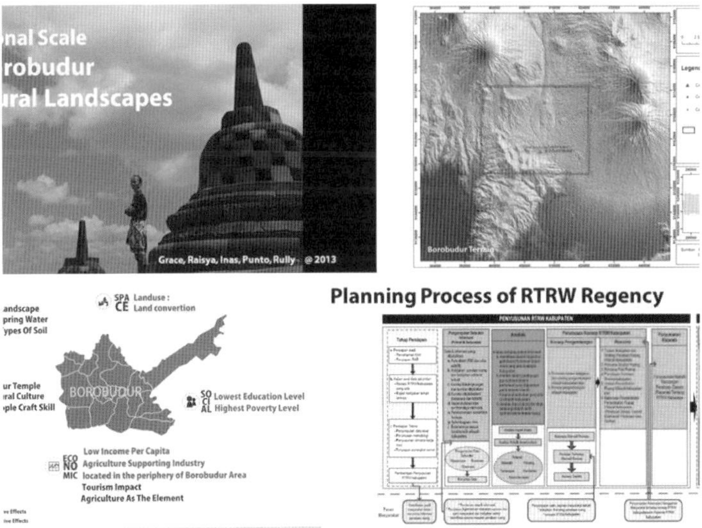

Figure 5.16: Final presentation slides by Regional Group, BFS 2013

- community initiatives
- support system
  - support for *saujana* heritage planning (involving scenery and vista, building design, historical landscape)
  - support for sustainable agriculture (involving community initiatives and agricultural activity).

Architecture Group

The Architecture Group made recommendations for:

- analysis
  - impact effect from media, which considers that modern architecture is more attractive
  - the mind set of people that using modern shapes, materials, and structures will increase their social status
  - the variety of functions that impact tourism economic capacity and the capacity of family members
  - the lack of education about the traditional architecture of the house
  - the addition of new functions and material (toilet, storage, additional rooms) based on needs
  - the lack of time for maintenance, so materials are changed for ease of maintenance (ceramics, bricks, etc.)
  - new materials are cheaper than local materials

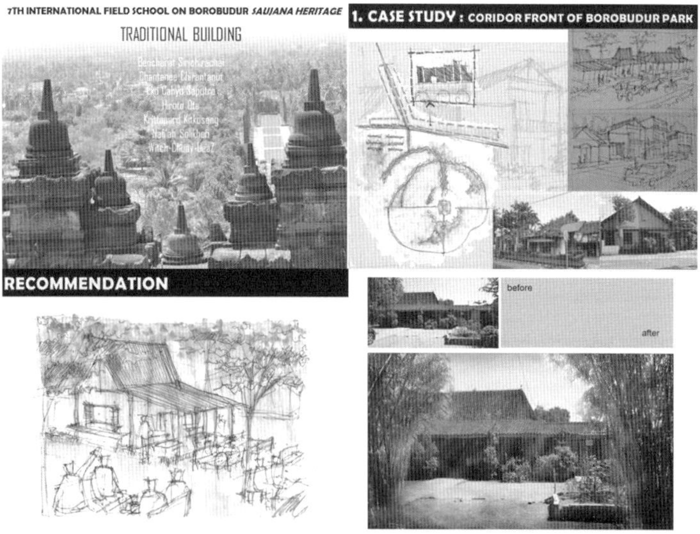

Figure 5.17: Final presentation slides by Architecture Group, BFS 2013

- strategy
  - provide education for the people to understand, and be proud to live in, the heritage area
  - acknowledge buildings that have good traditional architecture
  - acknowledge people who have good traditional houses
  - provide a map to guide local people and tourists ('learning by seeing')
  - provide documentation (surveys, measurements, drawings, etc. for publication), especially for local people
- guidelines
  - if architectural materials need to be changed, the first priority should be to use local materials
  - retain the pattern of the building envelope, shape, and structure (proportion, configuration)
  - additional components must be similar and in harmony with traditional components.

Temple Group

The Temple Group looked at community involvement in tourism activity in the Pawon Temple area and considered:

- problems
  - tourists come to Pawon Temple for a few minutes only to see the temple, not the villages around the temple
  - lack of information about Pawon Temple for tourists
  - potentials of the local community have not been understood and developed
  - tourism activity at Pawon Temple has been unable to provide an economic impact for the community
  - only a few local people are involved in tourism activity and benefit from it
  - there has been less concern for the community on tourism activity, although there has been high concern for the condition of the temple
- potentials
  - high concern of the community for the temple (high sense of belonging)
  - historical value that relates to the history of Borobudur and Mendut temples
  - good access to Pawon Temple from the main road
  - many traditional buildings and local vegetation in the settlement around the temple
  - community traditional lifestyle still exists (e.g. in Wanurejo village – traditional performance (*dayakan*, *jathilan*, *ketoprak*, *pitutur*), traditional crafts (gypsum statues, fiber work, stone carving, wood masks, *klithik* puppets, wood/batik puppets), home industry (brown sugar, tofu)
- conservation concerns
  - Pawon Temple is not the only tourism object in the area; the settlement is also an interesting place to visit
  - local people are willing to be involved in tourism to benefit from it
  - conservation should be conducted for the temple and the settlement

Figure 5.18: Final presentation slides by Temple Group, BFS 2013

- tourism activity should provide economic (income generation) and social (proud feeling) benefits to the local community
- developing community potentials
    - more local products (craft, home industry, local culinary specialty)
    - strengthening local traditional dance
    - designing crafts with a local identity (e.g. miniatures of Pawon Temple)
    - making more use of traditional houses for tourism facilities
    - making more use of local gardens for greenery, aesthetics, and consumption (e.g. papaya, rambutan, vegetables, medicinal plants, herbs)
    - introducing the Progo River and spring as a tourism object.

Village Group

The Village Group found potentials in villages surrounding Borobudur:

- Candirejo village – Watu Kendil, Banyu Asin, Watu Tambak, farming, vegetation, homestays, art performances, cultural activities
- Klipoh and Karanganyar – pottery, scenery, farming, art performances
- Maitan and Borobudur – scenery, art performances, traditional houses, home industries, farming
- other villages – scenery, art performances, traditional houses, home industries, farming.

The group also identified problems:

- lack of good collaboration between local people, stakeholders, government
- decreasing understanding of local culture

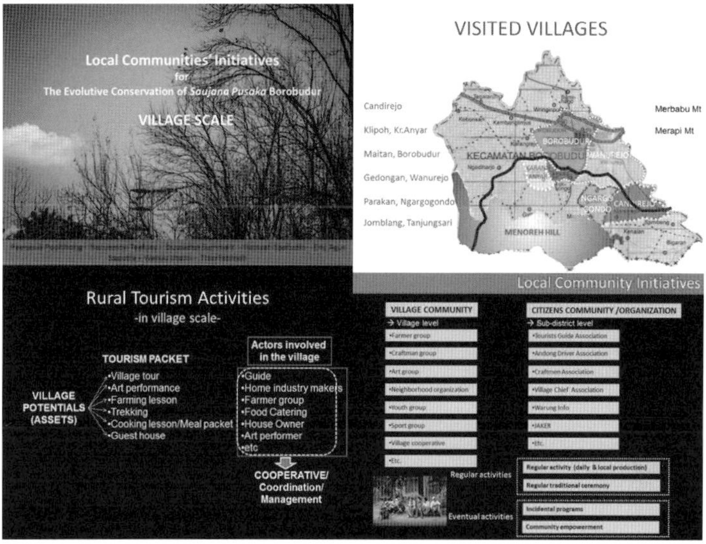

Figure 5.19: Final presentation slides by Village Group, BFS 2013

- excessive economic development, including many new buildings without permission
- decreasing farming areas
- natural disasters
- cultural shock
- garbage management
- transportation and circulation
- limited local resources
- management and organization – a need for more collaboration
- lack of knowledge in utilization of potentials
- lack of awareness to maintain and conserve the potential and heritage assets.

The idea of evolutive conservation on the village scale involves:

- understanding that changes cannot be stopped but can be controlled
- managing/controlling the village
- humans as agents of change who should have awareness and understanding of:
    - local activities
    - the need for regular meetings to provide an understanding of cultural values
    - the importance of childhood – children should be involved and taught culture and local wisdom through daily life activities from as young as possible
    - heritage education – to encourage pride in local culture (e.g. slogans and songs about the unique history)
    - the importance of awards and tokens of appreciation to people for good conservation (e.g. good renovations of traditional houses).

The daily life activities of the people have elements such as farming, local customs, local wisdom, traditions, and so on, which, if maintained in good ways, will lead to sustainable village heritage assets and the bonus of tourism.

The meaning of the Borobudur Field School for participants

Participation in the field school program involves living for a week in a village with the locals and meeting new people, and provides beautiful moments and memories.

The field school has different meanings for all participants, including the organizing committee and facilitators. Below are some comments from participants.

- KIMURA Yuta, first-year master's student at Graduate School of Urban and Environmental Engineering, Kyoto University, Japan (2005 participant):

> There was something precious in Indonesia!!
> In Indonesia, there are rich natures, hot but tasty food. Moreover people are kindhearted!
> I noticed how poor [the] Japanese skill of discussion in English was.
> We were entertained with food when we were investigating. Village people were very tender. I found that [the] Indonesian and Japanese idea about saving nature and landscape was the same.
> We were exhausted from the all-night studio-works, but I am glad to accomplish it.
> In this week, we could have strange experiences which we could never have in Japan.
> I was surprised and impressed…that we, foreigners, were invited to the traditional festival which is held only [a] few times a year. We learned the culture of Indonesian music as we were taught a *gamelan*.
> Actually, there are many people who resemble Japanese!
> We experienced what we could never do in Japan such as climbing a palm tree and catching a wild chicken.

- PUNTO Wijayanto, researcher at the Center for Heritage Conservation, Department of Architecture and Planning, UGM:

> Since beginning…the debate on conservation of the Borobudur temple, the uncontrolled transformation has become a major concern but remains unresolved. From the practical view, insufficient capacity of the governments to supervise the implementation of laws and regulations they developed has become the main reason.
> Question[s] should be…posed [about] filiations between the definition of historic monuments and heritage (cultural, natural or cultural landscape). Borobudur temple should be considered within a frame of our own concept, not occidental or other countries, where it enable[s] the modifications of

the basic concept of heritage. And it is during BFS, we can be involved in thinking about Borobudur Cultural Landscape for the development and the new orientations.

- Impressions from the 4th Borobudur Field School Participants:
  - in this [field school] I [had a] very good experience, thankyou…if I have chance in future I want to visit here again (Maeda)
  - when I sleep, my ear is still hear and concentrate on the lecture! I thank everybody…good experience participating in BFS. I recognise how my english is very terrible. I will study english more. And next time I will speak more clearly and discuss borobudur area (Han)
  - Thank you…I really want to know about the previous workshop[s]…it would benefit us more, [who] have only joined once…And more talking to the villagers more (Chi)
  - I eat very much, and there are many memories. The food is *delicious*! (Kana)
  - Best experience in my life. BFS should be held for 2 months!! (Ratna)
  - First time BFS, I just want to say in BFS we get everything, good friends, good food, good homestay, everything about good good good!! New knowledge, gogogo BFS! (Frida)
  - First time BFS glad in BFS – Good program I can learn en[g]lish more and get more friends – korean, japan, and local people. That's all (Riyanto)
  - I always wanted to join this since the begin[n]ing. This was my nature of my study. Age is not an obstacle!! All trainers and organizing committee [members] are very helpful. Try to assist me. I hope this BFS could spread more, not just between us but also to the other government, hopefully get bigger and bigger… Suggestion: already the 4th, not many people know here. Maybe more people… not only UGM but more diverse participants.
    Documented not only the picture but the specific class, so we can see its improving. Maybe [as a] source of energy, if [a] book [was produced] with very nice picture[s], maybe people will buy it and might cover the cost (Bu Ning)
  - this is [an] opportunity for study…and collaboration [with] local community. Another viewpoint: you have opportunity to conduct from many countries…I found new friends, without something like this, we would not have this collaboration, so please keep contact with each other, since maybe in the future you yourselves might do collaboration. Hopefully from now on we find new Idea whenever you have idea (Kanki)
  - new friends, travelling many laughs, thank you! (Yeni)
  - Good one – we need comments for new improvements in the near future, is it too long, to short, too hard – at this site its good we have a good sunrise!! (Rully)
  - We collaborated with many researche[r]s, and we might compile these works of these students/former BFS participants (Sita)
  - We have been organizing this BFS event…a long time. We have many valuable data and information. Let's start to use website to keep and maintain this information. It will help us to promote this event easier for the next program

(Titin)
- more foreign participants, and out of Java! (Sinta)
- very nice for me…thank you…first time get sunrise from borobudur. Hope we get more energy… (Maulana)

- Kamsiah Mohammad Bostock (Malaysian participant, 2012):

From the welcome dinner at Mustokoweni, hosted by Ibu Sita and her friendly team (Sinta Carolina, Priyo & Co) – to the wonderful breakfast picnic on Tuk Situmbu – the hill we had to climb in total darkness in order to reach the top in time to witness a spectacular dawn breaking over Borobudur on the far side of the valley, there were so many highlights.
The line-up of lecturers – Prof. Dr Kiyoko Kanki with her first hand experience of preserving the cultural landscape of Japan, Ir Helmi Murwanto who introduced the group to the ancient lake he discovered, and Jack Priyana who headed the local community movement to protect historical monuments – all had impressive credentials.
And the participants from Egypt, Hong Kong, China and Malaysia got along so well with the local participants from Jogja and Bandung.
The village of Candirejo was also well-chosen for home stays. I especially felt very lucky with the family who housed me – Ersyi and his beautiful sister, Erva – and their kind parents.
So I feel next to the whole experience of the Field School, the visit to the Borobudur monument pales in comparison – but of course, it made one appreciate all the more the culture that built Borobudur and still lives on.

- Priyo A. Sancoyo, UGM architecture student (Indonesian participant, 2012)

[From] 2–8 July 2012…I was with 24 people from various Asian and African countries…Learning and sharing knowledge, there are architect, writer, observer of culture, heritage conservationists students and activists. We are presented [with] the other side of Borobudur. Looking at the activities of people, try traditional Javanese gamelan and…bath[ing] in the river that divides the province of Yogyakarta (*Kali Progo*) was incredible. Not to mention the matter of the concept of heritage landscape conservation (*saujana*) delivered beautifully by various background sources, academics, architects, [people preserving the] Borobudur mandala, economists, geologists, and local guides who [were] very good on guiding us. This year the theme [was] the role of the community…in preserving the heritage area of Borobudur…

- Mathew Cheng, WWF manager, Hong Kong (participant, 2012)

Boro[b]udur Field School provides [a] unique experience in the region that focuses on offering practical solution[s] to enhance the management of an obviously significant cultural landscape. This is the opportunity to know and work together with local and regional experts in the field that I find truly enjoyable and meaningful.

- Organizing Committee member:

  Organizing an annual field school like the Borobudur Field School always gives new experiences, more and more knowledge on Borobudur and new perspectives on anything related to the temple and *saujana* heritage around it. It also enriched us with new knowledge, new experience for organizing even better field school in the coming years.

- Facilitator:

  The field school is a good opportunity to share knowledge and experience in the field of *saujana* heritage conservation, especially in Borobudur area and surroundings with people interested in the issues of the Borobudur Temple and its sur[r]ounding areas. There are usually dialogues created among facilitators and participants, as well as local people.

Conclusion

Organizing the Borobudur Field School for almost a decade has not only provided opportunities to meet new people from other countries, but has also provided knowledge and new perspectives on seeing Borobudur Temple not merely as a monument but as a center of excellence for the many people who come to visit and learn from it. The organizing committee must not only be able to arrange a field school program, but must have in-depth knowledge of Borobudur. Through the Borobudur Field School participants learn many things about Borobudur Temple, the people, and the culture, as well as the knowledge.

6 Conservation Strategy for the Future

Kiyoko Kanki, Laretna T. Adishakti, and Titin Fatimah

The Large Kedu Plain Context and smaller village areas

During the past ten years, the evaluation of the Borobudur Temple Compounds has become an active discussion among local communities, triggered by the commercial development plan of the PSJJ (*Pasar Seni Jagad Jawa*/Art Market Universe of Java) and the idea that the temples should not be regarded as three isolated sites but as a united landscape that includes vast areas of rural settings, as well as the temples. According to this idea, it is necessary to identify the characteristics and to recognize the stories of the cultural landscape.

Borobudur Temple is located on a slightly raised hill at the confluence of several rivers in the Kedu Plain and is surrounded by high mountains (several more than 3000 meters high). The characteristics of this basin area can be described as the continuing accumulation of assets from ancient times until the present. At the same time, each village and town holds such accumulated elements, which are recognized as the living, contemporary landscape.

The relationship between the Borobudur Temple Compounds and the contemporary surrounding villages and towns forms a united cultural landscape. There exist so many kinds of heritages from different eras in the past, which can be evaluated from different viewpoints. According to the time axis, many elements of the ancient eras survive today and, according to the various viewpoints, we can find, for example, geological or industrial meanings – namely, many value systems exist in the Kedu Plain context of Borobudur.

To summarize the achievement of ten years of the Borobudur Field School, we always focus both on the large basin and on the smaller village areas at the same time, and that focal point requires us to support local initiatives also both on the large basin and on the smaller village areas. Here we would like to review the achievement of each author in chapter 3, 4, and 5.

In Chapter 3, Murwanto, Purwoarminta, and Soeroso show the geological and geographical structures and features of the large Kedu Plain area, which can tell us the backgrounds of locations of the Borobudur Temple Compounds, as well as other temples, each village, land use, local industrial production, and so on. Moreover, we can imagine the old or ancient scenery of the basin and temples. Rahmi shows the characteristics of diverse items which compose the landscape of the large Kedu Plain and the village areas. These are the historical assets as well as resources of the attractiveness at each place in Borobudur. Punto then shows the necessity for the updating of regional planning, which could support the compositions of landscapes in the large Kedu Plain, and finally in Chapter 3 Priyana summarizes the total evaluations from the inhabitants' viewpoint and suggests conservation activities with the

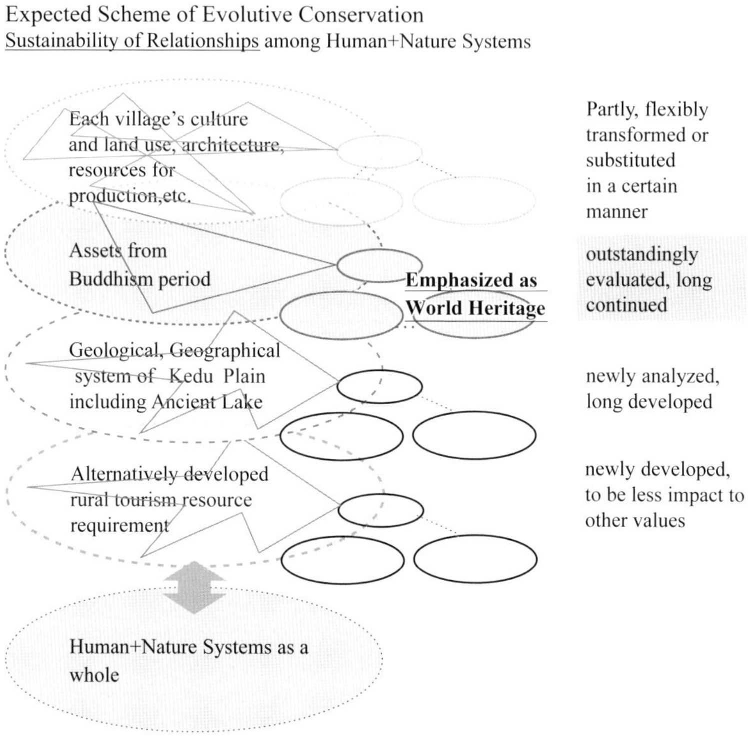

Figure 6.1: Various value systems of cultural landscape and the identification of outstanding world-class heritage value

recognition of the large basin and smaller village areas at the same time, as well as with the important local initiatives.

In Chapter 4 Fatimah, Utami and Tatak, Suparno and Kusumaningdyah, and Hatta show ways for the development of local initiatives. They describe the recent histories of organizational networks that cover the large Kedu basin area, as well as of each local village. Also, local initiatives for cultural landscape are expected to form a network both on the large basin scale and for smaller village areas at the same time. In this discussion, tourism management – decrease of the destructive impact of mass tourism and the introduction of managed rural tourism as supportive industry for the village – is very focused. In several case studies we can see the history of local empowerment supported by such a network.

In Chapter 5 we can recognize that BFS is the opportunity to connect landscape analysis, attractive village resource evaluation, active people, and organizations, including researchers and students. It is quite a tentative event – only one week per year on average. At the same time it functions like a certain experiment, which tries to introduce newly started or found

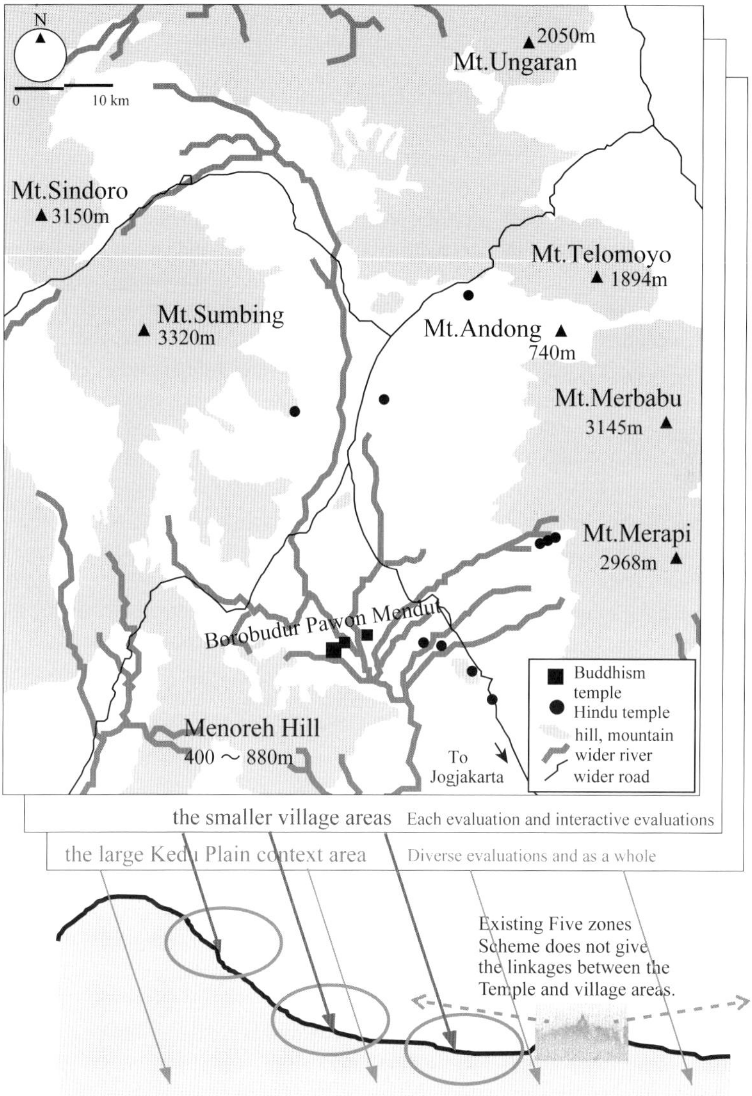

Relativizing the Borobudur Temple Compound in
the Kedu Plain Context

Figure 6.2: The village location and the whole context of the Kedu Plain features and activities to larger communities.

Here we would like to propose Figure 6.1, which illustrates the cultural landscape value system and how we can identify outstanding values of world heritage and other values. As we can see in Borobudur, an area of cultural landscape is the outcome of many kinds of values with many time layers and many viewpoints. The authenticity of an area can be described by many kinds of value systems. Those value systems are sometimes linked with each other, strongly or slightly, but are not the same as each other. If we can find the areas with outstanding value, such precious properties can be designated as protected world heritage. The documentation of the protected properties and their authenticity focuses on the outstanding value, and the designation will request preservation of the outstanding value. The difference between focusing on Borobudur Temple Compounds and recognizing the Kedu Plain context, including Borobudur Temple Compounds, lies in the interests and concerns of the value systems, mainly the outstanding value and the various value systems as a whole.

We can imagine the combination of the large basin area and smaller village areas with diverse value systems that link to the local initiative discussion. So far, views of the surroundings from Borobudur Temple, and views of the temple from the villages and towns, are likely to be focused, and now we have the image of each view in the Kedu Plain context, whether narrow or wide, which are to be evaluated. The description of the outstanding value of the Borobudur Temple Compounds cannot necessarily give the viewpoints of every place in the Kedu Plain. Each place is the outcome of several value systems, so we can decide the actions that can have some influence on cultural landscape by evaluating not only the idea of the Borobudur Temple Compounds but also several value systems related to the place.

By widening the scope of Borobudur towards the surroundings and by discovering the meanings of cultural landscape, we can create relationships organically in every step for the future.

Achievement and new problems

During these past ten years it has also been noticed that local communities and organizations are endeavoring to maintain, update, and create the characteristics of cultural landscape while sometimes facing difficulties in local industries or the inevitable transformation of tangible and intangible characteristics. Continuing to think and act for the future of the villages, with a concern for the known and unknown characteristics of the cultural landscape, is important for the sustainable development of the communities, as well as for the evolutive conservation of cultural landscape. Borobudur Field School started ten years ago, and the participants began with field surveys and discussions and by making handwritten maps of the case study villages. Since then, BFS participants have met several people who had started to search for the meanings of Borobudur as cultural landscape through their own academic or community-oriented interests. Over the ten years, BFS has asked more people to participate and to bring new viewpoints in finding the meanings of cultural landscape. BFS has connected the people and the various meanings of cultural landscape. Now, BFS itself is also to be evolutive, since there exist many problems for the sustainability of cultural landscape, some of which are rather new in Borobudur.

Plate 6.1: Tourists gathered in a village to watch the sunrise (photo: Kanki, 2013)

On the occasion of the Mount Merapi volcanic eruption and other volcanic eruptions, the temples and the areas have suffered heavily, and people from the local communities have volunteered and contributed to the recovery (UNESCO and National Geographic Indonesia 2011). Some important activities have been maintained for the sustainable development of tourism and can contribute to the tradition and environment of villages and towns. Now the next question is whether such activities are able to become a reliable industry for the communities in the near future.

Experiences in Candirejo village for alternative, community-based tourism have been highly evaluated. At the same time, such tourism activities can be realized by the non-community-based tourism sector, but village tourism is expected to be a community business on a good scale and to contribute to the village communities and their sustainability. There is still development of closed/private hotels in good locations that offer views of Borobudur Temple. Plate 6.1 shows a location that is managed by the village and offers views of the sunrise and Borobudur Temple. This is a better solution than constructing a private hotel because everyone can come here for a minimal fee. However, at the same time the number of tourists is increasing, so we should consider the environmental influence.

Since around 2013, the number of homestays has also been gradually increasing in several villages. It is unknown how this will influence existing community-based homestay businesses, such as those in Candirejo, in the near future. Community-based activities operate under competitive conditions and Borobudur is still under tourist development pressure.

The idea of Borobudur as cultural landscape has created networks of active people in local communities and organizations, and such people continually discuss and question such issues in the villages and convene meetings with colleagues. Such human activities keep searching for the next steps in the evolutive conservation of cultural landscape and community sustainability.

Abbreviations

BACC	Borobudur Archeological Conservation Center
BCA	Borobudur Care Association
BFS	Borobudur Field School
CHC-UGM	Center for Heritage Conservation, Gadjah Mada University
cm	centimeter
DPR	Dewan Perwakilan Rakyat (People's Representative Assembly, i.e. Parliament)
FLMB	Forum Lintas Masyarakat Borobudur (Borobudur Cross Society Forum)
FMSW	Forum Masyarakat Sadar Wisata (Tourism Awareness Community Forum)
FPD	Forum Putra Daerah (Local Genuine Generation Forum)
FRKPB	Forum Rembug Klaster Pariwisata Borobudur (Borobudur Tourism Cluster Discussion Forum)
GG	Gagas Gapura (Discussion forum)
HPI	Himpunan Pramuwisata Indonesia (Indonesian Tourist Guide Association)
ICOMOS	International Council on Monuments and Sites
ICT	information, communication, and technology
JAKER	Jaringan Kerja Kepariwisataan Borobudur (Borobudur Tourism Network)
JICA	Japan International Cooperation Agency
KOPARI	Koperasi Pariwisata (Tourism Cooperation)
KSN	Kawasan Strategis Nasional (National Strategic Area)
LEPEK	Lembaga Perekonomian Rakyat (Micro Economic Foundation)
m	meters
MAPAN	Masyarakat Peduli Lingkungan (Community for Environmental Awareness)
mm	millimeters
NPO	non-profit organizations
NRM-LCE	Natural Resources Management for Local Community Empowerment
P2WKSS	Peningkatan Peranan Wanita menuju Keluarga Sehat Sejahtera (Women's Role towards a Healthy and Prosperous Family)
PATRA-PALA	Indonesian Institute for Social Ecology and Tourism
PJWB	Paguyuban Jasa Wisata Borobudur (Borobudur Tourism Services Association)

PNPM	Program Nasional Pemberdayaan Masyarakat (National Program for Community Empowerment)
PRA	Participatory Rural Appraisal
PRL	Pertemuan Rebo Legi (Crafters Association)
PSJJ	Pasar Seni Jagad Jawa (Java Art Market/Universal Java Art Market/Art Market Universe of Java
PSWB	Paguyuban Sambya Waharing Boro (Association of Retailers & Vendors in Borobudur)
PT. TWCBPRB	PT. Taman Wisata Candi Borobudur, Prambanan dan Ratu Boko (Tourism of Borobudur, Prambanan, and Ratu Boko Temple Co. Ltd)
RT	Rukun Tetangga (neighborhood)
RTRW Nasional	National Spatial Plans
RW	Rukun Warga (harmonious citizens)
TANKER	Tim Anti Kekerasan (Anti-Violation Team)
UGM	Gadjah Mada University
UNESCO	United Nations Educational, Scientific and Cultural Organization
WI	Komunitas 'Warung Info Jagad Cleguk' (Community Information Center)
YBP	years before present

Bibliography

Adishakti, L. (1999), *Pengantar Konservasi Lingkungan Kota Berejarah* [Introduction to Environmental Conservation of Heritage City], Writing Project – Jakarta: Directorate of Higher Education, Republic of Indonesia.

Adishakti, Laretna T. (2003), Community Participation and Future Development of Borobudur Temple and Its Environment, paper presented at the Fourth International Experts Meeting on Borobudur, organized by Ministry of Culture and Tourism in collaboration with UNESCO in Borobudur, Magelang.

Adishakti, Laretna T. (2005), From Monument into Cultural Landscape Heritage of Borobudur, Indonesia, paper presented in the International Eco-museum Forum in Guiyang, Guizhou, China.

Adishakti, Laretna T. (2006), *Alam dan Budaya Sekitar Borobudur sebagai Kesatuan Saujana: Pusaka Saujana Borobudur, masih wacanakah?*, paper presented at the National Seminar on 'Borobudur, from the Past to Future', organized by the Committee of National Waisak 2550 BE/2006 M, Konferensi Agung Sangha Indonesia (KASI) in collaboration with Indonesian Heritage Trust, Jakarta.

Adishakti, Laretna T. (2008), *Konsep Rancangan Arsitektur Pengembangan Kawasan Pusaka Saujana Borobudur* [Architectural Planning Concept of Borobudur Cultural Landscape Development], paper presented at the National Workshop 'Re-thinking Borobudur', organized by the Department of Culture and Tourism in collaboration with the Department of Public Work, Jakarta, 27 May 2008

Adishakti, Laretna T. (2009a), Cultural-natural Expressions and Community Movement on the Saujana Heritage Conservation, presented at the International Workshop on Sustainable City Region co-hosted by Alliance for Global Sustainability, Trans-disciplinary Initiative for Global Sustainability/Integrated Research System for Sustainability Science, Global Center for Excellence for Sustainable Urban Regeneration, Tokyo University and Udayana University Bali, Bali.

Adishakti, Laretna T. (2009b), The Conservation Management of Borobudur and Surrounding Townscape, presented at the International Symposium and Public Lectures: Keeping the Past Public organized by the Faculty of Architecture Building and Planning, The University of Melbourne, Australia.

Adiyanto, Saryan et al. (2008), Annual Report of Candirejo Tourism Village Cooperative, Yearbook 2007, Magelang: Candirejo Tourism Village Cooperation.

Ahimsa-Putra, H. S. (2003), Twenty Years After – Economic, Social, and Cultural Impacts of Tourism in Borobudur, paper presented at the Fourth Experts Meeting on Borobudur, Magelang, Indonesia, 4–8 July.

Antara News (2010), Covered in volcanic ash, Borobudur closed temporarily, 6 November. <www.antaranews.com/en/news/1289042983/covered-in-volcanic-ash-borobudur-closed-temporarily>, accessed 13 December 2013.

Ask (2013), What is a bioregion?, <www.ask.com/question/what-is-a-bioregion>, accessed 11 December 2013.

Atmosumarto, Sutanto (2005), A Learner's Comprehensive Dictionary of Indonesian, London: Atma Stanton.

BTSS (Borobudur Travel Services Society) (2005), Member List of the Borobudur Travel Services Society, Borobudur: BTSS.

Backer, C. A. and R. C. Bakhuizen van Den Brink(1963), Flora of Java (Spermatophytes only), P. Noordhoff: Groningen, Netherlands.

Bakosurtanal (National Coordinating Agency for Surveys and Mapping) (2001), *Peta Rupa Bumi* [Topographic map of Indonesia: Magelang and surrounding sheet], Jakarta: Bakosurtanal, <www.bakosurtanal.go.id/peta-rupabumi/>, accessed 10 September 2014.

Berthommier, P. C. (1990), Étude volcanologique du Merapi (Centre-Java). Téphrostratigraphie etchronologie-produitséruptifs. PhD thesis, Université Blaise Pascal, Clermont-Ferrand.

Bimbaum, C. and C. Peters (1996), Guidelines for the Treatment of Cultural Landscape, Washington, DC: US Department of the Interior.

Birnbaum, Charles A. and Christine C. Peters (eds) (1996),The Secretary of the Interior's Standards for the Treatment of Historic Properties with Guidelines for the Treatment of Cultural Landscapes, Washington, DC: US Department of the Interior, National Park Service, Cultural Resource Stewardship and Partnerships, Heritage Preservation Services, Historic Landscape Initiative.

Bramwell, B. (ed.) (1990), Shades of Green: Working Towards Green Tourism in the Countryside, London: English Tourist Board.

Brown, V. and F. Leblanc (1992), The Ontario Heritage Regions Projects, Ottawa: Heritage Canada.

Buggey, S. and M. Nora (2008), Cultural landscapes: Venues for community-based conservation, in R. Longstreth (ed.), *Cultural Landscapes: Balancing Nature and Heritage in Preservation Practice*, Minneapolis: University of Minnesota Press, pp.164–79.

BTSS (Borobudur Travel Services Society) (2005), Member List of the Borobudur Travel Services Society, Borobudur: BTSS

CBS (Central Bureau of Statistics) of Central Java Province (2013), Central Java Province in the Figures: 2013, Semarang: CBS of Central Java.

CBS (Central Bureau of Statistics) of Magelang Regency (2003) Magelang Regency in the Figures: 2003. Mungkid: CBS-Magelang Regency Government.

CBS (Central Bureau of Statistics) of Magelang Regency (2013), Magelang Regency in Figures: 2013. Mungkid: DSA-Magelang Regency Government.

Calcatinge, A. (2012), The Need for a Cultural Landscape Theory, an Architect Approach,

Zurich: LIT Verlaag.

Committee on the Preservation, Development and Utilization of Cultural Landscapes Associated with Agriculture, Forestry and Fisheries (2003), The Report of the Study on the Protection of Cultural Landscape Associated with Agriculture, Forestry and Fisheries, Tokyo: Monuments and Sites Division, Cultural Properties Department, Agency for Cultural Affairs.

Cultural Properties Department (2003), The Report of the Study on the Protection of Cultural Landscapes Associated with Agriculture, Forestry, and Fisheries, Japan: Agency for Cultural Affairs.

Dahles, H. (2001), Tourism, Heritage and National Culture in Java: Dilemmas of a Local Community, Richmond, UK: Curzon.

Daldjoeni, N. (1984), Geografi Kesejahteraan II Indonesia [Indonesian Geographical History II], Penerbit Alumni/1984/Bandung. Kotak Pos 272, 56–62.

Darmosoetopo, R. (1998), *Hubungan Tanah Sima dengan Bangunan Kegamaan: Di Jawa Pada Abad IX-XTU* [Relationship between Sima Land and Religious Buildings in Java in IX-XTU Century], unpublished dissertation, Yogyakarta: Department of Archaeology, Gadjah Mada University.

Department of Communications and the Arts(1995), Mapping Culture: A Guide for Cultural and Economic Development in Communities, Canberra: Australian Government Publishing Service.

Directorate of Geology (1975), Geological Map Sheet of Magelang, Semarang and Yogyakarta, Bandung: Directorate General of Mines.

Droste, Bernd von, Harald Plachter and Mechtild Rossler (1995 ed.), Cultural Landscapes of Universal Value, Components of a Global Strategy, Gustav Fischer Verlag, Jena, Stuttgart, New York

Engelhardt, Richard, Graham Brooks, and Alexa Schorlemer (2003), Mission Report: Borobudur Temple Compound, Central Java, Indonesia: UNESCO-ICOMOS Reactive Monitoring Mission 16–20 April 2003, UNESCO-ICOMOS.

Farina, A. (1998), Principles and Methods in Landscape Ecology, London: Chapman & Hall.

Fatimah, Titin (2012), A Study on Community-based Cultural Landscape Conservation in Borobudur, Indonesia, unpublished doctoral thesis dissertation. Graduate School of Urban and Environmental Engineering, Kyoto University.

Fatimah, Titin, Kanki Kiyoko, Laretna T. Adishakti (2005), Borobudur – Recent History of Its Cultural Landscape - Toward the Sustainable Rural Development as the Landscape Rehabilitation - Paper presented at the Forum UNESCO - Universities and Heritage 10th International Seminar, Newcastle, United Kingdom, April 11-16

Fatimah, Titin and Kanki Kiyoko (2008), A study on the realization process of community based green tourism in Candirejo village, Borobudur, Indonesia, Journal of the City Planning Institute of Japan, 43–3, October: 517–22

Fatimah, Titin and Kanki Kiyoko (2009), A study on citizens' organizations relationship for cultural landscape conservation initiatives in Borobudur Sub-district level, Indonesia, Journal of the City Planning Institute of Japan, 44–3, October: 205–10.

Fatimah, Titin and Kanki Kiyoko (2012), Evaluation of rural tourism initiatives in Borobudur Sub-district, Indonesia: A study on rural tourism activities for cultural landscape conservation, Journal of Architecture and Planning, Transactions of AIJ, 77 (673), March: 563–72.

Fennell, David A. (2008). Ecotourism (3rd edn), USA, Canada: Taylor & Francis e-Library.

Fennell, David A. and Ross K. Dowling (eds) (2003), Ecotourism Policy and Planning, USA, UK: CABI Publishing.

Friedmann, John (1992), Empowerment. The Politics of Alternative Development. Cambridge: Blackwell Publishers.

Government of Magelang Regency (2000), Regional Spatial Balance of the Natural Resources (RSBNR), Mungkid: Government of Magelang Regency.

Gumisawa, Hideo (2007), On the Thought of '*gotong royong*': An Insight into Indonesian Nationalism (abstract), doctoral thesis, Tokyo University of Foreign Students, Japan

Hampton, M. P. (2005), Heritage, local communities and economic development, Annals of Tourism Research, 32 (3): 735–59.

Healey, Patsy (2003), Collaborative Planning in Perspective. In Planning Theory. Seymour J. Mandelboum, Liugi Mazza and Robert W. Burchell, Ed. New Jersey, Center for Urban Policy Research.

Hirata, Kazutosi (2003), *Kumanokodo Nakahechi Endo niokeru Keikan henka nikansuru Kenkyu –Bunkatekikeikan toshiteno Sekaiisan Baffazoonkanri--* [Study of the Landscape Transformation along Kumano Ancient Road Nakahechi – The Management in the World Heritage Bufferzone of Cultural Landscape], unpublished master thesis, Wakayama University, supervised by Kiyoko Kanki.

Hoch, Charles (1996). A Pragmatic Inquiry about Planning and Power", in: Explorations.In Planning Theory. Seymour J. Mandelboum, Liugi Mazza and Robert W. Burchell, Ed. New Jersey, Center for Urban Policy Research.

ICOMOS (International Council on Monuments and Sites)(2001), The Cultural Landscape: Planning for a Sustainable Partnership between People and Place, London: ICOMOS-UK.

Indecon (n.d.),<www.indecon.or.id/ecosites/index.html>.

Izumisano City Board of Education (ed.) (2008), *Hinenosho Chiiki no Bunkatekikeikan Chosa Houkokusho (Ogi and Tsuchimaru Chiku)* [Research report on Cultural Landscape of Hinenosho Areas (Ogi Village and Tsuchimaru Village)

JICA (Japan International Cooperation Agency) Study Team (1979), Republic of Indonesia Borobudur, Prambanan National Archeological Parks: Final Report, July 1979, Tokyo: Japan.

Jakarta Globe (2010), Borobudur Temple forced to close while workers remove Merapi ash, <www.thejakartaglobe.com/archive/borobudur-temple-forced-to-close-while-workers-remove-merapi-ash/>, accessed 13 December 2013.

Jaringan Pelestarian Pusaka Indonesia (2003), *Piagam Pelestarian Pusaka Indonesia* [Indonesian Charter for Heritage Conservation], in collaboration with ICOMOS Indonesia and Ministry of Culture and Tourism.

James, Jamie (2003), Battle of Borobudur, Time Magazine (Asia), 27 January.

Jamieson, W. (ed.) (1990), Maintaining and Enhancing the Sense of Place for Small Communities and Regions, Calgary: University of Calgary.

Jones, M. (2003), 'The concept of cultural landscape: Discourse and narratives', in H. Palang and G. Fry (eds), Landscape Interfaces: Cultural Heritage in Changing Landscapes, Dordrecht: Kluwer Academic Publisher, pp. 21–52.

Kanki, Kiyoko and Titin Fatimah (2006), Landscape Use Database System for the Shared Wisdom to Manage Cultural Landscape – Case Trial in Kii Mountain Range (Japan) and Borobudur Surroundings (Indonesia), 11th UNESCO Forum Universities Heritage, Florence, Italy, 11–15 September.

Kanki, Kiyoko (2011a), 2.2 *Bunkatekikeikan no Jusotekina Kachi tosono Keisho – Kumanokodo nimiru Keikanhozen heno Chiikidukuri Apurochi* – [2.2 Diverse Values of Cultural Landscapes and those Succession – Community Development Approach toward the Landscape Conservation in Kumano Pilgrimage Route --] , Architectural Institute of Japan (ed.) (2011), *Mirai no Kei wo Sodateru Chosen –Chiikidukuri to Bunkatekikeikan no Hozen* [For landscape of the future– Conservation of cultural landscape and regional development], Gihodo pub. ISBN-10: 4765525538.

Kanki, Kiyoko (2011b), Contemporary Cultural Landscape with Medieval Structure -Discussion on how to set up the management plan for cultural landscape (Osaka Pref. Izumisano City, Ohgi,Tsuchimaru) -, Architectural Institute of Japan, Annual Conference 2011,Rural Planning Committee Kenkyu-Kyogikai-Siryoshu-, pp.15-16, 2011.8

Kanki, Kiyoko (2012), Field School for the conservation of cultural landscape -The role of International Borobudur Field School-, Proceeding of Design Symposium 2012, pp.537-542, October 16-17 2012.10 (Kyoto), Architectural Institute of Japan and others

Krom, N. J. (1927), *Barabudur Archaeological Description* Vol. I, The Hague: Martinus Nijhoff.

Kuroda, M. (2004), Application of productivity and management tools for OVOP, utilization of unused resources and by-products: Case study of Indonesia Wild Silk Development Project, paper presented at the seminar 'One Village – One Product' Movement for Community Development, Chiang Mai, Thailand, 19 August.

Lane, B. (1994), Sustainable rural tourism strategies: A tool for development and conservation, Journal of Sustainable Tourism, 2 (1–2).

Lewis, P. (1979), Axiom for reading the landscape, in D. W. Meinig (ed.), The Interpretation of Ordinary Landscapes: Geographical Essays, New York: Oxford University Press, pp. 11–32.

Mason, R. (2008), Management for cultural landscape preservation: Insights from Australia, in R. Longstreth (ed.), Cultural Landscapes: Balancing Nature and Heritage in Preservation Practice, Minneapolis: University of Minnesota Press, pp. 180–96.

Miksic, J. (with photographs by Marcello and Anita Tranchini) (1990), Borobudur: Golden Tales of the Buddhas, Hong Kong: Periplus.

Moehkardi (2008), *BungaRampaiSejarah Indonesia Dari Borobudur hinggaRevolusi 1945* [Potpourri of Indonesian History from Borobudur until the Revolution of 1945], Yogyakarta: Gama Media.

Monier-Williams, S. M., E. Leuman, and C. Cappeller (1979), A Sanskrit–English Dictionary: Etymologically and Philologically Arranged with Special Reference to Cognate Indo-European Languages, England: Oxford.

Morishige, M. (2009), Revitalization of local community through local tourism development: Evaluation of the tourism policy in Yubari City in the viewpoint of community-based tourism, Advanced Tourism Studies, 5: 1–20.

Murwanto, H., Sutanto, and Suharsono (2001), *Kajian Pengaruh Aktivitas Gunungapi Kuarter Terhadap Perkembangan 'Danau Borobudur' Dengan Bantuan Sistem Informasi Geografis* [Study of Quaternary Volcano Activity for Borobudur Lake Development With Geographic Information System], Final Report DCRG, Ministry of Education, Indonesia.

Murwanto, H. (1996), *Pengaruh Aktivitas Gunung api Kwarter Terhadap Perkembangan Lingkungan Danau di Daerah Borobudur dan Sekitarnya, Jawa Tengah* [The Influence of Quaternary Volcanic Activities on the Lake Environment Development in the Borobudur Area and Its Surrounding, Central Java] Unpublished master thesis, Post Graduate Program, Gadjah Mada University, Yogyakarta.

Murwanto, H. and Sutarto (2008), *Geologi Situs Danau Purba Borobudur* [Geology of Borobudur Ancient Lake], paper presented at the National Seminar 'Re-Thinking Borobudur', organized by the Department of Culture and Tourism in collaboration with the Department of Public Work, Jakarta, 27 May 2008.

Murwanto, H., Y. Gunnell, S. Suharsono, S. Sutikno, and F. Lavigne (2004), Borobudur monument (Java, Indonesia) stood by a natural lake: Chronostratigraphic evidence and historical implications, The Holocene, 14 (3): 459–63.

NARC (National Archaeological Research Center) (1986), Prof. Dr. AJ Bernet Kempers, For Teacher: Dedication Disciples, to Commemorate 80 Years Old, Jakarta: Jakarta Archaeological Research Project, Ministry of Education and Culture.

NSW (New South Wales) Government (2011), 'What is a bioregion?', Department of the Environment and Heritage, <www.environment.nsw.gov.au/bioregions/BioregionsExplained.htm>, accessed 11 December 2013.

NWE (New World Encyclopedia) 2013, 'Sailendra', <www.newworldencyclopedia.org/entry/Sailendra>, accessed 11 December 2013.

Naveh, Z. (1995), Interactions of landscapes and cultures, Landscape and Urban Planning, 32: 43–54.

Nieuwenkamp, W.O. J. (1933), *Het Boroboedoermeer*, Algemeen Handelsblad, Denhaag, 9 September 1933.

Page, Robert R.(1998),A Guide to Cultural Landscape Reports: Contents, Process, and Techniques, Washington, DC: US Department of the Interior, National Park Service, Cultural Resource Stewardship and Partnerships, Park Historic Structures and Cultural Landscapes Program.

Palang, H., S. Helmfrid, M. Antrop, and H. Alumäe (2005), Rural landscapes: Past processes and future strategies, Landscape and Urban Planning, 70(1–2): 3–8.

Patton, M. Q. (1987), How to Use Qualitative Methods in Evaluation, Newbury Park, Beverly Hills, London, New Delhi: Sage Publications.

Perlez, Jane (2003), Borobudur journal, Buddhist monument and mall: Will twain meet?, New York Times, 27 February.

Pettigrew, A. M. (1990), Longitudinal field research on change: Theory and practice, Organization Science, 1 (3) (Special issue: Longitudinal Field Research Methods for Studying Processes of Organizational Change): 267–92.

Priyana, Jack (2013), Presentation at the 7th Borobudur Field School.

Rahmi, D. H. (2012), *Pusaka Saujana Borobudur, Studi Hubungan Antara Bentang lahan Dan Budaya Masyarakat* [Borobudur Cultural Landscape, Study on Interaction Between Landscape and Community Culture], unpublished doctoral dissertation, Gadjah Mada University.

Rahmi, D. H. and Setiawan, B. (1999), *Pengantar Perancangan Kota Ekologi* [Introduction to Ecological City Design], Jakarta: Universitas Indonesia Press.

Regional Water Company 'Tirta Dharma' of Magelang Regency (2005), Data Sources of Drinking Water that Are Managed or Not by the Company, According to the District in 2005. Mungkid: The Regional Water Company 'Tirta Dharma' of Magelang Regency Government.

Rossler, Mechtild (2001),UNESCO World Heritage Centre Background Document on UNESCO World Heritage Cultural Landscape, prepared for the FAO Workshop and Steering Committee Meeting of the GIAHS project.

Saldana, J. (2003), Longitudinal Qualitative Research: Analyzing Change through Time, Walnut Creek, Lanham, New York, Oxford: AltaMira Press.

Sariawan, Tatak (2012a), *Pengelolaan Home Stay Ala Desa Wisata Candirejo* [Managing Home Stay in Candirejo], presentation, June.

Sariawan, Tatak (2012b), *Candirejo Membangun Desa Wisata Berbasis Masyarakat* [Build Candirejo as a Tourism Village Based on Community], presentation, September

Sariawan, Tatak (2012c), *Candirejo Membangun Desa Wisata Berbasis Masyarakat* [Build Candirejo as a Tourism Village Based on Community], movie presentation (made by young local people), September.

Sarwono, E. (1988), The world of flora, hidden at the foot of the Borobudur Temple, Natural Sounds, 52: 14–19.

Schimdt, F. H. and J. H. A. Ferguson (1951), Rainfall types based on wet and dry period rations for Indonesia with Western New Guinea, Verhandlingen, 42.

Silalahi, Monika L., et al. (2003), A Memory of Candirejo Village, Borobudur, Magelang, Central Java, Indonesia, NRM-LCE Project, Magelang: JICA & PATRA-PALA Foundation.

Soekmono (1976), Chandi Borobudur. A Monument of Mankind. Paris, TheUnesco Press.

Soekmono (1976), *Candi Borobudur* [Borobudur Temple], PT Dunia Pustaka Jaya.

Soeroso, Amiluhur (2007), *Penilaian Kawasan Pusaka Borobudur Dalam Kerangka Perspektif Multiatribut Ekonomi Lingkungan dan Implikasinya Terhadap Kebijakan Manajemen Ekowisata* [Valuing Borobudur World Heritage Area in a Multi-attributes Framework of Environmental Economics Perspective and Its Implications toward Ecotourism Management Policy], unpublished doctoral dissertation, Yogyakarta: Postgraduate Program, Gadjah Mada University.

Soeroso, Amiluhur (2012), National Strategic Area, Presentation at the 6th Borobudur Field School.

Stefanica, Mirela and Maria V. Gurmeza(2010), Ecotourism – model of sustainable tourist development, Studies and Scientific Researches (Economic Edition), 15.

Suhandi, Ari S. et al. (2003), Master Plan of Tourism Development of Candirejo Village, Candirejo village, Magelang: PATRA-PALA/INDECON.

Sumukti, T. (2005), *Semar: Dunia Batin Orang Jawa* [Semar: The Inner World of Javanese],

Yogyakarta: Galang Press.

Sustainability-now (2013), ‘Why bioregional approach?’,<http://sustainability-now.org/bioregionalism.htm>, accessed 11 December 2013.

Sutikno, H., Murwanto, and Sutarto (2006), The environmental assessment of regional geology at Borobudur, Magelang Regency, Central Java Province, paper presented to University of National Development ‘Veteran’ Yogyakarta.

Suwarsono and Alvin Y. So (1991), *Perubahan Sosial dan Pembangunan di Indonesia* [Social Change and Development in Indonesia], Jakarta: Penerbit LP3ES.

TAS (Tranquil Abiding Shop) (2013) ‘What is Bodhi?’, <www.tranquilabidingshop.com/what_is_bodhi.html>, accessed 11 December 2013.

Taylor, Ken (2003), Cultural landscape as open air museum: Borobudur World Heritage Site and Its Setting, Humanities Research, 10 (2): 51–62.

Theobald, William F. (ed.) (2005), Global Tourism(3rd edn), USA: Elsevier Inc.

Thompson, G. F. and F. R. Steiner (eds) (1997), Ecological Design and Planning, New York: John Wiley & Sons.

Tribun News (2010), *Inilah Foto-foto Kerusakan Candi Borobudur* [These are photographs of temple destruction], 7 November, <www.tribunnews.com/regional/2010/11/07/inilah-foto-foto-kerusakan-candi-borobudur>, accessed 13 December 2013.

UNESCO (1994), Operational Guidelines for Implementation of the World Heritage Convention, Paris: UNESCO World Heritage Centre.

UNESCO (2012), Operational Guidelines for the Implementation of the World Heritage Convention, WHC 12/01, July 2012, Paris: UNESCO World Heritage Centre, <http://whc.unesco.org/archive/opguide12-en.pdf >, accessed 10 September 2014.

UNESCO (2013), Borobudur Temple Compounds, <http://whc.unesco.org/en/list/592>, accessed 10 December 2013.

UNESCO World Heritage (2003), Cultural Landscapes: The Challenges of Conservation, World Heritage Papers 7, Paris: UNESCO World Heritage Centre.

UNESCO and National Geographic Indonesia (2011), Borobudur – The Road to Recovery: Community-based Rehabilitation Work and Sustainable Tourism Development, Jakarta: UNESCO.

Van Bemmelen, R. W. (1949), The Geology of Indonesia: General Geology of Indonesia and Adjacent Archipelagoes, vol. IA, The Hague: Government Printing Office, Martinus Nijhoff.

Van Bemmelen, R. W. (1952), *De Geologishe Geschiedemis van Indonesie* [Geological History of Indonesia], Den Haag: NV Uitgerverij, W.P. van Stockum En Zoon.

Vink, A. P. A. (1983), Landscape Ecology and Land Use, London and New York: Longman.

Von Droste, Bernd, Harald Plachter, and Mechtild Rossler (eds) (1995), Cultural Landscapes of Universal Value, Components of a Global Strategy, Jena, Stuttgart, New York: Gustav Fischer Verlag.

Wearing, Stephen and John Neil (2009), Ecotourism: Impact, Potential and Possibilities (2nd edn), Burlington, MA: Elsevier.

Whitten, T., R. E. Soeriaatmadja, and S. A. Afiff (1996), Ecology of Java and Bali, Singapore: Periplus.

Wikepedia (2103a), ‘Java Eagle’, <http://id.wikipedia.org/wiki/Elang_jawa>, accessed 15

December 2013.

Wikepedia (2103b), *Taman Nasional Gunung Merapi* [Merapi National Park], <http://id.wikipedia.org/wiki/Taman_Nasional_Gunung_Merapi>, accessed 15 December 2013.

Wikepedia (2103c), *Taman Nasional Gunung Merbabu* [Merbabu National Park],<http://id.wikipedia.org/wiki/Taman_Nasional_Gunung_Merbabu>, accessed 15 December 2013.

Winarni (2006), *Kajian Perubahan Ruang Kawasan World Cultural Heritage Candi Borobudur* [Assessment of Spatial Changes in Borobudur Temple World Cultural Heritage Site Area],unpublished master thesis (in Indonesian). Gadjah Mada University, Yogyakarta.

Zakharov. A. O. (2012), The Sailendras Reconsidered, Working Paper No. 12, Singapore: Nalanda-Sriwijaya Centre, Institute of Southeast Asian Studies, <http://nsc.iseas.edu.sg/documents/working_papers/nscwps012.pdf>, accessed 11 December 2013.

Index